Money and Energy: Weathering the Storm

Money and Energy: Weathering the Storm

C.V. Myers

Soundview Books
Darien, Connecticut 1980

Portions of the material in this book have appeared in *The Coming Deflation,*
by C.V. Myers, published by Arlington House, 1976.

**LIBRARY OF CONGRESS
CATALOG CARD NO.: 80-50032**

Myers, C.V.
Money and energy.

Darien, Conn.; Soundview Books
241 p.
8002   800109

ISBN 0-934924-00-7

Printed in the United States of America

To all non-conformists with the mental courage to believe what they think and the moral courage to say so - for they are the watchdogs of freedom.

CONTENTS

INTRODUCTION

Today, everyone knows we're in a money and energy mess.

Hardly anyone has any real idea of how we got into it, or how we can get out.

Corporation president or factory worker, we are all beset by common questions, common uncertainties, common anxieties. There's a good chance —we all recognize it—that everything we've ever worked for is going to go right down the drain. How can we preserve what we've worked so hard to get?

Does it make sense to buy stocks or sell? Buy gold or silver coins? Save or spend? Buy Swiss francs or works of art or anything we can get on the theory that *any* kind of goods will keep going up in price while the value of our money keeps going down, down, down?

It's scarey.

And it should be.

A storm is gathering. A storm of hurricane violence. There's no way to avoid it and no place to hide. How do we protect ourselves? And what will we have to deal with when it's over? What kind of wreckage will we face?

I believe that you can't intelligently protect yourself unless you know what caused the storm, how to plot its course, and how to estimate the probable damage.

That is what this book is about.

As you start to read, you may find yourself thinking about the crash of 1929, and how, with World War II, we finally managed to get over it.

It would be dangerous to believe there is a fully parallel solution today.

But there *is one* parallel—a root cause common to both '29 and the situation today—Bloated Debt. Throughout monetary history, the uncontrolled growth of debt has always reached a point of collapse. In 1929 the trigger for collapse was the stock market. Today, the trigger could be any of a number of other factors.

To isolate them, we must first understand that the situation today is very much worse than it was, and for two reasons. First, the 1929 debt load did not even approach the mammoth world-wide debt of 1979. Second, in 1939 we had an abundantly cheap and almost unlimited supply of energy.

Today, both our industry and our military power are dependent on a source of energy half way around the world. Most of it must pass through a 2-mile strip of water, the Gulf of Hormuz. Think of that gulf as your oxygen tube, with some unfriendly fellow standing by with a pair of scissors. How good are your chances?

It is no exaggeration to say that the energy problem confronting Western civilization is a threat to its very existence. What most people do not realize is that a large part of the energy problem arises right out of the money problem —out of inflation itself.

Money and energy have become inseparable.

ENERGY AND MONEY

Oil-producing countries have been withdrawing their real wealth, safely stored in the ground, and trading it for a constantly shrinking asset—paper dollars. They foresee the day when, their wealth dissipated, they will be left holding nothing but promises of doubtful worth. By changing oil into currency, their natural resource is depleted. They don't need the money now. Why should they make the exchange except to oblige the West?

So the sinking value of money is a vital cause of swiftly rising oil prices. It is also a very good reason for the oil producers to curtail production beyond their own immediate needs.

Since the U. S. produces only half its energy requirements, it faces the greatest danger in its history. The energy problem and its possible solution are inextricably intertwined with the money problem. And the money problem is our overpowering load of debt.

DEBT

Through various manipulations, the government has been able to blow up the debt bubble to many times its earlier size. When it bursts, the result will be so much the worse.

In the summer of 1929, we didn't know which or whose pin would bust the bubble, and we don't know which pin it will be now. It could be real estate. It could be the falling dollar. It could be an oil embargo—or something entirely unforseen.

We fell into the depression because of a basic illiquidity—an extension of credit beyond the capacity of the system. When the highly margined stock market broke, it set off the whole disastrous chain of events.

Yet in 1929, we still had behind us two great sources of strength that are not available today—for the simple reason that they have been used up. We had a residual liquidity, the accumulated savings of the American people. And we had the energy, whenever we cared to call on it.

When the break came, capital of great strength simply went into hiding. It was immobilized by fear. Liquid corporations refused to expand. Liquid banks would only lend to those who were already liquid. Liquid municipalities guarded their savings. Money refused to take a chance, and money was the decisive factor because we were on a money economy.

Today, we are on a credit economy. If you had any money in the thirties, it was your own. Today, the credit in your bank account is somebody else's debt. Through over-application of Keynsian principles, calling for governmental heating and cooling of the economy, real money has disappeared. We have used up whatever real wealth we had in 1929, and mortgaged ourselves far into the future.

Fifty years ago, people who owned their own homes *owned* them—or at least owed only a little on them. To buy a home with ten percent cash down was unheard of and unthought of. Even cars were mostly paid for. In 1979, nothing is paid for. People still owe money on last year's vacations.

In 1929, the vast structure of credit, built on the credit card system, had not been invented. Today, this is an additional burden of debt.

The Great Depression ended with World War II. At that time the country was loaded with savings, with real hard cash, sweat-earned wealth. The depression didn't endure those terrible years for the lack of wealth behind the economy, but because few were prepared to risk that wealth. The rich knew what happened when money was lost—they had seen their friends jump out of skyscrapers, or go bankrupt. The less affluent knew what happened when money was lost—they went hungry. Rich, poor or middle class — all shared a common fear, and the result was a nation-wide contraction of capital.

Cash was king, and the best thing to do with it was to hang on. Interest rates were low—two or three percent—but at least they were safe. Safety was all-important. If someone wanted you to lend him money to develop a gold mine, you wanted to see twice the amount in gold first. Why take chances?

It took a war — the greatest the world had ever known—to pry the money loose and to end the depression. As a remedy it was not intentional, but intentional or not, it was a remedy that worked. War changed the rules. If private money owners would not spend, the government certainly would. With the government buying, private money came out of hiding. The huge War Bond issues were quickly subscribed. Jobs mushroomed. Factories went up overnight. With money in their pockets, and coming in regularly, people splurged. Everybody needed *something*.

In short, war opened the money chest. *But war could not replenish it.* And now that money is gone.

So the Great Depression and its aftermath of World War II provide us with no valid solution for getting out of our present mess, for several reasons. Among them, we simply do not have the residues of wealth to draw on. They have been used up and mortgaged far into the future, into our children's future.

It is a future that grows increasingly bleak as our debts continue to mount. One critical example:

Millions of workers have paid billions of dollars in Social Security payments so that they could be looked after in their old age. *That money has already been spent by the government.* In return, the government has given the Social Security Fund an IOU. What happens when payments become due (as they rapidly are)?

The money will simply be (and is being) collected all over again from the current working force in order to pay off the retirees who have paid in the first instance and are justifiably expecting security. But as the population grows older, a shrinking army of workers will have to pay for a growing army of retirees.

How long can the younger people afford to pay both for their own retirement and for the retirement of those whose money has been squandered by the government? Someday, inevitably, we will be told that the debt is hopeless.

I have said—and hold it to be true: *It is a natural law that a debt will always be paid; if not by the one who borrowed it, then by the one who lent it.*

In the case of Social Security, let the creditors beware.

OIL

To understand the worsening energy situation, we must clearly understand the following:

1. The global oil supply — where it comes from and where it is being consumed.

2. The immediate and near term effect of the 1979 revolution in Iran.

3. The implications for the U. S.

4. The down-to-earth expectations of national supply and price.

The following report (as of early 1979) tells the story.

The Global Supply

The world is now using 60 million barrels a day. The U.S., with five percent of the population, is using one-third of the daily supply, and the price is the cheapest of the industrial countries.

The oil demand in the Free World is 50 million b/d; in the Communist World 11 million b/d daily. The biggest producer in the world is U.S.S.R. with 11 million b/d. But Russia has shown no real increase in the last three years, and has put its Eastern partners on notice that they will be cut 1.4 million b/d over the next four years; making them new potential bidders for Mid-East oil.

The second largest producer is the U.S.A. with 9 million bbls. daily (half of what it uses). The third is Saudi Arabia with normally 8.5 million b/d, but temporarily running 9.5 to 10 million b/d. Iran was running third, exporting nearly 6 million b/d, but at the moment?

Here are some recent statistics on the world situation as compiled through efforts of John S. Herold Inc., leading world oil analysts and Bosworth Sullivan of Denver, Colorado.

Country	Current Demand	Current Prod.	Imports	Reserves in Billions Barrels
U.S.A.	19	9	10	30
Western Eur.	14	2	12	27
Japan	5	0	5	0
	38	11	27	57

(These are the big users. They have to buy 27 million b/d. Most of it comes from 20 million b/d produced in the Middle East. Now look at the rest of the picture with emphasis on the exporters.)

Country	Current Demand	Current Prod.	Imports	Reserves in Billions Barrels
Saudi Arabia	0	10	Exp. 10	160
Other Mid-East	1	7	" 6	150
Africa	1	6	" 5	60
Latin America	4	5	" 1	50
Iran	1	1	" 0	67
Canada	2	2	" 0	8
Other Free World	3	3	" 0	20
	12	34	" 22	515

World oil shortage — 5 million b/d.

The first frightening fact is this: The big industrial nations import two-thirds of their oil. Of the 27 million b/d, a full 20 million comes from the Middle East. When Iran was exporting 6 million b/d, we were in balance.

Except by the grace of Saudi Arabia and some African countries like Libya, we are 5 million b/d short. Actual shortage (not shown in table) however, in March was about 3 million b/d. (For perspective, realize that the big Alaska pipeline is flowing 1.2 million b/d.)

The present world shortage is being made up out of inventory. *When that disappears, we can expect a worldwide cutback on the use of oil.*

Since shortages always result in higher prices, we must expect to see an oil price of $18 to $20 a barrel this year—placing a severe strain on all economics and threatening zero growth.

Moreover, there is no guarantee Saudi Arabia will hold exports at 10 million b/d, which is 1.5 million more than it wants to produce.

In March 1979, world renowned oil consultant, Walter Levy, said: "*If any mid-east country halts its oil production, the United States and the Western World have had it.*"

He also said that with demand outstripping supply, OPEC oil prices will increase by as much as $10 a barrel. And if oil prices reach $20 a barrel by year's end, the U.S. balance of payments will soar from *$45 billion to $65 billion*. The effect on the dollar would be too horrible to contemplate. (By late summer they had already reached $18.00 a barrel.)

❁   ❁   ❁   ❁   ❁

The question may well be asked: Couldn't the suppliers produce more? Well, yes, to some extent.

Going full out, *Saudi Arabia* could produce 12 million b/d, but she is showing more signs of retrenchment; talks of cutting back to 8.5 million b/d. Any more would come at a very high price.

Other Middle Eastern countries could produce 8 million b/d instead of 7, but are already producing some of that to fill the Iranian shortage.

Iran might produce 5 million b/d instead of the current 4 million, but that is not to be counted on at all.

Fact is the 5 million b/d shortage worldwide was caused by the shutdown in Iran December 25th, 1978.

Africa could—if it went full out—produce 1 million b/d more.

(In other words, if all the oil wells in the world would go full out to oblige the U.S. and other industrial countries—and if Iran sold 2 or 3 million b/d—we would have as much oil to use as we did up to December 25, 1978.)

Canada, Mexico and Western Europe are producing all they can. Mexico is producing 1.3 million b/d. It hopes to double that by the end of 1980. That doesn't help much now, and percentage wise it will help very little over the next few years.

People who talk about Mexico as another Saudi Arabia also are dreamers. Mexico has big reserves, but no one knows how big. And it will take some years to bring them on the market.

❁   ❁   ❁   ❁   ❁

What about China? Charles G. Masters of the U.S. Geological Survey says this: "It will take ten years to have a good idea of how much oil China has, but I think it will be measured in tens of billions of barrels, not hundreds of billions."

Worldwide, geologists have a pretty good idea in broad terms where we stand compared to where we have been:

There are 600 sedimentary basins in the world outside of the *deep* oceans that *could* contain oil. Of these, 240 have been found not to contain enough oil to produce, and 160 are producing.

Consulting geologist, Keith Hubb, says the 200 unexplored basins lie in deep water, near the poles or where drilling conditions will be harsh.

The point is, China may have very substantial reserves of oil, but they will be of little or no use to us during the crisis of 1979 and into the next five years.

What about the *U.S.A.* itself? In 1978 it found 2 billion barrels of new oil; better than the 1.75 billion of 1977. But with consumption at 20 million b/d — that two billion, if it could be produced all at once, would last the U.S. only a little over 3 months. In reality, such reserves are produced over the course of some 15-20-or more years. U.S. never found more than 3 billion a year in its heyday.

Is the U.S. working hard enough to find oil? Well, in 1978 it drilled 48,161 wells compared with 32,893 in 1974, and 29,467 wells in 1970.

Total footage read like this: 1970 — 142,431,000; in 1974 it was 153,164,000; and 1978 chalked up 229,149,000 feet.

And all this time the daily production capacity of the U.S.A. has declined from 10 million b/d to 9 million b/d, and reserves have declined.

Recently several leading oil companies have expressed pessimism over Baltimore Canyon, which had also been hailed as a great new bonanza. Repeated wells have found the structure empty. All we have got so far is one good gas discovery.

The second frightening fact is that 447 billion barrels of the Free World's total of 515 billion barrels is located in the Middle East and Africa—Arab or Arab affiliated lands, either unstable, militarily weak, or vulnerable to Russian domination. Of this, 380 billion of prolific production lies dead center in the Middle East. That outlet is principally the Gulf of Oman in the narrow opening of the Strait of Hormuz.

Early 1979 Iran choked off 6 million b/d. The best we can expect this year (or maybe long thereafter) is 4 million, leaving the 2 million as a shortage. We must depend on the Muslim countries to make this up, and to be *willing to take depreciating paper dollars in exchange*. Will they, especially, in view of the overuse and underpricing of oil in the U.S.?

PRICES OF REGULAR GASOLINE (Feb. 1979)
(Source — John S. Herold Petroleum Outlook)

Country	$ Per Gallon	Country	$ Per Gallon
U.S.A.	.70	England	2.12
Phillipines	.84	Brazil	2.13
Canada	1.05	Switzerland	2.15
Taiwan	1.50	West Germany	2.22
Singapore	1.52	Denmark	2.35
Belgium	1.84	Norway	2.43
Spain	1.85	India	2.45
Austria	2.10	France	2.74
		Italy	3.53

THE BURSTING BUBBLE

We have taken a quick overall look at the two major factors that have caused our current mess—overblown debt and under-abundant energy.

The balloon cannot contain itself much longer. We are facing the collapse of the credit markets, a flood of bankruptcies, and the advent of the worst depression in the history of the world.

The next question: how do we get out of it?

To answer this, let's first examine in greater detail the history and causes of the morass in which we find ourselves.

SOME GUIDELINES

Literature about money often seems meaningless because its terms of reference are meaningless. What precisely does a *billion dollars* mean? One million dollars a thousand times over doesn't bring it much closer to home. Look at it this way:

1. If your government borrows a billion dollars, it has borrowed five dollars on your behalf. (There are 200 million plus people in the U.S.A.). You now owe $5.00.

2. When the U. S. piled up red ink of $50 billion dollars in 1977, it signed you up for a debt of $250. If you are the head of a family of four, the government borrowed $1,000 for you to pay back, and to pay interest on.

How will you be asked to pay all this? Through your taxes. How did the government borrow the money? By selling its securities, or IOU's, which run for various terms. The government will have to buy them back when they mature. Meanwhile, the government will have to pay interest on them.

Where will the government get the money to buy back its IOU's and, meanwhile, pay interest on them?

In two ways. One way is to borrow *more* money. That is, issue new securities to pay for the old ones. Of course, that just postpones the day of reckoning and swells the bill for interest. The government might even have to sell more securities just to pay the *interest* on the old debts.

The other way is to boost taxes—your income tax, taxes on the company you work for, excise taxes on phone calls you make, or cigarettes you smoke, or liquor you drink, or things you buy. Tariffs on imported cars and the like. Of course, this is the only real way out. But will Congress dare to raise taxes enough to pay on the debt? Will you allow them to? Could you pay your taxes if they did?

3. From 1975 to April 1978, the government increased the national debt from about $495 billion to over $746 billion. That's $250+ billions. Whether you know it or not, your family of four went into hock for $5,000. *Your* family? Who else? On who else's credit does the government borrow but on the credit of its citizens? At eight percent compounded, you will pay about $400 interest annually on that debt.

If you don't pay, the debt simply increases to $5,400. Whatever other debts you chalked up from 1975 through 1977, don't forget to add this one.

4. By this means, your government now has total indebtedness approaching $800 billion. ($798.733 billion in January 1979) And interest rates are up. That's

roughly $4,000 against you if you are single, or $16,000 against your family of four.

5. *Every infant born faces a debt of $4,000* the moment it lets out its first yell. No wonder it yells! Unless the debt interest is paid by the government (through taxes), the debt will be $8,000 when that child is ten years old; $16,000 when he is twenty; $32,000 when he is thirty; $64,000 when he is forty; $128,000 when he is fifty; $256,000 down the line if he quits work at age sixty. *That's if the government does not borrow another cent for the next sixty years.* That's also figuring ten percent simple—not compound—interest, and assumes that nothing changes for the worse. A rather dangerous assumption.

6. For the moment, consider the country at large. It will help you to arrive at an assessment of the monetary situation.

The national public debt is now nearing $800 billion. Suppose the government never borrows another net cent for the next sixty years. Interest will double that debt to $1600 billion in ten years; $3200 billion in twenty years; $6400 billion in thirty years; $14,800 billion in forty years; $28,600 billion in fifty years; and $51,200 billion in sixty years. *Fifty-one trillion dollars!*

Assuming no more net borrowing, the annual interest on the debt in sixty years will be in the neighborhood of five trillion dollars. (Who wants to live in *that* neighborhood!) Today you pay government annual interest of $41.6 million (as of first quarter, 1979). In sixty years you pay interest of nearly a thousand times as much. Preposterous and impossible! Isn't it clear that such a structure must collapse?

As you read, always try to relate the huge figures to yourself. Keep in mind one billion dollars is five dollars to *you.* Any and every financial commitment by your government is on behalf of you and in your name. Who else?

                    *   *   *   *   *

Whether you are at the top of the ladder or just starting on the first rung, you must be shaken by these thoughts. More so by the fact that the financial press, while it copiously publishes the statistics, jealously guards and conceals their meaning.

Whatever your position, you may have a family and hopefully you have a future. An understanding of what *has* happened and what *is* happening may help you to deal with what *will* happen. A well-informed public may still save America from a monetary catastrophe. If not that, at least this book may help you to save yourself.

1. CHANGED PEOPLE IN A NEW ERA

History is made up of tidal movements. They are not recognizable as such while they are going on; only in retrospect do they become discernible. Thus we speak of the Age of the Pyramids and the Glory of Egypt. Even earlier we recognize the Stone Age and the Bronze Age. We see the Grecian Age of enlightenment, the age of the Roman Empire, the Middle Ages, the Industrial Revolution.

Within the ages there are eras. These eras are extended periods of certain prevailing ideas. The time of the Crusades was such an era. It was fashionable for staunch Christians to teach the infidel Turks what they had better believe.

There was the era of expansion of mighty empires. Nations sought to acquire lands in all corners of the earth, and to exploit them, and to bring them under the central flag. This practice was quite acceptable. The era of imperialism persisted right into the twentieth century.

But while these eras were in progress, they were hardly recognizable. Probably no newspaper wrote about the Industrial Revolution as it was progressing. Only later do we see that it represented, indeed, a revolutionary change in the mode of human existence on the earth.

Less talked about is the era of the gold standard, where for nearly two hundred years the British pound was absolutely as good as gold and could be freely exchanged for gold by anyone at any time. The real gold stood behind the pound. It was the era of the greatest monetary stability and progress in the history of the world up to that time.

World War I marked the beginning of the era of credit on a massive scale. The world was prosperous. Savings were large. All that was needed to get the money to fight the war was to borrow on these holdings. Owners were issued certificates—called bonds—that were simply a promise to pay back the real wealth that was being borrowed. Because these bonds were believed to be as good as money, and the money as good as gold, they were transferable at face value from person to person, or country to country.

This massive debt, however, came to roost in the late twenties when it was discovered that the real wealth represented by the bonds could not be paid back in full. Britain had to back away from the gold standard. The inflation of that period reduced the value of the debt and was a partial repudiation of the debt.

During World War II the same process was repeated on a vastly larger scale. Moreover, the accumulation of debt did not end with the war; it accelerated as the winners and losers alike undertook to rebuild the horrendous destruction.

Instead of paying off the debts accumulated by the fruitless efforts of war, governments had to rebuild. They also wanted to expand; so they borrowed more, issued more bonds. Debt piled on debt.

The only limit to debt is a limit of confidence.

As long as the instrument of debt—printed money or bonds—continues to be accepted at face value, it can be circulated from person to person and country to country. When there is no longer enough private money to buy more bonds, the Federal Reserve manufactures the money. And the new bonds circulate—just as counterfeit money would—along with the old bonds, which when issued, represented real money, in other words, real commodities, articles or service of real value. They no longer do.

Quite unwittingly we were moving into a NEW ERA. It was the era of inflation. So great was the confidence of the brave new after-the-war world that it seemed as if this could go on forever. The following line of thought became fashionable: What does it matter what we owe? Business is good. We owe this debt to ourselves. And as long as we have growth and prosperity, who cares what figures are on paper?

This type of thinking remained popular over a protracted period.

It was downright unpopular to suggest that someday these debts might have to be paid off. That would take the money out of the banking system! (When a debt is paid off, that amount of money, originally issued simply by a book entry, is canceled out). Taking the money out of the system would have reduced the money supply, causing a contraction of business. In no way could business be allowed to contract, so government came up with a new answer: if debts *had* to be paid off—just print more money to pay them. No one seemed to bother to ask who would *buy* the new debts. And even if someone *would* buy, what would he buy *with* when nearly all of the *real* wealth had already been used as an instrument of credit?

And herein lay the seeds of the collapse. Because when all the real wealth had been gathered together and committed, the expanded money could do no more than water it down. We had a gallon of real whisky. When there was no more real whisky to add, the governments and the moneymen added water. For a long time the watered-down whisky was passed off as real whisky. As long as no one tasted it, or demanded an analysis, it worked just as well as the real whisky. So now we had two gallons of whisky and later, because we were getting into trouble with wages and costs, we added another gallon of water. Now we had three gallons, but really, still, only one gallon of whisky.

By 1978 this process had continued to the point where we had five gallons of money, which was really worth only one gallon. Almost without exception everything needed by human beings had increased in price between four to six times. A nickel cup of coffee was now worth thirty cents. A $1,000 car of three decades ago was now worth $5,000; a $10,000 home of 1940 was now worth $50,000 or more. We had simply watered down the whisky.

Without knowing it we had, because of World War II, and continual expansion of our social programs, entered into a new era—a third of a century of inflation.

This was not the first time that the human race, having become prosperous, had overextended itself and imagined that prosperity was a God-given and eternal right. It had happened with Genghis Khan. It had happened with Babylon. It had happened with Rome. It had happened with France. It had happened with Germany. The result was, without exception, consistently, identically, and unalterably the same—collapse of money as a medium of exchange.

The new era, this latest era of inflation, differed from the others in two important aspects. Firstly, it was massive—worldwide—and on a scale never before dreamed of. This was possible because of the invention of the credit mechanism of bonds, IOU's of various types, made prevalent in the U.S. by the Federal Reserve System that had been empowered to create money simply by book entry; and by the use of the Gold Exchange Standard that virtually doubled the amount of credit previously available for one ounce of gold.

All of this tended to conceal the unbelievable mass of credit.

The second difference was the vastly improved means of communication and, therefore, of propaganda. As long as the newspapers believed that the process of inflation could continue without disaster, there was a good chance the public would believe it, especially when there never seemed to be any penalty for the accumulation of credit. The magician can make you believe that he has ten rabbits instead of one, as long as you don't demand actual delivery of the rabbits. And so we had the invention of Special Drawing Rights—or, as it was so inanely named, "paper gold."

The name itself would have been enough to alert a man out of the Bronze Age to suspect that something was fishy. But with all of the economists and the highest monetary authorities believing in the fantasy, and propagating the fantasy through the public press, the population, still eating beefsteak and driving big cars, began to believe in the fantasy too. Money need not *be* anything. As long as the proper figures were written down in the proper book, money at the central bank level was unlimited.

Historians in future years will find it hard to believe that supposedly sane adult people could fall for such a crazy scheme. But humanity moves in waves of fashion. And when it is fashionable to believe that paper is in every respect substitutable for gold, then you will be very unpopular if you should take the opposite view, even if you try to prove it by setting the two substances side by side. They will call you unenlightened—you just haven't caught up with modern times. Obviously a lot of important money disagreed; in 1974 gold reached $200. By 1978 the whole world was beginning to realize that paper was transitory. The resulting uneasiness was responsible for the October 1979 monetary crisis that sent the dollar plunging to new lows all around the world. By now billions of the world's people have been reawakened.

They *know* that we have, indeed, been swept up in an era of inflation. They may *not* know that this era is in a terminal condition; and that the inevitable result of the termination of vast inflation is collapse. But they must try to determine what we shall face in this era of collapse and plan as well as possible to withstand the enormous social dislocations that will accompany the collapse of money.

The vastness of the changes facing our civilization and our mode of life will tax your imagination before you have finished.

PRECIPITATION WITHOUT WARNING

A book about money—if it is to be worth a reader's time—must be of practical value. Few are interested in the theories of money or the academic considerations that so fascinate the professors and economists who formulate economic policy.

Unfortunately, it will be hard to accept the practical conclusions drawn here unless, first of all, we understand the fundamentals that are the very bedrock of the economy, and therefore of money; by extension they are also the fundamentals of the social structure of our country, and of the world.

Almost anyone could see by reading the newspapers in 1974 and 1975 that we were building up to some kind of drastic adjustment. The bulk of the population had faith that the planners in the backrooms had the situation well in hand and were already planning to implement the blueprints that would set us back on an even keel. Apparently this is not the case. Thus far, it seems that the planners have no idea how to restore equilibrium to the international monetary situation, and consequently to the various western economies. It is becoming painfully obvious that these men are stumbling forward one step at a time, hoping against hope that some as yet unforseen development will take place to extricate them from a deepening morass. Therein lies the cause for alarm and the reason why individual financial survival demands understanding first of all, of the conditions that have brought us to the brink of a monetary collapse.

Moreover, there is an urgency to our understanding.

Readers may remember, from early chemistry courses, that adding a solution of weak sodium hydroxide to a strong solution of hydrochloric acid, bit by bit, could continue without making any noticeable change. It would be very easy to think the process could go on forever. But sooner or later there came a critical point. When that critical point arrived, suddenly the solution changed. The clear liquid was now a cloudy mass. The precipitation had taken place instantly.

Inflation in the economic system is like adding a weak solution of sodium hydroxide. Its early introduction results in no visible difference. The process can be continued by degrees to the point where the whole population begins to accept inflation with complacence. After all, it hasn't wrecked us yet, why should we think it's going to later on? Why not learn to live with it?

This became the generally accepted attitude through the late sixties and early seventies. We must learn to live with inflation.

But by 1974, a keen observer could see that we must be reaching the point of saturation, and therefore nearing the point of precipitation. With interest rates above twelve percent, how could building go on? How could a wage earner expect to pay off a home, a car, and all of the other so-called necessities? How could business expect to expand without continually higher prices? It didn't. We had the worst recession since the thirties.

The stock market had been in decline since 1966. Although it still stood at 850 in 1974, compared with 1000 in 1966, few people stopped to consider that inflation during that period had amounted to more than one-third and that, therefore, the 850 level of the Dow Jones was actually more like 650. *When D.J. hit 580 in late 1974, its real value was more like 380 compared with the value of 1000 in early 1966.* When by late summer 1979 the D.J. still hovered around 850, it looked like it had recovered well from that old low of 1974 (D.J. 380). But continued inflation since 1974 now made 850 equal to barely more than 400 in 1966 dollars.

This was first pointed out in the graph reproduced on Page 18 (MFE Newsletter, April 1975). By 1976, *Wall Street Week* had wakened to the illusory nature of the Dow Jones. By 1978 various publications all over the country were showing similar graphs giving the real value of the Dow Jones. By October 1978 in terms of purchasing power, the Dow Jones was down to its level of 1913.

The quoted value of the stocks on the New York Stock Exchange had depreciated two-thirds in real value! During eight years of inflation and continually higher prices and continually higher wages, we had, nevertheless, been sinking deeper in an inexorable downtrend. But the stockbrokers, with their noses deep in detail, didn't recognize it. The public didn't recognize it. That's why the chemical mix hadn't precipitated.

Well, what if it should precipitate?

When the weak solution of inflation has been added to the economy so that it reaches the critical point, we have the precipitation of credit.

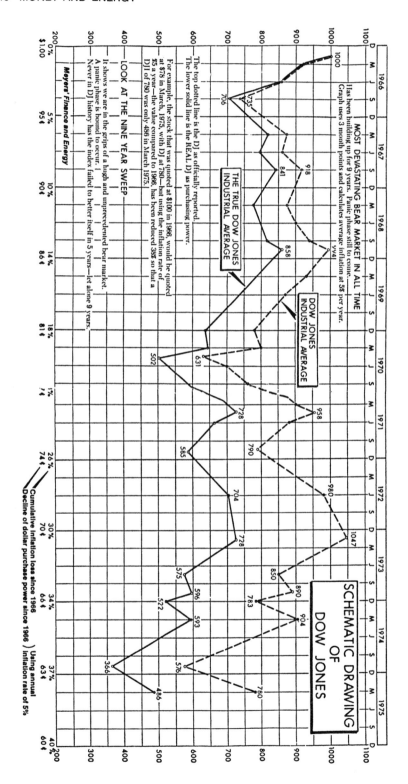

MOST DEVASTATING BEAR MARKET IN ALL TIME
Has been building up for 9 years. Panic phase still to come.
Graph uses 3 month points and calculates average inflation at 5% per year.

THE TRUE DOW JONES
INDUSTRIAL AVERAGE

DOW JONES
INDUSTRIAL AVERAGE

The top dotted line is the DJI as officially reported.
The lower solid line is the REAL DJI as purchasing power.

For example, the stock that was quoted at $100 in 1966, would be quoted
at $75 in March, 1975, with DJI at 780—but using the inflation rate of
$5 a year—the value compared to 1966, has been reduced 38% so that a
DJI of 780 was only 486 in March 1975.

LOOK AT THE NINE YEAR SWEEP—
It shows we are in the grips of a huge and unprecedented bear market.
A panic phase is bound to occur.
Never in DJI history has the index failed to better itself in 5 years—let alone 9 years.

Meyers' Finance and Energy

SCHEMATIC DRAWING
OF
DOW JONES

Cumulative inflation loss since 1966) Using annual
Decline of dollar purchase power since 1966) inflation rate of 5%

THE GREATEST BEAR MARKET IN THE HISTORY
OF THE WORLD WAS CLEARLY VISIBLE BY 1973

The above graph, published in 1976, is purposefully not updated here. The final reading of 780 in March 1975 compares with a final reading 805 on December 31, 1978. However, during those three years, inflation had increased by another twenty-five percent. The real reading of the Dow Jones at the end of 1978 (on the basis of value) was more like 402.5 compared with the 858 high of 1968.

When the interest rates get high enough, the borrowers have to scamper to borrow more to serve the interest on their debts. But in this era of credit and inflation there are many more borrowers than there are creditors. The debt load is enormously larger than the assets. Corporations in America owe 90 cents on every dollar of assets. But with the spiraling interest rates, the servicing of a debt of 90 percent threatens to destroy the asset.

There are several signs that precipitation is imminent. In 1971 we had the near bankruptcy of Lockheed, which nearly triggered the bankruptcy of the Bank of America. The situation was only saved by an act of Congress. The government of the country had to use taxpayer money to keep one corporation from going bankrupt. Then we had the Penn Central, the largest corporation of its kind in the world. Again the same remedy. In 1974 we had a severe warning when the Franklin National Bank, one of the largest in the United States, had to call on the Federal Reserve System to keep it solvent. The frightening thing about the event was that the news was allowed to get out at all. Normally banks will pitch in to save another bank in order to maintain confidence in the banking system. The banks of the United States either were unwilling or unable to assist Franklin. The Federal Reserve had to help the Federal Bank Insurance system (FDIC) to do it.

New York City began to fight off bankruptcy in 1976, pleading to the Congress of the United States to bail it out. It looked like large banks and thousands of bondholders would be left holding the bag. In the end, the Federal Government guaranteed New York City Bonds on the premise that New York would balance its budget. On the basis of this guarantee, the city struggled on, but it was becoming increasingly clear that New York will never balance the budget, and that its huge debt will never be paid.

By September 1979 the wolf was back at the door; Chrysler Corporation being the wolf and the White House the door. The close calls with credit precipitation by New York, Penn Central and Lockheed were to be tested again, for a Chrysler failure would endanger the banks thereby posing the threat of national liquidity on a grand scale.

There is another lesson to be learned from the chemistry lesson.

After the solution of hydrochloric acid has reached the stage of precipitation, it will not matter how much more hydrochloric acid is used. You can pour in five gallons. It will have no effect. Once the solution has been precipitated, it cannot be *un*precipitated by the addition of more hydrochloric acid.

Once inflation has precipitated the credit structure, no amount of additional inflation can bring it back. It can be poured in till hell freezes over. When credit has collapsed, no amount of inflation can restore it.

The end product of the precipitation of credit is deflation.

Simply expressed, deflation means getting back to the things—and the values—that are real. We find that the prices prior to the precipitation were far too high. So now we are back at lower prices. That means that the money we have—if we have been fortunate to hang on to money—will now buy much more than it would before the period of precipitation. The precipitation of credit has caused bankruptcies far and wide. This has reduced the money supply. It has reduced the money in circulation so drastically that all of the goods and services combined are worth much less in numbers of dollars than they were prior to the precipitation.

This is bad news for any creditor. It is bad news for the overextended banks of America. It is bad news for the heavily stock-invested pension funds. It is bad news for debtors who may be called to pay, because unless they can pay they will find that they have become a part of the precipitation, which is bankruptcy.

During late 1974 and 1975 the chorus of those predicting continuing inflation was becoming louder and louder. The only hope for avoiding precipitation was the hope that the critical concentration was still a long way off. If everyone would believe that, perhaps confidence could be retained so that indeed the critical level could be further delayed. And miraculously it was.

But history tells us there is inevitably and always a critical level to inflation—a level at which the precipitation of credit occurs. In advance, the precise point is almost impossible to know. But one thing we know for certain, when it comes we will be living in a different "solution," in a new economic climate. In short, the environment in which we have thrived will suddenly have been transformed into something totally different. The era of inflation and debt will have disappeared. Some will be ready, *most will not*, to face new circumstances.

Let us see if we cannot arrive at some fundamental conclusions that, hopefully, will preserve our wealth and our substance, by seeking the understanding that puts us in a position to act with confidence and—once those actions have been taken—to weather the storm.

The energy crisis brought the American population up short. Within a few months, inflation had precipitated a worldwide energy dilemma. Few realize that the cause of the crisis was inflation. The oil-producing nations were reacting to their discovery that the store of value they kept in the ground was being depreciated quickly on the surface once they had turned it into dollars. As long as they kept it in the ground, it retained its value. Once it was pumped above ground, it lost value. As long as they didn't need the cash, it didn't make sense to produce the oil except at four times the price.

But no news announcement from Washington ever bothered to explain that the depreciating U. S. dollar was the direct cause of the energy crisis. Nor that the higher price of oil would mean a higher cost of living—and that the higher cost of living would mean a reduced living standard for all people of the United States, unless somehow the United States could produce more with which to pay for the raw materials from abroad. And further, that a contraction in the standard of living, with the attendant reduction in spending and borrowing, could only mean unemployment and lower profits for corporations. Such conditions would, of course, precipitate the calling-in of loans. People who are desperate to pay their loans to avoid bankruptcy would have to pay even higher interest rates.

That is precisely what happened.

2. THE NATURE OF MONEY

Money is stored-up labor—the fruit of sweat, put into cold storage. But if it deteriorates in storage, who is going to save it? If you could only be paid off in tomatoes, would you bother to work in order to save? Your currency would only rot. A collapsed monetary currency rots in much the same way.

The collapse of a currency is not a new event in world history. It has happened countless times. When a currency collapses it ceases to operate as a medium of exchange, and trade reverts to barter.

Unremitting inflation of a currency has resulted invariably, inevitably, monotonously, and without exception in the collapse of the currency.

It's strange that a cause-and-effect relationship as old as Babylon, one that has never varied, could be so repeatedly challenged—that presumably intelligent men could be led to believe that they somehow had stumbled on a method that could reverse natural law.

Universal and natural laws are well known to everyone—from peasant to king. If the king drops a stone from between his fingers it will always go down. It will never go up. It will never go sideways. The peasant knows this equally well. There has never been an exception to this law in all of the history on this earth. In outer space it may work differently, but we're concerned with life on earth, and with earth-bound economics. Like gravity, economics is predictable.

There are a number of truths we know about it.

You cannot consume more than you produce, unless you (a) take something away from someone else, or (b) unless you get him to lend it to you. In the case of (b) you must pay it back. If you do not pay it back, you have either confiscated it, or you have tricked him into turning over to you without compensation that which was his. In any case, the excess of your consumption over your production had been at the expense of another man, who consequently had to consume less.

This brings us to a fundamental moral law of our civilization. *No man may be permitted to take by force that which belongs to another man.* In other words, *Thou Shalt Not Steal.*

Without this cornerstone of conduct—without this prohibition—our Western society would be vastly different. We would have total anarchy. We would constantly plunder one another. Ten—not even two—people could not cooperate to build a shelter—because, when it was finished, the stronger would take the shelter for himself and turn the weaker one out.

So, underlying the structure of our society is the recognition of private property—the inalienable right of a man to keep what is his even though he may not have the physical strength to defend this right.

As our society developed, men willingly submitted to certain restraints in order to make life better for all. They agreed that any of their members violating this cardinal rule would be punished. Not too long ago the cattle owners of the West collectively hanged rustlers from the branches of trees for the violation of this law of private property.

Without this law, liberty, and prosperity are impossible because every man would live in fear that the fruit of his effort would be taken from him. Also he would only exert effort to obtain essentials from day to day. To try to accumulate a *Store of Value* would be pointless.

From this, then, we may say: You can only consume more than you produce at the expense of someone else; and if you do, you will eventually be punished.

In other words, consumption in excess of production will always result in a penalty for someone. This is true for a person, true for a group, and true for a country.

Thus it is clear that one country cannot, in aggregate, consume in excess of its production except with a resulting penalty to another country.

When you have said this, you have said that no nation in the world can run a balance-of-payments deficit without paying it back or without the consequences of its excess consumption having been paid for by others. The question of who will absorb the penalty is the basis of the current confrontations—and the unremitting crises in the world.

With this in mind, we can now more clearly define the nature of money.

A STANDARD OF MEASURE

Man's desires to acquire goods and to hoard them beyond his present needs are unlimited. His desire to acquire the services of other humans is likewise unlimited, since such services can be used in the acquisition of further goods.

But we have seen that the acquisitiveness of man would result in anarchy unless restrained; and so that acquisitiveness in organized society finds expression in the form of trade.

He acquires a thing he wants by giving up something of his own, or by performing a service. The more he performs for others (work), the more things he can acquire. If, by chance, he has an unusual talent, it may be that for the products of an hour of his time he can engage someone of a lesser talent for a period of two or three hours. So, in a free society, one man's productivity may be higher than the productivity of another; in that event, he will end up with more worldly goods and services.

But how can such things as the differential productivity of two men be measured? It can only be measured in goods, in *things*. How can this exchange (barter) of goods proceed in a smooth and orderly manner? The answer is the use of a standard of measurement. And that is the first function of money—a medium of exchange.

The most reliable understanding of money occurs at the lowest level of labor. We all understand that we want to acquire certain goods and services and that we are the sole dictators of the amount of effort we will exert to acquire these wants. So, in the final analysis—regardless of all the monetary experts—the people will become the dictators of price.

To understand that in depth, we should have the outlook of a laborer, a producer, a small farmer, a carpenter. The more closely we think like those who sell only services (e.g. engineers and doctors) the less we comprehend. When we reach the top pinnacle of political and monetary theory, we shall have lost contact with the earthly meaning of money.

And so, in your imagination, I want you to join with me upon an adventure.

We shall suppose that we are going to form a new colony on some hospitable but uninhabited isle. There is a boatload of us, and we are taking along with us every conceivable commodity and every type of worker as a cross-section of our society. We start with all of this.

We call our country *Freedonia*.

When we have finally disembarked on the island, someone suddenly remembers that we have forgotten to bring any money. We have the price lists, everything — and a list of who owns what — but no money.

On our consignment list of property, every person has been accredited with an equal share of commodities, both necessities and luxuries. For example everyone has in the storehouse an ownership of three cans of pipe tobacco, although many do not smoke. Everyone has two bottles of perfume. I have soon smoked up my pipe tobacco, and I ask my wife what am I going to do. She replies that Jack Jones, who likes candy, ran out of candy, and he worked for several hours for Mr. Smith who was building a sunporch and who did not like candy, and got, in exchange, candy from Smith. Perhaps I can do the same for pipe tobacco.

I say no, I do not want to work for Smith; I will trade my accredited perfume with Mrs. Doe for pipe tobacco that she does not use. When I go to Mrs. Doe she does not want to trade with me because she does not want any more perfume, but she does love canned peaches. We have eaten our canned peaches. So now I must hunt for someone else who does not care for canned peaches, but who likes perfume. I must trade my perfume for the canned peaches, which then I, in turn, take to Mrs. Doe and offer for the pipe tobacco.

This is barter. This is the way primitive trade took place. It was cumbersome, and organized society advanced slowly under the system. An immense amount of effort was wasted in matching the customers of trade. It's obvious that our new colony will not function very smoothly under this system, although we have collectively all the goods that we need.

The elected leaders confer. Someone says that since we have all the prices and the values and a complete inventory of all the materials, we will manufacture our own money to the exact extent of the materials we have. We will make this in denominations large and small to accommodate any size of purchase. All of the materials will be placed together in a storehouse, and taken from the ownership of all the people. All of the people will be given their credit (money) to the extent of their ownership in these materials.

Now I do not have to search out Mrs. Doe at all. I can go to the storehouse and for the prescribed amount of money I can immediately purchase my tobacco.

The leaders have also decided that since money could be so easily lost or misplaced, a clearing house for money itself would be in order. All or any of us may place the money we have received into our accounts in this clearing house or bank.

We have made a terrific stride forward. All of the time and effort expended in the search to match buyers and sellers can now be applied to production. We can use this time to build more shelters or swings or umbrellas or whatnot—greatly improving our comfort and, therefore, our standard of living. This plan seems to be working out very well.

After a while we find that we have assets—things—commodities we have grown in the garden—beyond the original amount of money collectively deposited in this bank, and we are being hampered in the matter of exchange because of a lack of money to match the expanded amount of goods. Prices have been going down. Either they will continue to go down as the volume of goods increases, or we shall have to have more money.

Again a meeting is called. We find prices have gone down about ten percent. So we decided to increase the money supply by ten percent. We have discovered that to make this colony work smoothly we shall continually have to increase the money supply as the results of our labors increase the goods.

We adopt this policy, and now we are in high gear. There is no limit to the amount of hours a man may work and produce, and thus earn more of this money with which to buy more goods that have been also produced by others. Although our money supply has increased, prices remain perfectly stable. Money is functioning smoothly as a medium of exchange.

It was the discovery of money as a medium of exchange that led to an enormous advance in civilization and to the harnessing of the power, abilities, initiative and the ingenuity of man. All of his talents were put to work for the collective benefit of all, although each man was able to retain for himself the fruits of his own labor.

Note that it was completely unnecessary for the leaders of this colony to pass a law that this money is legal tender and must be accepted as a payment of debts. Such a law would have been superfluous. Natural law is in operation. Each and all of the colonists know that all of the other colonists are anxious to acquire this money. It is not necessary to force it on anybody. It represents real goods. *It is in fact real wealth.* It is not just a symbol of wealth. It is wealth itself in a *different* and *convenient* form. Real money is a highly desired medium of exchange, and it *is* wealth.

Note too that it will not be necessary to have any laws regulating the price of items. If those who grow potatoes in their gardens grow more potatoes than the aggregate collective demands, they will not be able to sell all those potatoes. The result will be that some offer potatoes at a lower price. This brings down the price of most of the sellers of potatoes. Under these circumstances some housewives will say, "We will eat more potatoes and fewer turnips which have been in short supply this year." So the potatoes are consumed at the lower price, and the price of turnips, which had risen beyond the year before, begins to recede to the normal price. The producers of the community are responsive to these conditions and regulate their crops accordingly.

Any controls by the state or the elected representatives of our new state would be superfluous and disruptive.

This machine is operating like a dream.

Also notice we have no gold or silver. People are able to buy gold and silver jewelry in the stores, but it is not a functioning part of our monetary system. Up to this point there has been no reason to introduce gold and silver money, or any kind of backing for the money. The backing for this money is the actual commodities in use. Each piece of money is actually a warehouse receipt. There is no need for an intervening medium.

Herein lies the basis of the argument of so many people that gold is unnecessary in the functioning of a monetary system. At this stage, they have won the argument. But this society has not finished growing. There are new developments to come. And certain laws have not, up to this point, come into play.

3. A STORE OF VALUE

In our Freedonia, money is a highly reliable store of value. We know that the money we save today can be used tomorrow or next year to buy exactly the same value in goods that it will buy today. This is true because the money supply is kept constant with the amount of goods available. As long as this condition is maintained, we can have complete confidence in this money—even though it is only paper. For, in truth, it is much more than paper, it is the actual *warehouse receipt* of goods *physically* existing.

Unfortunately and unknowingly we have picked up a few crooks in our excursion to this new colony. Any society contains some crooks—people who will try to acquire the assets of others, if not by force, then by subterfuge.

It has not gone unnoticed by these crooks that the printed pieces of paper money can be reproduced. With the help of some smart managers and good technicians, these crooks set up a clandestine printing press and begin to produce apparently identical money. This money finds its way into circulation. The fake five-dollar bill will buy every bit as much as the real five-dollar bill. Now our system begins to malfunction.

If we had a million dollars representing the goods and services, and our crooks produce one hundred thousand dollars of bogus money that becomes intermixed with the real money, we have a money supply ten percent in excess of our warehouse receipts. It is clear that if more money bids for the same goods, the price of the goods goes up. If ten men have one dollar to buy ten bags of flour, and if someone slips each one of them an extra dollar, the price that can be paid for the flour under competitive bidding will rise. In general this doesn't happen right away, because some of the money is placed in savings accounts, but before long we will notice a rise in prices.

The crooks have now obtained for themselves a claim on ten percent of all of the physical goods of our colony. The loss has been suffered proportionately by all members of the colony. Without the use of force, our crooks have managed to steal from us all. The result is the same as if the goods had been taken at gunpoint. We are witnessing the beginning of the breakdown of society, the introduction of an element that, if allowed to continue, would end in anarchy.

This must be stopped. If it is not stopped the counterfeiters will continue to make money until they own twenty percent, thirty percent—or, eventually, all of the assets of society.

Fortunately we have some fairly smart detectives in our colony and they have observed that some of the circulating money has a tiny smudge in one corner that differentiates it from the real money. Now the society is alerted. These bogus bills are picked up as they are returned to the bank, and destroyed. That has only half solved our problem, because the goods that were bought with the bogus money are still in the hands of the as-yet-unknown crooks. The rest of the society has suffered a loss of these goods.

Finally, the clandestine printing press is discovered and the conmen are brought to justice. The only difference between these and other thieves is the identity of the victim. Here the victim is all of society.

The most important point here is that while this counterfeiting was going on the money supply had been increased over and above the value of the goods, and consequently prices had increased. We had inflation.

The introduction of this inflation was a shock to our money system. It meant that the dollar saved the year before could no longer buy what it could have bought then. The quality of savings had been impaired by ten percent. Our confidence in our savings had been correspondingly damaged. Many of our population began to say: "If the money we save will not be as good next year as it is now, we had better buy more of the things we want now, and save less."

Actually we have just been introduced to inflation. If we stop it now, no permanent damage will have been done.

We have survived a crisis. Once more we move on confidently and industriously under conditions where every man may keep for himself the produce of his labor and the fruits of his ingenuity.

Before too long it becomes apparent that some sections of our society are prospering much more than others. The more able and the more industrious men are well off, while the less able and the lazy are poor. Some are living next to the poverty line. Time shows us that the second class is growing faster than the first class.

Now this is a democratic society and our policy makers obtain their posts by election. Some keen politicians quickly perceive that the votes of the poor outnumber the votes of the well-to-do. The experience of the counterfeiters has not gone unnoticed. If counterfeiting could just be legalized by a certain few who run the government, money could be manufactured to distribute as alms to the poorer part of the society. If these politicians could get enough votes to put them in power, they would be in a position to pass a law permitting a certain increase in the money supply by the government.

Accordingly, these politicians direct their campaigns toward the larger and poorer segment of the colony. Their message is that the society is very rich, that the present government is favoring the well-to-do; as a whole the colony is well able to provide a decent standard of living for all. If they are elected there will be benefits to the poorer sections of society regardless of whether their poverty arises from ill health or simply because they are incompetent.

When these politicians obtain office they find only two methods by which they can fulfill their promise. One is to tax those who produce, and thus *legally* take property from those to whom it belongs and give it to those to whom it does not belong, *or* print more money and deliver the excess supply, in benefits, to the less productive sections of the society.

Both of these alternatives produce exactly the same result. As the counterfeiters were bandits ravaging others illegally, these politicians are bandits ravaging members of the society legally.

Once these people have been firmly installed in office they begin to pay themselves handsome salaries and to peddle their influence. They make very sure that they deliver on their promises to the poor in order to count on those votes at the next election.

The process that has begun may not ruin the society for some time, but the inevitable end of the policy is a continual depreciation in the values of the money and an impairment of the money as a store of value. Those who have enough shoes but who wish to save to buy a pair of shoes tomorrow will find, when tomorrow comes, that the money they have saved will only buy one shoe or will buy a pair of shoes of half the quality. This produces a very strong feeling *against* saving.

Meanwhile these new politicians have invented interest and loans. The depreciation of the value of money has caused a reduction of effort and a reduction of total productivity. In order to "get the economy rolling again," their answer is to make loans to those who wish to build houses and expand their businesses. In order to loan additional money they have to resort to the printing press. This money, of course, does not have the backing of goods. For a time this causes great prosperity. With these loans people hire labor to build roads and houses. Labor is scarce and hourly rates go up; and so on down the line. In spite of the fact that prices are constantly rising, the printing press of these legal bandits turns out enough money so that the society is still moving ahead, and the man on the street says of the rising prices: "So what, I am better off than ever before. If this is the result of inflation, I'm in favor of it."

Simultaneously with the invention of the loans comes the invention of interest on the loans to pay for the *risk*. The additional money needed to meet interest demands an even larger money supply. Interest mounts year after year and interest mounts on interest. The U.S. Government had to provide over thirty billion dollars to pay the interest on its debt in 1975 alone. But note the speed of growth. In 1978 interest was approaching $50 as a result of compound interest, and interest on additional debt.

It now becomes necessary to create even more money to keep up with the interest—or, on the other hand, to tax at a higher rate to pay for the mounting debt built on interest.

We have launched into an era of full-fledged inflation, and already, before the society realizes it, we are in a position where it will be extremely painful to halt. For one thing, all of the interest that has accumulated is in the form of money that is in *excess* of goods and services available. Loans from the banks are in excess of goods available in Freedonia. If lenders get scared and call these loans, business will go bankrupt and people will be out of work. But printing more money will keep the wolf from the door for a while.

Halting this inflation is going to throw the society into a recession, and consequently a political furor. Politicians who spell out the truth will be denounced as cruel people, unsympathetic to the plight of the poor and deliberately promoting unemployment and poverty. These people will not be able to gain office.

It is becoming pretty obvious that the inflationists are in the saddle and that it will be impossible to unseat them. The process will go on—erratically perhaps—until they are destroyed by the collapse of the economy and a starving population beating at their doors with clubs and pitchforks. If the process is allowed to go on long enough, it will end in revolution with all its attendant chaos.

This has happened in history many times, and the process first gets under way when money begins to lose its store of value.

It is exactly here that most kings, dictators, and even democratic governments go astray. While constantly aware of the mandatory function of money as a "medium of exchange," they conveniently forget the equally important function of money as a "store of value."

That's because the deterioration of the "store of value" requirement does not show up at once, and, by the time it does show up, the temptations toward inflation have become so strong that it is easier to further reduce the store of value by a tiny percentage than it is to check the inflation.

The store of value depreciates so gradually at first that no noticeable complaint arises. The increase of the depreciation is insidious. The population, like the patient camel, doesn't mind the addition of just one more pound on its back, then two pounds, and eventually ten pounds. But as surely as the back of the camel will eventually break, so will the currency of that society eventually collapse.

In this process money has gradually deteriorated from representing real and existing wealth in its function as a medium of exchange into representing only an exchange *vehicle*—irredeemable in wealth, but circulated and accepted because of an overhanging confidence from its *past*. When finally it reaches a point where confidence fails and it is liable to be rejected in payment of a debt, the politicians are forced to pass a law that demands that people accept it at the face value imprinted upon it. They call it *legal tender*.

By Government edict it will bear the following inscription, which appears on the currency of the United States today, "This note is legal tender for all debts, public and private."

Notice how this was unnecessary in the early history of Freedonia. It follows, therefore, that when real money exists, coercion is unnecessary. Correspondingly, when real money loses value because of dilution through legal counterfeiting, coercion (legal tender) becomes necessary. When coercion is necessary, liberty is in retreat.

Notice that when natural laws were not suppressed, liberty was in full bloom. Coercion was unthought of. The penalty for inflation is the *loss* of the "store of value." So the penalty has been paid by those who have saved, and by those who have lent to the government and to others.

The nature of money is such that when it is ravaged by inflation, it correspondingly loses its store of value, so that a continually accelerating inflation is necessary to maintain the same purchasing power—and that it is not possible to stop the inflation without a collapse of inflation (drastic deflation).

The inflation in the Western world today has accelerated to the point where this *collapse* is a foregone conclusion.

4. BRIEF HISTORY OF INFLATION

Inflation is an expression of the universal desire to have something for nothing, and of the power of politicians to fulfill that desire simply by printing money. It is also a manifestation of our natural inclination to rationalize—to convert wish into belief.

Thus, inflationary tendencies are rooted in our nature, similar to greed, fear, and lust. Inflation is an aspect of nature in operation; it has been with us since money was invented as a medium of exchange. We can therefore expect to be plagued with inflation forever.

Stability—once re-established—will always be adulterated by a new army of wishful politicians. Once started, inflation always rises to a climax and the climax is always the same—collapse.

Money was used by the Babylonians at least 5,000 years ago; and with the help of hard money and the confidence resulting from hard money, Babylon became the center of world civilization and power. The city of Ur was a city of gold. It's interesting to observe that while Babylon attained grandeur via hard money, it reached even greater grandeur as it debased its money. But the debasement also brought its end.

The king of Ur devised a scheme for wealth much greater than the wealth of his limited gold. As a custodian, he issued receipts—IOUs—and loaned out at interest the great wealth from the treasury of Ur. The stimulation of the doubling or the tripling of the wealth gave rise to visions of world powers as it produced the then-known world's greatest BOOM.

But as this immense purchasing power swelled, the claims on gold increased until they exceeded the gold. Foreign claims as a result of imports, plus domestic claims, exhausted the gold supplies of Ur. Still the IOUs circulated. After a long time the swollen volume of IOUs caused people to demand more of them. Inflation was in full swing.

Undaunted, the Babylonian facing the fact that it took more money to buy the same goods, continued the expansion. He still had lots of silver. Adroitly, he extricated himself by a very neat device. He declared that the value of silver was equal to gold.

For some time Babylon advanced on a currency of silver equivalent to gold. But an uneasy feeling that this situation was not quite solid caused people to demand real silver faster than they had demanded real gold in the beginning. Soon there was no silver.

The next step was to declare that copper had a value equal to silver. This didn't work as long. It served rather as a confirmation of the decline in the value of money, and the collapse was at hand. Now, with its back against the wall, Babylon moved to its last retreat. It declared that lead had a value equal to copper.

Then Babylon fell.

So human nature was not so very different in 2000 B.C., than in 1968 A.D., when the world's most affluent and most powerful nation declared that *paper* had a value equal to gold, and actually got other countries to agree to issue *paper gold* as a reserve asset of world money under the dignified name of Special Drawing Rights.*

Babylon's gold and silver had fled to other lands. Assyria became the great center. Later Persia. Alexander the Great took Persia's gold, and Greece briefly replaced Persia.

The same gold and silver later helped build the mighty empire of Rome, but eventually there too the coin-clipping started. The debasement of Rome's currency led to the refusal of its legions to perform as soldiers, which led to the collapse of the Roman Empire.

---

* Special Drawing Rights (SDR's) — SDR's are special credits entered on the books of the International Monetary Fund in favor of its member nations, which they may use in purchasing foreign exchange from other member nations who have deposits in the Fund. The idea of creating SDR's was agreed on by ten countries — U.S.A., U.K., Japan, Canada, Sweden and the Common Market (France, West Germany, Italy, Belgium and Netherlands) at a London meeting Aug. 27, 1967. The agreement was signed by the I.M.F. governors at Rio de Janeiro Sept. 28, 1967. Finance Ministers and state bank officials met at Stockholm March 30, 1968 and drafted a plan to be ratified by the 107 members of the I.M.F. On April 30, 1968, President Johnson asked Congress to approve the plan and it passed PL 90-349 as an amendment to the I.M.F. agreement. I.M.F. members were asked to accept SDR's proportionate to their allocations in the I.M.F. on the understanding that they could exchange these for convertible currencies to pay for foreign purchases at the rate of 1 SDR = $1.00. Since they were bookkeeping reserves without any gold backing, they were called paper gold. A number of countries declined to join, and some still have not joined.

Without exception, and throughout the trading history of mankind, the substitution of watered-down money for real money, and the continuing dilution, has marked the end of affluence and, later, influence.

Probably the three greatest *Declarers* in the history of civilization have been Babylon, Kublai Khan, and the U.S.A.

The Great Khan, ruling, with absolute authority, the largest kingdom ever known to man, stretching from Hungary to the China Sea, *declared* money at will and put his absolute power behind the declaration.

The writings of Marco Polo in the thirteenth century, as it turns out, described two monetary systems separated by 700 years. For "Kahn" simply read "U.S.A." Marco Polo wrote:

"It is by this means that the Great Khan may have, and in fact, has more treasure than all the kings of the world. These pieces of paper are issued with as much solemnity and authority as if they were pure gold or silver, and on every piece a variety of officials whose duty it is, have to write their names and put their seal. And the Khan causes every year to be made such a vast quantity of this money, which costs nothing, that it must equal in amount all the treasures of the world.

"With these pieces of paper the Khan causes all payments on his account to be made, and he makes them pass current universally over all his kingdom (country) and possessions and territories, and whither-so-ever his power and sovereignty extends. And nobody however important he may think himself, dares to refuse them on pain of death."

It will be distressing for the money managers in Washington to read that the Great Khan (with all his power) could only make this last for 27 years. Paper money issues of 1260 depreciated one-fifth by 1287. At that time the Great Khan recalled all monetary units and gave one new one for five old ones.

In another 80 years his empire had collapsed.

It is interesting to note that since 1944, about thirty-five years, the U.S. currency has deteriorated in purchasing power about five to one and so far, this exceeds Kublai Khan's record by eight years. The Great Khan, of course, could put whole cities to the torch if they refused his money. U.S. propaganda, extolling the virtues of the paper dollar, has evidently been more effective than the sword and the fires of Kublai Khan. Nevertheless, if we are to be realistic, we must seriously doubt that the day of the big exchange can be far off.

Or so it seems. But hold on for a minute! It has been widely assumed that the solution devised by the Great Khan will be the inevitable solution to the inflation of the U.S. dollar—an exchange of several old ones for one new one. I myself was among the first to propose that this would happen, but I had not thought deeply enough.

When there is a massive overhang of credit, totally beyond any means of repayment—that credit must eventually be liquidated. There is no escape. The credit can be liquidated by one of two means. The first was that of the Great Khan—wipe it out by declaring the value of the debt to be only a fraction of what it was originally. A man had lent a hundred dollars. Now we say we will give 100 of the new dollars for 500 of the old dollars. But you who lent the money will get 100 of our currency, which, of course, is the new dollars. That is one way.

The second way that the massive debt can be liquidated is through bankruptcy. That is to say, default. A man lent a hundred dollars. The debtor goes broke and says to the man simply, "I'm sorry—I can't pay you back—I don't have any money."

The first answer means increased inflation. The second answer means deflation; that is, bankruptcy and depression. The great argument remains: which route will be taken to liquidate the massive and plainly impossible structure of debt—deflation or inflation? The former—the route of the Great Khan—would be the easier. But there is one fundamental difference between the position of the U.S.A. and that of the Khan. He was the absolute ruler of all the lands where his currency circulated. The U.S. currency circulates throughout the world and is the basis for all world money; but the United States does not have the sovereign power to pass laws for the countries beyond its borders. To date, the might of the United States has been used via implication and polite threat, a matter of propaganda rather than guns.

It has been the military power of the United States that has given credence to its threat to withdraw its troops from Europe—laying countries defenseless before Communism—unless the dependent countries of Europe should continue to accept the engraved-paper promises. Germany had to buy billions of irredeemable dollars.

Kublai Khan's money was made "official" by the signatures of officials whose duty it was to affix their names. If you will examine the currency in your pocket, you will find that it is the law of the land that "This note is legal tender for all debts, public and private," and you will see that certain officials have affixed their names—George P. Shultz, John A. Connally, Henry H. Fowler, David M. Kennedy—all of them monetary replicas of the officials of Kublai Khan.

It seemed that the fall of the Roman Empire taught mankind a lesson to remember: subsequent to that epoch inflations have nearly always resulted only from war. War necessitates an unbalanced budget—more politely known today as deficit spending.

War causes the ruler, or the government, to speed up production and to decrease relatively the amount of consumer goods. This puts everybody to work at higher wages without producing a corresponding amount of consumer goods and services. Unless the government coffers happen to be bulging with savings, it must create new money; and since there are no goods and services to match the new money, prices go up and inflation has commenced.

An example of this kind of inflation were the worthless assignats of France that blossomed and survived for seven years, from 1789 to 1796. Since this is not a history book we need not go into the details except to note that the result of the inflation once again was the collapse of the money.

The most dramatic modern example of the ruins left by the fires of inflation—once out of control—was the German inflation of the 1920s. To understand it you must understand a basic characteristic of inflation. *The decline of confidence in money accelerates faster than the decline in value of the money—once the confidence decline is in full swing.*

The decline of confidence is usually triggered first by the repeal of gold convertibility. This makes a few citizens suspect something is fishy. Inflation starts slowly here and builds as the feeling of insecurity grows.

Germany lost the war in 1918. In the following two years the government doubled the money supply. But prices had increased by five times; the public was discounting the value of money faster than the government was printing it; the erosion of confidence outpaced the erosion of value. The public feared the depreciation of its savings and, to protect them and to maintain some real value, it began to exchange its money for *things*, bidding prices up higher and higher.

By the end of 1920 prices had increased 14 times. But there they reached a plateau. They had reached a point where people thought they were ridiculous. The buying stopped; the money stabilized for about six months. But by about the middle of 1921, people became nervous again. Nothing had happened to confirm the stability of commodities at these levels. For no reason that one can nail down, a new spending spree started in the last half of 1921, and in this six-month period the value of money fell drastically as the printing presses raced to produce enough money to match the prices that were being bid higher and higher. It now took 37 marks to buy what one mark had bought at the time of the armistice. Money had lost two-thirds of its value in six months.

In the next six months, by January 1923, money went up 2,785 times. Now there was no hope. The inflationary fire was raging in full force. Money, as a store of value, was no longer even a concept. It was better to have a cow today at a high price than perhaps only a leg of lamb a month from now. In the next six months money went up 194,000 times. And in the following four months, by November 1923, it had gone up 726 billion times.

One mark at the time of the armistice would have bought as much as 726 billion in November 1923. Every German was a billionaire.

All bonds, all savings, had been wiped out.

During the time of the medium inflation a doctor borrowed from the bank and bought a dairy herd. Three months later he sold one cow and paid for the herd.

This isn't likely to happen again, but it serves as an object lesson in what public psychology can do to money that isn't backed by anything *real.*

The money managers of Germany were upset. "The public has always trusted our paper promises! Why have they stopped now? It's *irrational!*"

"Irrational!" echoed the treasury officials of the United States when unredeemable dollars swamped the money markets of the world.

It is important to remember that if the money had any intrinsic value, or was redeemable for any amount of intrinsic value, this never could have happened. The only irrationality on the part of the public was that it fled from the money a little faster than was necessary.

At the height of the German inflationary storm money was losing value every hour. Factories paid their workers three times a day, and wives had to be Johnny-on-the-spot to collect the husband's money to get to the grocery store to buy some food before the prices again doubled the next day. But, alas, the shops were empty!

What farmer would sell his goods—his beef, his milk, his potatoes—for money that tomorrow would be worth half as much as it was today?

What worker would arise at seven in the morning to sweat for eight hours to receive money that would buy nothing tomorrow?

The economy was in complete collapse.

The monetary wizards of the United States have been propounding and repeating the old saw that the value of the dollar relies upon the productivity of the nation rather than upon any intrinsic worth. But the German case makes fools of them. Germany enjoyed productivity, but the increasingly worthless paper mark destroyed that productivity and destroyed the economy.

If Kublai Khan was the model for the U.S. Treasury's method of monetary growth, Hitler was the prototype for its philosophy. It was Adolph Hitler who said, January 29, 1937:

"For the nation does not live from the fictitious value of money but rather from the actual production from which money itself gets value. This production is the real business of our currency and not a bank or treasury full of gold."

What he did not say reverses his words: Money is the measurement of the net production. It is the scale.

U.S. Treasury Secretary Blumenthal repeated almost these self same words in 1978.

There is no doubt that gold itself does not make a nation rich. There is hardly any less doubt that it *measures* the wealth of a nation.

There is little doubt that, under the strictest restraint, money can function both as a medium of exchange and as a store of value, as we saw in Freedonia. Unfortunately there is also little doubt that, without the *discipline of a commodity* (gold), managers and politicians will inevitably tamper with the money supply in pursuance of the human frailty to want something for nothing, and the human ability to rationalize a wish into a belief.

5. THE NATURE OF INFLATION

Just as the nature of money is a reflection of human nature, so is the nature of inflation.

It is part of the nature of man that his desires are without limit; as opposed to other species, whose desires fall within the limits of food, shelter, and reproduction. Since man's desires are limitless, his want for goods is limitless, and therefore his want for money is limitless.

He has come to learn that money means goods and the services of others. In his normal life it has never occurred to him that if the money he receives is in excess of the available goods, that money cannot, of course, represent goods. So the general public never realizes that inflation is taking place until it experiences inflation's consequences in the market place. The natural reaction to this is to demand higher wages. The higher wages, if granted, only increase the amount of money—*but not the amount of goods*—unless production increases correspondingly. So the addition of that inflationary purchasing medium has done nothing for the worker.

And it is a fact that an artificial increase in purchasing *media* cannot be of the slightest benefit to the collective population. But successive increases in purchasing media, and resulting price increases, cause the population to begin to have less respect for the money. Thus we see the inception of a vicious circle that, once begun, can rarely be checked without a return to a total quantity of money *commensurate* with the total amount of goods and services. This always means a temporary contraction or recession, or, in extreme cases, depression.

Governments don't usually have the courage to accept the remedy. Instead they temporarily fool the worker by creating additional purchasing *media* and gradually set themselves up for an inevitable fall.

Since the time lag is considerable between the commencement of inflation and the final collapse, the politicians in power are not inclined to worry about the future. Their main aim is a pleasant present.

When John Maynard Keynes*, who advocated deficit spending, was reminded that someday we would have to pay off the enormous debt, his reply was, "Someday we will all be dead." He failed to mention that the upcoming generation wouldn't be dead, and the people who were now lending money wouldn't all be dead by the time its value had depreciated. It was typical of money managers and politicians, and typical of human nature, to defer the bad effects to the future.

Since it is human nature for those in power to resist the painful steps necessary to halt inflation, the tendency always is first to condone it, then assist it; until, finally out of hand, it prepares the ground for its own collapse.

History amply proves this thesis. A few politicians and bankers will make an effort to correct the situation, but, as soon as they see the face of the upcoming recession, they lose their nerve and go for the palliative of increasing the money supply, which temporarily once again satisfies the workers.

President Nixon, in 1969, vowed to control inflation and balance the budget. In six months he was confronted with a crashing stock market and the threat of bankruptcy throughout the nation. The vision of the upcoming disaster arising out of the long inflation would have been enough to deter even a mighty Caesar. Nixon and his banker, Arthur Burns, raced to push the button that would start the printing presses rolling again. From 1970 to 1974 we saw the greatest increase in the money supply of the world since money had been invented. The grim reaper confronting the United States was nothing short of chaos. But as the country was gripped with recession, the previous increases were made to look small. Then when the recovery came, under Carter, the budget deficits, instead of decreasing as one might have thought, had to be increased further to keep the recovery going. Consequently, we had the biggest splash of red ink in U.S. history in the years 1977 and 1978. In three years, back to back, we piled up government debts of $150 billion. We had come to the point where in order to delay Armageddon we had to guarantee it.

So far we have seen, and we can conclude, since it is almost a natural law arising from human nature, that *inflation, once established, will always accelerate—when it is under the arbitrary control of human beings.*

Arbitrary control of the money supply can only take place under conditions of fiat money. † It can never happen when money is exchangeable for a commodity, for the simple reason that the authorities—unlike Jesus—are

---

* John Maynard Keynes, 1883-1946. English economist and monetary expert. During the Great Depression, recommended government deficit spending to promote employment. Author of *The General Theory of Employment, Interest and Money,* (1936).

† Fiat Money — Paper money which is made legal tender by government fiat, or decree. It is not redeemable in any fixed amount of gold or silver.

unable to make a hundred fishes out of one or, indeed, even 101 fishes from 100.

Having understood that inflation is as certain as death and taxes when the money supply is under the control of mere men, we can now read the following from the *Encyclopaedia Britannica* with a degree of enlightenment:

> Until the 1930s, inflation had been generally regarded as an infrequent problem ... no important inflation or deflation had in fact occurred for more than a hundred years before 1930, except as the consequence of war ...
>
> One reason and probably the most powerful, for the infrequency of major inflation or deflation before the great depression of the 1930's was the widespread use of the gold standard. This system limited the issue of paper money and bank deposits to the level which the public, able to exchange money freely for gold, was willing to hold instead of gold.
>
> Free gold convertibility under the gold standard proper, or a fixed money-to-gold ratio set by legislation as an alternative, was completely effective (except when abrogated in wartime) *in setting limits to the power of government to acquiesce in inflation.*

It is no coincidence that during a century of stability the king of money in the world was the British pound; Britain was on the gold standard and the pound was fully and freely convertible to gold. The hundred years up to 1914 saw the greatest industrial growth in the history of mankind. Generally speaking it was characterized by falling prices rather than by rising prices. A million dollars left as a bequest in 1820 was still worth a million dollars to the grandchildren at the dawn of the twentieth century—and more. But a million-dollar bequest of 1940 was worth no more than $300,000 by 1970; and no more than $200,000 by 1975. It's no coincidence that in the first case the world was to all intents and purposes on the gold standard, and in the second case the world was on the gold-exchange standard.

The enormous difference between these two systems and the deceptiveness of the second in its early stages will be discussed in the next chapter.

It should be clear by now to any reader that man, by his very nature, is not to be trusted as the custodian of the money supply, and that for the benefit of all mankind an immutable discipline must be imposed. The only immutable discipline is a commodity. In 5,000 years the most satisfactory commodities have been either gold or silver.

A primary argument against gold has always been that it is utterly stupid for men to fritter away their time in the bowels of the earth digging up gold and processing it, only to bury it again in vaults. Gold is superfluous to human needs and its production is a waste of time. You cannot eat gold.

You cannot eat a Fairbanks Morse scale either, but there is no other way to keep your butcher honest. There could be no trade without the use of millions of scales and rulers. These are safeguards to honesty, safeguards against avarice. Immutable measurements are mandatory if trade is to advance, and gold is a most convenient measurement.

As for storage, a million dollars at the $35 price* occupies but one cubic foot. All of the gold in the world, saved since the dawn of time, amounts to about 80 billion dollars and can be stored in a room 50 x 50 x 32 feet. Of course at $210 per ounce, we store $480 billion.

The Central Banks can put their present total of gold in a room 25 x 50 x 32 feet.

---

* $35 per Troy ounce.

6. THE GOLD STANDARD

Let us return to our colony, and let us, this time, imagine 10 million dollars of gold at $35 per ounce, representing all of our goods according to our price lists. Let us imagine that we had set up a council to administer our money, and agreed that we would print paper certificates equivalent to the amount of gold and redeemable in coins of gold to whoever might demand them.

As soon as our people found they could always get the coins in return for the paper, and knew without question that the coins were there, they would prefer the paper because of its convenience. Even if, at times, they became distrustful and demanded coins in place of the paper, ready fulfillment of demand would instantly demolish any misgivings. Reassured, citizens would, as a matter of convenience, quickly drift back to the paper.

As our society produced and progressed and built more houses and grew more crops, we would find ourselves with goods in excess of money. In that case one of three things would have to happen.

a. The price of commodities would gradually go down—nothing wrong with that. Money that had been saved would buy more.

b. We would have to increase the value of the gold. If we had 25 percent increase in goods we would have to increase the value of the gold twenty-five percent, and have a 25-percent increase in the money supply. If we had doubled our store of value collectively, we would have to double the money supply and therefore double the price of gold.

(This gives the lie to those who say that there is not enough gold in the world to back increased commerce and increased productivity. Nonsense. It's only a matter of arithmetic. It's a question of assigning a monetary value to gold commensurate with the goods and services available to the society. There is absolutely no such thing as insufficient gold to make a gold standard work— except in the case where all of the people might be demanding the coins. In that event the coins might be too small to handle, requiring admixture with an alloy for practical use.)

c. If we didn't want prices to fall, and if we didn't devalue the money, we would simply have to increase the supply of gold by finding some.

Surely this ought to be clear to our economists. Unfortunately it isn't. But history demonstrates that it's true.

Consider the following from *Chambers' Encyclopaedia*:

> In epochs when the national economy was dependent upon supplies of a money metal, inflation was only possible if relatively exceptional quantities of the metal became available—as in Europe, and particularly Spain, between 1550 and 1650, on the arrival of the produce of the silver mines of Spanish America.

This was an unusual event in history and the increased availability of silver couldn't last. As soon as the increase stopped, the resulting mild inflation was also throttled. Runaway inflation was an impossibility.

The encyclopaedia continues:

> The possibilities of considerable inflation of this kind diminished, so that the gold discoveries of the second half of the nineteenth century, although of unprecedented size, had only small and gradual effect on price levels.

The truth is that production of precious metals can't take place fast enough to cause serious inflationary problems, whereas the production of fiat currency, produced by the whim of man, can proceed at any speed desired.

The encyclopaedia continues:

> Where, however, currencies take the form of inconvertible paper, and can thus be expanded at will, no natural limit exists to their inflationary possibilities ... The need for additional currency commonly arises from the exigencies of an unbalanced budget, and since such exigencies occur most acutely in time of war (when also, supply of consumers' goods tends to fall) severe inflations are usually found to arise out of war-time conditions.

If our colony were to find that a hitherto-unexpected population intended to attack it—perhaps destroy it—it would be necessary, in the interest of the safety of all, to prepare for war. Workers would have to drop many of their constructive projects, even to the extent of leaving the fields, to make spears and swords and, if possible, guns and bullets. The production of these laborers would add nothing to the general goods and services available and desired in the normal life of the colony.

These laborers would nevertheless have to be paid, even though the fruits of their labors could not be sold. It would be necessary either to borrow the savings from our people or to issue more money against the gold (inflation) to keep this war effort going. If the war lasted a long time, extra taxes would have to be imposed and the savings increasingly consumed. The injection into the purchasing media of more than the equivalent of the total usable goods and services could not help but make all the money worth less, and thus reduce the value of all savings of the society. That would be the price our colony would have to pay to defend itself.

The net result would be a reduced standard of living during the war and even thereafter, to make up for destruction and wasted effort.

But as long as we remain on the gold standard, with our paper redeemable in the metal, albeit in smaller quantity, confidence in the money could not be stampeded and the inflation could not go unnoticed. When the war was over, our monetary situation would return to normal. All prices would be higher, as a result of lost production and of destruction during the war.

However, it would be possible that during the war itself we might not experience much inflation, despite the increased money supply. Production of goods would have declined to the point where wartime rationing was necessary. The wages of our workers and our warriors, over and above the goods available, would go into savings. When the war was over the people would want to spend their money, and they would bid up the prices of available goods in the market place, and that is where we would notice the inflation resulting from war.

Still, in all, in the case of a gold-backed currency, the entire population would be aware of the true devaluation of the currency as a result of war. As long as the government did not increase the money supply beyond the new rate necessitated by the war; as long as it would publicly announce the value of the dollar compared with the gold reserve, no ruinous inflation could result, simply because no more money could be created.

Gold would have performed an incalculable service by its validation of the measurement of the price we have paid for defense.

Our colony would find that since one of its dollars would (as a result of the war inflation) buy fewer goods at home than it bought before the war, it would also buy fewer goods in the countries with which we might be trading. The value of the dollar would be established domestically. Whatever that value turned out to be, it would be solid; and other countries would trust it.

However, if after the war we industriously rebuilt our nation, we would find that our efforts were gradually increasing the volume of goods once again until they equaled what they had equaled before. As the goods increased in our colony, and as we did not, under the gold standard, print bogus money, we would find the price of things actually coming down, as the total volume of goods rose in relation to the total volume of money. By our industry we should recover to the point where our money had the same value in goods as it had before the war.

In all of this time we should have known exactly where we stood through an immutable and precise measurement of our wealth, as precise and impartial as the Fairbanks Morse scale—the commodity gold.

And there, in a nutshell, you have the reason why the political leaders of a country that is going downhill despise gold—*its ability to measure and to clearly announce the results of their management.* In a country that is making real progress, politicians usually come to love gold, as they did in the United States until the early 1960s.

There was never a greater gold-hater in the world than Adolf Hitler. The value of German money was enforced by law. He was still able to produce a miracle. The value of the German mark was, for a period, even solid outside the country. Antigold people will point to this sometimes as an example of the superfluous nature of gold. They haven't seen the whole picture.

When a large part of the productive capacity of our colony is diverted toward unproductive ends, and when we have to create money to pay these unproductive workers, it is a natural law that there are fewer commodities available for the population per unit of money. You have inflation whether you like it or not, and either one of two things must happen:

a. the price must go up;

b. the purchase of commodities must go down.

Authoritarian states chooses the second because it masks the adulteration of the money. Goods are strictly rationed. Unable to buy goods, the workers turn the money into savings. The excess money becomes *backed-up* in bank accounts—unspendable. Prices can stand still if there is no increase in the volume of goods purchased.

At this point they do not recognize that the "saved" money is without substance because there are no goods in the marketplace to represent it. The inflation has been there all the time, but it does not emerge until the savings are released into the marketplace in competitive bidding for limited goods. Only then do they find that the "saved" money that gave such comfort in their bank books was really an *illusion.*

Fiat money has fooled the population.

7. GOLD CAN CAUSE INFLATION

For a hundred years following the wars the economy in the land of Freedonia was strong and stable. The mines of the country produced just about enough gold to keep up with the increasing productivity of the land. As long as this balance was maintained they had neither inflation nor deflation. For more than a hundred years a dollar was always worth a dollar.

If a boy earned a dollar chopping wood when he was ten years old, and if he had put that away in a piggy bank and forgotten about it, he could recover it when he was seventy years old and buy the same necktie that he would have bought for a dollar when he was a boy. Had he put the money at interest he would have earned something each year, because money was lent in the land of Freedonia for sound business enterprises.

Money could always be lent for goods on their way to market. For instance the farmer, with wheat in his granary, could borrow on that wheat, because it was known to have real value, and it would sooner or later reach the warehouse. It was considered to be goods on the way to market.

It was possible even to borrow money to buy seed grain if the farmer already had his farm and his horses and his plow and a reputation to back him up. The seed grain would probably become grain and could be considered goods on the way to market.

In the decades to follow, however, this concept of banking would be wiped out. They would stretch it to include an advance to buy the machinery to plow the land to seed the grain, to harvest the grain, to bring it to market. Then later on, in the days of heavy speculation and easy credit, this would be extended to buy the land on which to plant the grain with the machinery purchased on credit to be eventually harvested and brought to market.

But in the days when Freedonia was strong and the banking system was stable, loans were always repaid. The money supply always represented the goods and services in existence as they increased or decreased. No one got rich through speculative land deals, nor through the clever manipulation of other people's money. But shoe factories sprang up along with mills and mines, and a growing fraternity of merchants to distribute these products to the population.

This is not to say that the Freedonians were satisfied. They always wanted more, and wanted it quicker. They always needed and wanted more money than they had. There was always a complaint about the scarcity of money. Imagine the rejoicing then when, one day, the news came that gold had been discovered in the far eastern corner of the country. So rich was this discovery that nuggets could be lifted from the surface. The excitement was electric.

With all this new money, thought the Freedonians, everyone would be rich. Everyone could buy all he needed. And so the mines began to hum; and the gold began to pour into the vaults of the Freedonian treasury as it issued currency for the gold.

Alas, the dream was short-lived.

All that happened was that when the gold supply was doubled the money supply had also been doubled, but the amount of goods and services available had not increased a bit. In a very short time it became clear that it now took two Freedonian dollars to buy what one Freedonian dollar had bought before the gold discovery. Those who had cashed in early on the gold had benefited, of course, but generally, and in the country as a whole, the consequences of the gold discovery produced more harm than good. While the early birds had benefited, it had been at the expense of others.

This great discovery of gold had really amounted to the same thing as if the Freedonian government had suddenly decided to double the money supply without any backing.

That has happened at least twice in our recorded history. Alexander the Great was the first to suffer from an excessive accumulation of gold. He raided the vaults of every country he conquered and sent the gold home to Greece. Money was issued to match this very fast accumulation of wealth. The result was inflation, and a bad one.

It happened to the Spaniards after they discovered the great gold hoards in the new world (the discovery of gold in South Africa had a similar, but lesser, effect).

All this is to show that there is nothing magic about gold and, therefore, nothing magic about the Gold Standard.

The *reason* that gold has served monetary stability so well is that it is so scarce, and that its production is quite stable and quite slow. It acts as a great balance wheel. No other metal or commodity can fill this bill.

Today the discovery of gold in the amounts found by the Spaniards in the new world would have very little effect on the world, because *percentage-wise* it would be such a small part of the money supply. In those days, percentagewise, it was a very impressive factor.

It is very important to recognize that those who back the gold standards are not simply nuts who have a sort of *religion* relating to gold. Gold could as well be nothing more than black coal, or iron, as far as the gold standard adherents are concerned. They believe in it only because a lot of it cannot easily be found, and therefore it acts as the stabilizer par excellence.

8. THE GOLD-EXCHANGE STANDARD

To this point we have been discussing basics with a view toward understanding the conditions existing in the United States today and throughout the world. If we can accurately assess and clearly evaluate the reality of the current conditions we may be able to get a reading on the direction in which we are moving and to see whether we are running into an obstacle, or over a cliff.

If we were to find that this inflation will continue until it collapses, that would be very valuable information on which to base our investments, and indeed to plan our lives—because in this modern society the population has been promised so much, and has been led to expect so much, that the collapse of inflation and the resulting depression, would most certainly touch off violent resentment from the masses.

The foreclosure of mortgages and the closing of banks, the destruction of savings, and riots on a scale never before imagined could, under the right conditions of mass psychology and mob violence, result in conditions similar to those of the French Revolution.

Probably the first reaction of the government to pacify the raging public will be to print enough money to keep the banks in business and stimulate employment to where workers could pay their rent and feed themselves—even though this new influx of inflation could only worsen and intensify the dying convulsion of the present era, the age of inflation.

That term (the Age of Inflation), owes its name to the most astute economist of this century, Jacques Rueff.* Rueff traced inflation's roots to the gold-exchange standard and philosophized more than ten years ago that unless the system were corrected it would destroy our Western civilization.

The gold-exchange standard is a 50-year-old invention. It grew out of the inflation following World War I, when it was discovered that there was not nearly enough gold to back the large new quantities of money in circulation. Rather than face the fact that money had lost purchasing power, the authorities thought to remedy the situation by conserving gold.

So the gold-exchange standard was, from the moment of its birth, a gimmick. There was a deficiency in the quality of money. The gold-exchange standard was invented to *cover it up.*

Had a fundamentalist been in charge of the Genoa Convention of 1922 the inflation tree would never have been planted. For it was in its beginning an outright defiance of natural law.

The Genoa Convention† proclaimed that you can dispose of your cake to others without losing any yourself. (If I lend you $2,000, that is $2,000 for you to use—it must mean that I am not now able to use that $2,000 for myself. The Genoa Convention defied that proposition).

The United States dollar and the British pound had come to be accepted as the equivalent of gold. The Genoa Convention said that since these currencies are as good as gold and are interchangeable with gold, they may be held in the reserves of Central Banks and be considered in every respect the equivalent of gold.

There is hardly any doubt that the fathers of this convention were blind to the Frankensteinian nature of the infant they then released upon the world. Not for a moment did they dream that fifty years later their naive creation would smite them with such unremitting fury that the very foundations of civilization would rattle.

To understand this fully it is convenient to return to our highly prosperous country of Freedonia. Let's say Freedonia has a hundred million ounces of gold valued at $35 per ounce. Its total money supply then is $3,500 million in its checking accounts and currency.

If Freedonia had spent $100 million in a foreign land, its currency would of necessity be reduced by exactly $100 million. It might happen this way:

The foreign land, having received the Freedonia dollars from tourists or what not, presents them to the Freedonian Treasury for gold. The Freedonia

---

*Jacques Rueff — French economist. Author of *The Monetary Sin of the West*, N.Y. MacMillan Company, 1972. Called upon by de Gaulle to recommend measures for the stabilization of the French franc; de Gaulle accepted virtually all of his recommendations. As a result, the franc turned around overnight, and France was able to effect convertibility of the franc into all major currencies a few months later at the end of 1958.

† Genoa Convention — This Convention was never adopted, but was recommended by the financial committee of the International Conference which met in Genoa, Italy in 1922 to consider problems of post-war reconstruction. The Convention was intended to economize on the use of gold by the introduction of the gold exchange standard or an international clearing system.

Treasury turns over $100 million of gold to that country. Since Freedonia is on the gold standard, it could not possibly have that $100 million for itself any more. Its gold supply, and therefore its total money supply, has been reduced by exactly that amount. It now has $3,400 million.

Perhaps Freedonia was well able to afford this loan—or this expense, or this war—as the case might have been. The point is that while the money was being used in another country, *it was taken out of use in Freedonia*. The money supply in total among all the countries remains the same.

But under the gold-exchange standards invented in Genoa, that old-fashioned principle no longer applied.

Freedonia could spend the $100 million in Atlantica and Atlantica would immediately take this money into its central bank reserves and it would spend this money in other countries for perfume or guns or whatever, and other countries would accept it because it was as good as gold. Actually it wasn't. Atlantican currency was *only converted into Freedonian currency*. Freedonia still maintained, at home, the same amount of money it had spent abroad, but the money it kept at home had gold reserves to back it. The money spent abroad didn't. Thus the total money supply had been *doubled* in relation to gold.

So this $100 million, while it went abroad to be used for spending at the same time stayed home to be used for spending.

This was precisely what happened in the United States after both wars, and this was the gold exchange standard. It simply doubled the money supply.

The effect was electric. Credit was greatly increased on the other side of the Atlantic, without cutting down on the credit on this side. The more British pounds and U. S. dollars that were lent and spent, the greater became the credit. Much of the money returned and was spent in Great Britain and the United States, increasing still further the money supply in these two countries—making money very plentiful.

Where, at one time, it was difficult to build a house with only fifty percent cash, and fifty percent borrowed, now a man might build with only forty percent or perhaps thirty percent. At any rate, the more money that was issued the greater was the credit available; the bigger were the loans men could receive with which to build houses, start businesses, buy luxuries, and so forth.

Why wouldn't there be a boom?

As the available money was multiplied in the banking system, large funds were available for investments of every kind, including the stock markets all around the world. The bidding went higher, then higher, then higher.

Once people began to see how easy it was to make money, more of it was placed in the stock market. There was general euphoria. Stock prices became related less to value than to a guess as to how much the next guy would pay to get the stock to sell later at a still higher price to someone else.

No one suspected it couldn't last. No one suspected we were building up to 1929. Prosperity was, in fact, so well assured that there was no longer need to pay the full price for stocks. Obviously they weren't going to go down. So it came to be that you could buy a stock for a hundred dollars, and borrow at least $50 on it from the bank. You paid the bank interest. Later the stock doubled. Everyone was happy.

Natural law had been abridged.

With everyone making money, credit was further expanded. Margins were reduced until at last you could buy a hundred-dollar stock by only putting up $10 of your own money.

It is not the purpose here to go into the stock market crash of 1929 and the depression of the 30s. These were in fact sharp reminders that natural law had been violated. The bankruptcy of a huge Austrian bank sent out tidal waves like the eruption of a volcano in a small lake. There was the fall of the empire of Kreuger, the match king. One fall brought on another. Millionaires on Wall Street were knocked over like so many match sticks. Enormous paper fortunes went up in smoke.

As it turned out, those who thought themselves so rich had only been rich in thought. They had been rich in figures that were written in ink on some paper.

It had all been a grand illusion.

The insight into the nature of the gold-exchange standard must from the beginning be credited to Jacques Rueff. This French economist saw it instantly for what it was. But he had to be wrong. Weren't the events of the 20s proving what a great success the gold-exchange standard was?

Jacques Rueff was to see the event occur again, but not until much later, because in 1934 President Roosevelt went back to the gold standard. By devaluing the U. S. dollar he made it fully convertible internationally into gold. In order to do this he had to deprive U. S. nationals of their right to own gold—a right of which they were wrongfully deprived until January 1975. By this time gold had reached $200 an ounce, and their opportunity for gain had been lost.

Many, or even most, of the economists writing on the subject of 1929 and the depression of the 30s, were obtuse enough to blame it on the gold standard. If these men had spent all of their lives learning how to be wrong, they couldn't have been more successful. The gold standard was merely the specific remedy—if a tough one — for the damage done by the gold-exchange standard, which had so seduced the economists.

In his book *The Crisis of World Inflation* William Rees-Mogg, editor of the *Times* of London, states, "Prices in Britain were very stable for the two hundred and fifty years after the Restoration with the exception of the Napoleonic period. *It is quite plausible that prices were about ten percent lower in 1913 than in 1661.*"

Any depressions or booms during the quarter-millennium of the gold standard had been minor waves on a stable monetary sea. Deflations and inflations were never more than ripples. They never could be more, because the discipline of gold snuffed out every unreality almost as soon as it arose. You could not fool yourself into thinking you were rich when before your very eyes you could see the gold pile shrinking.

9. THE BUST OF THE BOOM

No one could have told the speculators of 1928 and 1929 that the stock market would lose 90 percent of its value. They listened to the same slogans then as fell on the ears of the speculators of 1974, "Merrill Lynch is BULLISH ON AMERICA."

As the stock market got top-heavy, ever larger volumes of buying were required. Once it moved into reverse, enormous amounts of capital were required. It became fashionable to be "BULLISH ON AMERICA"—as if the degree of a man's patriotism could be measured by the extent to which he was willing to place his funds on the line. If you didn't want to bet on the stock market going up, you were next thing to a cop-out. You were not bullish on America. It wasn't exactly treason, but it took a pretty low type of character to be bearish on America.

That was the implication, and it demonstrates the irrationality of the investment community. It is an irrationality unfortunately that spreads to the monetary community, and even to the monetary managers.

In fifty years that much hasn't changed.

When the crash came it dealt with the inflationary abominations swiftly and effectively. When a stock selling at a hundred dollars goes to $10, ninety percent of the money supply in that share has simply been wiped off the face of the earth. And so billions upon billions were stripped from the money supply. The billions of inflationary hot air that had been pumped into the balloon were suddenly let out.

It was a good thing, because had it gone on the end of the binge could have only been worse.

It was an example to the world of what would happen if ever again it should apply this Alice-in-Wonderland philosophy—the gold-exchange standard.

When the citizens of the U.S.A. offered their gold certificates that guaranteed one ounce in gold, or ten ounces in gold, written above the great seal of the U.S.A., the gold window was slammed down on their fingernails. All of the solemn promises were repudiated. The seal of the U.S.A. was revealed to be a farce.

This truth was not publicized, nor was it barely allowed to be thought. The official repudiation had to be cloaked in the terms of "the common good." So bankrupt was the country and the world that repudiation had to be followed by confiscation.

In 1934, Roosevelt ordered not only the cancellation of all gold contracts, but also that every citizen of the United States turn in his gold to the United States Treasury. He stripped the population of gold.

Now it was time for the edict that the currency notes were legal tender, and it was written upon them that they could be redeemed in "lawful money" of the United States. It was never defined what "lawful money" was. Later on, in the 1960s, even this meaningless redemption clause was removed from all the notes so that all they amounted to was a statement claiming that the piece of paper on which it was written was indeed legal tender, and if the holder owed a debt to anybody, the creditor would be required to accept the note at face value in payment of the debt—no matter how much the purchasing power of the note had depreciated.

The "good as gold" currency was only a memory.

To thinkers of the present day the question must arise, however: who was responsible, Roosevelt, or his predecessors, the men at Genoa? Both must bear a share of the guilt.

Roosevelt had no choice but to devalue the dollar because it simply no longer represented the former standard weight in gold. There was just too much currency out against the existing gold. But instead of repudiation he might well have considered a devaluation of a larger scale so that the money supply and the gold supply would again be brought back into equilibrium, and internal convertibility preserved. The grand seal and the honor would have been retained to the highest degree possible.

People who go into bankruptcy and who simply do not have the assets to cover their debts, but who pay every last cent they can, are not in disgrace. But those who repudiate are never more to be trusted.

Roosevelt devalued the dollar from $20.67 for an ounce of gold to the point where it took $35.00 to buy an ounce of gold; and prohibited the trading of gold internally in the United States. External balances among countries still had to be settled by gold. There was no other way to settle them, because the gold-exchange standard had collapsed. There was nothing left but the gold standard. It was not a positive choice for Roosevelt; it was a last retreat. So, during the depression, the gold standard was in force. It did not *cause* the depression; it was *preceded* by the depression.

Nevertheless the gold standard, being in force, got the blame for the depression. It was as if a country, after fighting for some years, was about to lose a war, was about to be destroyed—and then brought in some general who barely prevented it from being destroyed but who could not produce a victory. So the country would blame this last general for the disastrous war. There was no way the gold standard could miraculously pull the world out of the morass into which it had been thrust by the gold-exchange standard.

The milk had been spilt. The gold standard could not sponge it up again. There never had been that much money in the first place. The prosperity always had been a pseudo-prosperity. Under natural law there was no way the world could come out rich from the destruction and wasted effort of war. But, instead of paying the price during the 1920s, the world paid the price during the 1930s.

The gold-exchange standard had simply delayed and, in doing so, intensified the penalty of war.

Economists will write for fifty years opposing theories of the intricate causes of the great depression, completely failing to understand that it was nothing more than the manifestation of a natural law: which means that if a stone is released it will drop; if a hand intervenes to delay the drop, it will still drop as soon as the hand is removed. The gold-exchange standard was the hand.

The depression was the price of the war and the additional penalty for trying to cover it up.

There is always a penalty for deceit—even with yourself. Anytime you fool yourself you will pay a penalty.

The enemies of the gold standard will point back to the depression, emphasizing that it still wasn't over in 1939 at the beginning of World War II; that we had, in fact, slipped again into depression in 1937. Had it not been for the stimulus of the war, they say, the gold standard might have kept us in depression forever.

No one knows when the depression would have ended. It is probable that even the years of depression had not yet paid for the massive devastation of World War I, including the almost incalculable amount of labor that was totally lost to consumer goods.

What we do know is that World War II unleashed another tidal wave of credit, far greater than the first. And that the result is that virtually all of the money in the world is debt. The $10 bill in your pocket is someone else's debt; nobody has paid this bill either.

10. ERA OF INFLATION IS BORN

The inflation of the 20s was too short-lived to classify as an era. It was an interlude—a ten-year cancellation of the gold standard. The victorious powers tried the inflationary remedy. It ended in a bust. So they had to reverse themselves in 1934 and go back to the gold standard in America. The pound had been discredited and practically destroyed. The United States' dollar emerged as the world's most desired currency—a money still as good as gold internationally, albeit at a reduced price.

War presented the financiers with little problem. Even in our ideal colony of Freedonia in its early stages—operating on the gold standard — the mustering of resources for war was relatively easy. That is because in time of war people will willingly support their country with their savings. They will accept depreciation of their money. There is always this argument: If we lose the war, what good will our money do us? It is after the war that the money problem arises. It is after the war that the price of the destructive expenditures must be reckoned.

Many people, therefore, expected a depression after World War II. They simply could not see how we could lose so much time, waste so much effort, destroy so much—without paying the bill. We hadn't been that well off before the war. Surely it wasn't natural that all this waste could take place and then leave us better off than ever, richer than ever before. If one were to believe that, he had to accept a new axiom: *"destruction brings wealth."*

People couldn't believe that, and they expected a depression.

By the fall of 1978 we hadn't had that depression yet. In thirty years we have had nothing but booms as a result of the war. Apparently the war has produced an enormous prosperity, and if we want to be prosperous we must keep on destroying.

We destroyed and wasted hundreds of billions of dollars collectively, and now are we better off than before?

Doesn't make sense. But here is the living proof—thirty years of world prosperity. How come?

You and I know that the bill owed doesn't go away. You and I know that a quart of milk spilt is a quart of milk less. A farmer knows that if one of his fields is burned up, he has lost that much grain—no matter how much money the bank is willing to lend him, or for how long a period—even thirty years.

How did this 30-year miracle occur? The answer is simple:

The gold-exchange standard! The Bretton Woods Agreement.*

In 1944 the powers met at Bretton Woods and constructed a new monetary system for the world. Well, not exactly. It was the self-same system they had put forth in Genoa in 1923.

Bretton Woods was built on two fundamental planks. One was the international convertibility of the dollar into gold at $35 per ounce. The other was a system of fixed parities by all countries as measured against the dollar, as measured against gold. But look at what has happened.

At Bretton Woods the powers all agreed that the U.S. dollar — backed by nearly 25 billion in gold in the U.S. Treasury — was certainly as good as gold. Any and every foreseeable demand could be amply met, and more. Who would look forward to a day when the United States would spend so much more than it earned that it would accumulate debts with these other nations equivalent to its entire gold pile? More fantastic still, who would look forward to the day when it would incur debts even $10 billion in excess of its gold pile — yes, $20 billion — yes, $50 billion — yes, and by 1973, $80 billion, and by 1975 more than $100 billion. By its printing presses it would produce an amount of international debt certificates equivalent to three times the entire gold pile of 1945. What is more, it would have received goods and services for this created money. What is more, it had no way to pay for those goods and services already received.

But in 1945 who could look forward to such a day?

And so the gold-exchange standard, started in Genoa in 1923, which in ten

---

*Bretton Woods—United Nations Monetary and Financial Conference held at Bretton Woods, New Hampshire, in July 1944. Established the International Monetary Fund and the International Bank for Reconstruction and Development, a world system preceding the organization of the United Nations in San Francisco the following year. The members of the I.M.F. contributed to it gold and local currencies, and obtained the priviledge of buying foreign exchange from the fund on a quota basis. The I.M.F. governed international exchange rates between currencies under a system in which the U.S. dollar was convertible into gold at $35 an ounce Troy and other currencies were exchangeable for dollars at rates agreed on with the I.M.F. In addition other central banks were free to use gold as an alternative to the U.S. dollar.

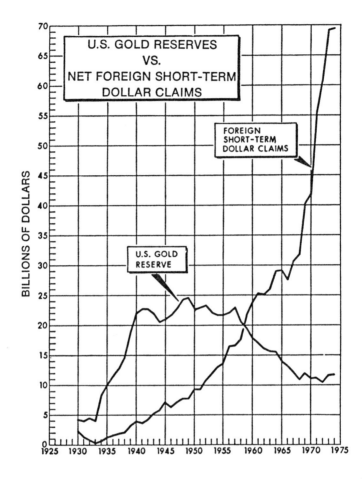

This graph shows the solid solvency of the United States Treasury in 1950—holding $25 billion in gold with only about $6 billion of outstanding claims. If all the creditors at once had converged on the U.S. gold pile they would have been paid off and the U.S. still would have has $19 billion in solid gold.

By 1960 the gold pile had declined to equal the outstanding claims and the United States — technically speaking — moving into insolvency. Kennedy recognized the dangerous trend and made dollar stability part of his election platform.

The Johnson administration could be aptly termed the era of stimulation: U.S. Treasury and administration officals closed their eyes to the danger of the expanding debt.

In 1968, following the Washington agreement, Central Banks agreed not to buy or sell gold and were pressured to promise not to ask for gold. As a consequence the U.S. gold stock remained stable thereafter. But the debts mounted to $60 billion by the end of 1971, and by the end of 1973 had reached an estimated total of between $80 and $100 billion, which was eight to ten times the existing gold stock. The price of gold would have to be multiplied eight to ten times for the United States to become barely solvent again—in other words to recover to the position where it stood in 1960. The frightening prospect of an 800 percent devaluation caused the United States to continue to resist gold convertibility, and to push the acceptance of imaginary money such as U.S. printing-press dollars and Special Drawing Rights.

short years led to the most terrible depression in history, was in 1944 simply hauled out of storage, refurbished, painted up, and put back into action under a new name — Bretton Woods.

The United States could spend hundreds of millions for the reconstruction of Europe, and the dollars would not come back to the Treasury to be redeemed for gold. So while the United States was spending this money abroad, it was at the same time spending it at home. Its money supply was not reduced by the amount of money it gave away or spent.

For $10,000 it could build a $10,000 house in Duluth, and at the same time a $10,000 house in Dresden.

The dollars were trusted in Dresden. The thing that people didn't see was that *someday*, somebody, somewhere, might become nervous about those dollars and — when he tried to use them to buy an equivalent amount of goods from someone else — he might meet reluctance to accept them at face value. At that time he would send them back to the United States and ask to be paid off in gold.

This is exactly what happened.

In 1968 when all the powers combined could not withstand the surging world demand for gold at $35 per ounce, Bretton Woods was smashed. World gold sales were stopped. The fracture was papered over under the now infamous Washington Agreement.°

Nixon closed the gold window for good in 1971 when he refused to pay out gold for dollars at any price, thereby voiding condition number one of the Bretton Woods Agreement, which provided for international convertibility of the dollar into gold at $35 per ounce.

On March 12, 1973, the six countries of the Common Market broke the last vestige of a fixed relationship when they decided to float their currencies one against the other internally — and the dollar could do whatever it wished. The dollar would, in fact, be measured *against* them. If Bretton Woods was killed in 1968, 1972 was the official burial. As of this date, there was no single, universal monetary system in the world. There was no longer anything against which the world's currencies could be measured. Prosperity itself was in question. And all this stemmed from the gold exchange standard. What was wrong with the miracle known as the gold exchange standard?

What was wrong with it was that it was, from the first, a trick. There was nothing wrong when Jesus made many fishes out of two fishes. If — as we are told — the story is true, many fishes actually appeared and filled the bellies of the people. But when the magician makes many rabbits out of one rabbit, it is

---

° Washington Agreement - On March 17, 1968, the U. S. and six other nations belonging to the London Gold Pool (Switzerland, Netherlands, Italy, England, West Germany, Belgium) plus the International Monetary Fund and Bank for International settlements announced that they had agreed not to sell any more gold to private buyers, but only to governments and central banks. In such official transactions the price of $35 an ounce would be maintained, but no attempt would be made to fix the price on the general market, which would depend on supply and demand. This was known as the "two-tier gold price system."

merely sleight of hand. It is a *deception*. And that is what was wrong with the gold-exchange standard.

What people did not foresee was that when the United States refused to pay gold as it had pledged, the gold-exchange standard would be dead. The IOUs would not be collectible. The last guy with the money was like the guy at the end of the chain letter.

It was in fact a monstrous universal chain letter.

How such a thing could come about and go on was illustrated in one of the *Myers' Finance & Energy* newsletters in the section called the "Quiet Corner," July 18, 1969, here partially reproduced:

> I have said that U.S. money is debt money. Some are puzzled by this: find it hard to fathom. Will you join me with your imagination for a moment?
>
> Suppose that I am Howard Hughes. You are my creditor and I give you an IOU for one hundred dollars. (A check on the bank is an IOU of course). You give this to your service station mechanic. He accepts it readily. Howard Hughes can issue untold thousands of one hundred dollar IOU's, instantly acceptable anywhere.
>
> Let us now suppose that Mr. Hughes does issue a million, even two million IOU's of a hundred dollars. People don't even bother to take them to the bank; they are just as good as money; just the same as money. With the confidence in this great empire, imagine these IOU's circulating freely. But these bills are large denominations; and wherever he can Mr. Hughes gets his men to pick them up and reissue ten dollar notes on green paper with his signature. Thus let's say we have one hundred million dollars in Hughes' currency. Is it money? That depends.
>
> If Mr. Hughes is indeed a solvent as we thought, it is money. But whether it is money or not, it amounts to one hundred million dollars of Hughes' *debts*. Does it not?
>
> Now suppose that Mr. Hughes has in the meanwhile engaged in ruinous ventures in airlines in China, movies in Italy, etc. Suppose he has lost and mortgaged his various plants and properties. Now is this Hughes' currency money?
>
> No it is not. It represents Mr. Hughes' debts. It is debt money. It is DEBT masquerading as money. Economists give this a very good sounding name — MONETIZED DEBT.

The U.S. currency in your bank accounts today is exactly that: the monetized debt of the United States. The notes are convertible to nothing by the government itself; not wheat, not iron, not even straw. The United States Treasury will give you absolutely nothing for any of them except a replacement of another piece of paper. The substance, two billion ounces of silver and $25 billion in gold, that once backed these pieces of paper has disappeared. But you say, "Look at the great productivity of the United States. In its productivity lies its wealth." You are right.

But did you stop to think that this productivity does not belong to the government? Rather to the people. That the vast scores and hundreds of billions spent by the government has been collected from the people and that the government gave the people IOU's. The IOU's are government bonds and they are the currency.

The government alone owes this money, and the government has nothing in its vaults to back it up.

Federal Debt of the United States in Billions of Dollars

Term	Years	Total Debt	Growth Rate
36 years	1879-1915	2 billion	Stable
16 years	1916-1932	18 billion	1 billion per year
10 years	1932-1942	71 billion	5.3 billion per year
10 years	1942-1952	260 billion	19 billion per year
10 years	1952-1962	348 billion	8.8 billion per year
10 years	1962-1972	442 billion	9.4 billion per year
2 years	1972-1974	495 billion	21.5 billion per year
4 years	1974-1978	746 billion	63 billion per year

Federal debt stayed steady at 2 billion from 1875 to 1915 — 40 years

Federal debt grew 258 billion 1916 to 1952 — 36 years

Federal debt grew another 235 billion 1952 to 1974 — 22 years

FEDERAL DEBT GREW 251 BILLION 1974 TO 1978 — 4 YEARS

How did it get so big?

Say the government sold a billion dollars of thirty-year bonds in 1930. In 1960 it sells $3 billion worth of thirty-year bonds. It uses one billion to pay off the original buyers of 1930. It borrows the other two billion to work with. The newly borrowed two billion will be paid off thirty years from now *If* the people of the United States thirty years from now still trust the government enough to buy more bonds. If they don't trust the government the present lenders will get nothing.

The government does not have anything in its vaults with which to pay off its debts.

The government has never repaid the money it spent and lent for World War II. It just borrowed from U.S. citizens and then borrowed again (bonds) when bills came due. So what you have is debt money. It circulates mostly by force. It is called "lawful money" and "legal tender." Did anyone ever have to write those assurances on a silver dollar or $20 gold piece?

The truth is that, regardless of any laws, your savings account in the bank is a debt. The $10 bill in your pocket is a debt. More money is created when more money is borrowed (lent) by the government or the people. If people or banks quit lending or borrowing money, available money stops growing. When you pay or default on a debt, available money shrinks. Massive bankruptcies mean massive shrinkage. Massive shrinkage is deflation.

When this will happen no one can be quite sure. But happen it will. Debt money is the product of the new era—the new age—that began with the Bretton Woods agreement of 1944. The reason the government did not have to pay off the cost of World War II was that it borrowed most of the savings of all the people and paid the bills with that. But having done so, it still owed the people in the form of bonds and fiat currencies. It has never paid the people—except to borrow from new generations to pay off the old generations. It is operating because all of the people of the United States *Believe* that a debt bearing the signature of the government is as good as gold—or at least as good as U.S. money. But it is not.

The United States Government operates like our imaginary Howard Hughes who has squandered all his assets but still operates because people *believe* his IOU's are good. But remember, Howard Hughes' IOU's are just as good as real money as long as people *Believe* that Howard Hughes still has his assets. When they find out he does not, the Hughes money collapses.

So the prosperity following World War II ushered in an era of plentiful money. Jacques Rueff hit it on the nose when he called it the era of inflation.

The money was sent to Europe, and the same money was spent in America, and all the savings of the people that had been collected in bonds and taxes were used, and have now been consumed.

The era that was launched in 1945 increasingly encouraged, as it progressed, the expansion of credit. If people were to save and pay off their debts, they would buy fewer washing machines, automobiles, etc. This in turn would cause a slowdown in the factories. This could bring on unemployment. Unemployment would result in the default of debts and in seizures of property. If that process ever got started people would sell out of the stock market, producing a crash, margins would be called, and more stock market sales would be necessitated. The whole monetary process would go into reverse.

Once launched upon this era of inflation, the only salvation was to keep it going. Each year the interest on the national debt was mounting until in 1973 the interest required nearly $24 billion of Mr. Nixon's $257 billion budget, and well over $30 billion on Mr. Ford's $350 billion budget of 1975, and well over $40 billion for Mr. Carter's $435 billion budget of 1979.

The meaning of all this is that the debt continues to build astronomically on a foundation that was never meant to carry it, and that is now cracking and caving in under the enormous weight. The money supply must keep on increasing, even if only to pay the interest. Never mind a thought of paying off the principal. That by now has become forever impossible.

All this means that the money supply will have to continue to increase to avoid the dreaded bust. But it means that the dreaded bust will not be avoided.

11. CHANGED PEOPLE IN A NEW ERA

The tremendous flood of money couldn't help but have its consequences upon the social structure and on the basic attitudes of the people. They jubilantly welcomed the era because they simply did not understand what was going on. How could they? The government and the press assured them that humanity was now launched into a new age when there would be plenty for all. So confident were the policy makers that they had discovered the endless fountain of money, they even passed a law called the Full Employment Act of 1946. It prohibited unemployment, as if the government had so much power that it could actually prescribe the degree of prosperity of the country.

The people believed that they were living in a changed world—and they became a changed people.

And why not! Whereas once you had to lay out substantial cash (savings) to buy a car, now you were urged to buy one with no down payment at all. Whereas once you had to pay it off in a year, now you could pay it off in as much as two or three or five years. Whereas once you had to have fifty percent for the price of a bungalow, now you needed only ten percent. And finally, by 1972, if you had $500 you could buy a $20,000 house with $500. But by early 1975 you were not able to buy any house at all, because the savings and loans associations had no money. The chicken was coming home to roost.

Up to then the mortgage companies had been happy to lend the money. Why not? After all, wasn't there a law that said that unemployment had been banished—just as King Arthur had banished snow from Camelot. That being so, no mortgagee would ever be without work, or at least enough social security to make his payments.

As a consequence the generation that became teenagers in the late fifties and early sixties were brought up to believe that credit was a desirable way of life. They were brought up to have what they wanted now, and pay later; whereas earlier generations had been taught to save first and buy when they had the money. What a drastic change! And it came about almost unnoticed.

Those who didn't want to work found that they could do almost as well on unemployment insurance. Their weekly checks of course, were being paid by those who were willing to work. Any surplus unemployment contributions went into the government coffers in Washington. But this money was not saved. It was written off as a debt of the government and the money spent for other things, including Vietnam or other social benefits.

By the end of 1977 the Social Security Fund was in danger of going under. That simply meant that people who had paid into it had supplied the money for the retirement of those employees who had preceded them, but wouldn't be able to get any themselves. The principal reason was because the government had already spent the money. So it was necessary to jack up the Social Security contributions significantly. Millions of workers set aside each week a portion of their earnings in the form of pensions for their old age. But this money was not saved either—it was invested. The pension funds themselves bought government bonds, which are debt instruments. Pensioners will eventually lose all or most of their contributions unless the government can continue to sell bonds to pay off the savings it has already consumed.

Let me repeat: Not a dime of the social security payments that millions of workers have made has been put away. It has all been spent. Not a dime of their employers' contribution has been put away. All has been spent.

The Social Security "contribution" went into the Treasury's general fund along with all other taxes and was spent.

The Social Security payments made in 1978 were all bogus dollars created by the Federal Reserve because there was no fund, and because the budget was already in deficit, and there was no other way to make the Social Security payments.

If a man's taxes this year were $2,000 and his Social Security payments were $1,200, then he paid $3,200 taxes, not $2,000.

He will never get the Social Security payments he made. If he gets paid at all it will be from future taxes of people still working when he quit working. His money is long gone.

If the American people revolt against this deception — and resign from it — there will be nobody left on the scene to pay anyone.

There are resignations now: states, cities, counties. They can resign from the fund, and observing what a poor deal it is they are leaving it. Including New York City, more than two hundred and fifty such have resigned—hundreds— even thousands may follow.

These losers mean a shrinking army of workers to pay for a growing army of would-be pensioners.

Every Social Security payee of such bodies leaving the fund loses his whole "contribution to his retirement" when his state, city, etc. withdraws.

It's clear that Social Security is as crooked as a chain letter. It's worse, because your Social Security number makes you falsely believe you are connected with the fund. But your Social Security number gives you no claim on, and has no contact with, any fund anywhere.

The amount of an individual Social Security payment has no bearing on a person's "contributions" (really taxes). It will be what Congress says it can afford.

Any private pension or insurance scheme of sound base would give you much greater benefits than your Social Security. If such a company spent the money on something else and didn't put it away in a trust, they would all be jailed for fraud.

The government is under no contractual obligation for payments to its citizens. Yet it pretends and encourages them to think they are saving for their old age.

When Congress tripled the maximum 1977 "contribution" from $1,930 to $60,092 by 1987, it was nothing more or less than a tax increase under guise of a "benefit" which may never happen. Congress can cut at will the amount anyone gets, or raise at will the age at which one starts to get it, 65-68-69-70-?

The only amount of money a person could be sure of until late 1978 was a $275 burial fee. Now it seems that, too, is to be abolished to enable Carter to cut the budget; despite the fact that this burial has already been paid for.

People are living longer. The crowd coming up for benefits is ever larger. The baby boom population entering the labor market has peaked. So fewer workers must work harder and longer to pay more recipients. But can they be sure when they quit there will be enough people left working willing to pay enough high taxes to pay *them* any pension?

Social Security is a cruel *tax hoax* masquerading as *personal savings.* The lie has lulled contributors away from saving anything for themselves on the belief that their savings were being funneled into Social Security for their old age — the so-called system.

There is no fund and there is no security!

As in every other aspect of our life, we have nothing but debts.

This new era of inflation has made a business of selling debts, much as Proctor & Gamble has made a business of selling soap.

"Why pay now, when you can pay later?" The credit card business has mushroomed. Banks advertised their free credit cards. Others promised that you could run an overdraft without worry. And still others that you could borrow on a heavier scale and defer payment longer than you could with some other bank.

Private debt spiraled in sympathy with the public debt, and both hit astronomical levels. Under the social climate of the era of inflation no one saw anything wrong with this. The public tended to welcome it. After all, wages were constantly going up as the inflation continued. And prices were constantly going up. This was a great boon for the man with debts! If he had borrowed money ten years ago, the constant inflation meant that he paid back in materially reduced dollars, thereby repudiating part of his debt. That was fine for about ten years, but by 1978 the whole thing was getting scary. In this single year consumer borrowing jumped 50 percent. Four-fifths of all U.S. households were in debt. Many were using their pay checks just for debt.

At the same time mortgage borrowing leaped 54 percent. In the 1960's it usually increased at $15 billion per year. But in 1978 it jumped $100 billion.

What really scared the pants off European economists was that during the recovery years of 1976 and 1977, *when U.S. public debt should not have grown at all*, it actually shot into the stratosphere, *jumping from $495 billion to $745 billion!*

In 1978 each child, as it came from its mother's womb, was responsible for paying $4,000 with continuing compound interest. The government had signed him up for it.

This utter irresponsibility on the part of the government could only undermine the morality and integrity of the people.

So the era of inflation involved more than money. It involved a deterioration of moral fiber. When a government steals from its people, what can it expect of its citizens?

We have seen from our society of Freedonia that the entire social structure will fall unless men can be secure in the knowledge that they can retain what they have earned. Undermine the right of private property and the right to retain it, and you have struck a blow at morality. And you have proclaimed, "Let us all plunder one another!"

The age of inflation produced a dry rot that began to destroy the timbers under the social structure soon after the ending of World War II. By 1973 the timbers under the economy were rotten. Still the building stood. Still the building looked beautiful. And those who did not wish to know about the timbers and the foundation, refused to cast their eyes at the base of the building. They only looked at the beautiful painted walls and the great shining glass windows, and they said, "All is good. Look at the building. What a beautiful building we have built!"

In other words the age of inflation, having produced a public immorality, guaranteed its extension by that very immorality — at least for a time. For a trend, once in motion, does not stop of its own accord. Only later will its own accumulated internal flaws bring it to a halt.

Henry George, a thinker far ahead of his time, wrote in 1879 in his book *Progress and Poverty: "For in social development, as in everything else, motion tends to persist in straight lines, and therefore where there has been a previous advance, it is extremely difficult to recognize decline. Even when it has fully commenced there is an almost irrestible tendency to believe that the*

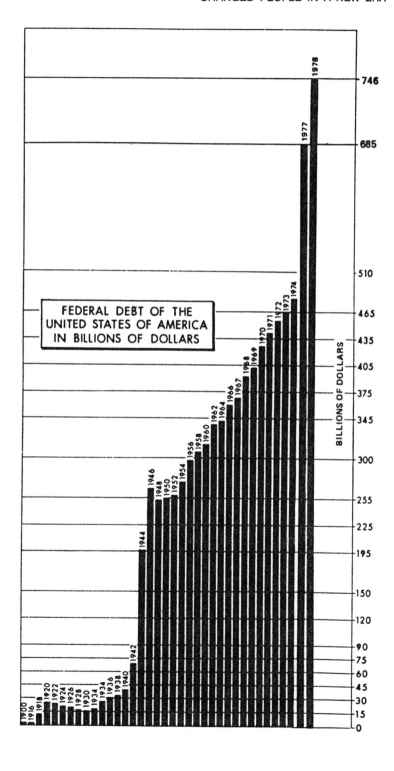

FEDERAL DEBT OF THE
UNITED STATES OF AMERICA
IN BILLIONS OF DOLLARS

forward movement, which has been advancing and is still going on, is still advancing." George also believed that the moral breakdown of society started from the top and he said:

"The most ominous political sign is the growth of a sentiment which either doubts the existence of an honest man in public office or looks on him as a fool for not seizing his opportunities. That is to say, the people themselves are becoming corrupted."

Inflation has destroyed the old-fashioned virtue of thrift. Why save if what you save will constantly evaporate? It has destroyed the old-fashioned virtue of ambition, for why work harder when the man next to you lags behind and earns exactly the same amount as you do? It has destroyed the idea of pay as you go, for those who pay as they go are the suckers; those who pay later pay off with cheaper dollars.

And of course this could not have happened in a short period of time. The gold-exchange standard of 1923 to 1934 did not produce an immorality in the population. That could only happen over the course of a generation or more, which Jacques Rueff has rightly called THE AGE OF INFLATION.

And since inflation will not stop of its own accord, and since it cannot be stopped except at the cost of a deflation, its continuation is certain until it brings about a collapse of the economy and a collapse of social order. As 1979 dawned, the structure was beginning to tremble.

All of this has been evident for some time. It could be told by the criteria as outlined by Henry George* when he said: "Civilization has begun to wane when, in proportion to population, we must build more and more prisons, more and more alms houses, more and more insane asylums."

---

* Henry George—American economist. Believed that a single tax on land would meet all the needs of government. Author of *Progress and Poverty* (1879)

12. INTERNATIONAL TENTACLES

The reader is bound to have reached a stage by now where he will be wondering rather urgently how much longer this inflation will continue, when it will come to an end, how it will come to an end, and what, if anything, he can do to protect himself—not only from the economic repercussions of the collapse of inflation, but also from the social consequences of the economic collapse. To attempt even an intelligent *guess* in answer to these questions it is necessary to understand the international implications.

It is the international aspects of inflation that have allowed inflation to thrive so long. The length of its life will be found to have been an important determinant of the severity of the collapse and the duration of the collapse.

Never before in history was inflation able to endure for such a lengthy period. Never in history did it encompass the world. The reason is that never before in history did we have a gold-exchange standard, at first condoned and then, of necessity, supported by the world. Previously the jaws of inflation frequently crushed a single country. Never before were the jaws so huge that they could grip the globe.

The greatest currency the world has known—the greatest lubricant for industry and trade and prosperity—was the British pound. Its use encircled the world, but it was based on the gold standard. During the age of the gold standard, inflation was never able to raise its head more than an inch before it was knocked down again.

When all of the countries of the free world endorsed the gold-exchange standard in 1944, they set the stage for the most massive fall in the history of man — a fall that would make the very gods tremble. When all the countries set their sails by the U.S. dollar, the flotilla had embarked on a voyage into the sea of oblivion.

It worked this way:

The reserves of a country represent its profit position. They are like the savings of a man. They are a guard against a rainy day. If the crops are bad in the country, the reserves can be called upon to buy imports. So the reserves of a country are extremely important.

When the reserves of a country are the currency of another country, the first country becomes necessarily dependent upon the health of the second. The United States dollar became the reserve currency of the world. Holdings of United States dollars became the protection of those countries against a rainy day. If the dollar was durable those piggy bank savings were secure. The value of the reserves of other countries would vary according to the value of the United States dollar.

Once the countries of the world included masses of United States dollars in their reserves, it was to their interest to preserve the integrity of the dollar. They had been trapped into a position where they had to save the dollar to save their own necks.

France was the first country to see that the dollar was so far gone it would eventually have to tumble. The French logic was that if the dollar will have to tumble, better it tumble early than late. For the longer the deterioration of the dollar continues, the worse will be the plight of everyone when it falls.

General DeGaulle, in the mid-sixties, with unerring vision, started a policy of changing French reserves from dollars into gold. Some may blame him for contributing to the fall of the dollar. That would be foolish. A currency falls because it is sick of itself. Had the dollar been sound it would simply have shrugged off this paltry attack.

Unfortunately for the world, DeGaulle was thwarted by internal problems in France in May of 1969. His efforts to establish a solid base for world money had to be abandoned. Thereafter the weakening paper giant was propped up again, fed some more stimulant, and pushed out into the arena looking better than ever.

DeGaulle saw that the constant increase of debts of the United States was a trend that was likely to continue. He observed what was plain for anyone to see, that the debts of the United States well exceeded the gold supply. Everyone knew that the world's monetary system was based on the idea that any outstanding dollars could always, without question, be changed to gold. DeGaulle saw that this day was nearly over. He knew that it was only a question of time until the nations would clamor for gold for their dollars. He also knew that by that time the United States would have manufactured so many more dollars that the situation, when it came eventually to crisis, would be infinitely worse.

To understand fully the development of the international lack of confidence one must go back to 1961. For sixteen years—since Bretton Woods—the United States alone had guaranteed the gold validity of its outstanding dollars. But in that year, when the debt exceeded the gold, the public of the world became alarmed and began to trade dollars for gold at a premium, yielding $41 dollars for an ounce of gold in place of the $35 guaranteed maximum price by the United States. The United States had to call for help. It asked the major nations to deposit a large amount of gold into a joint pool, and jointly to inform the world that all of these big countries would stand behind the price of gold at $35, and would sell gold in unlimited quantity to all takers. These nations, already holding sizable numbers of dollars, and hoping for its stability—even France—gladly cooperated. The free market price of gold dropped back to $35.

But the sickness was inherent, although it was progressing slowly. By 1968 the United States gold supply had dwindled to about $10 billion and the debts had risen to well over $30 billion. The demand for gold all over the world was growing. Still the gold pool sold to all comers. But this was becoming alarming. Realistically, France perceived that in the market place of the world, under free conditions, an ounce of gold was worth more than $35. France dropped out of the gold pool. Although this was kept secret, the run on gold continued.

The internal paper currency of the United States amounted to about $40 billion, and there was a law that said that this currency had to be backed 25 percent by gold. That meant that the entire remaining U.S. gold stock of $10 billion was committed to the pocket currency in circulation. There was need also to increase the pocket currency. The United States was at an impasse. It could not print any more folding money unless it increased the price of gold, for it only had about $10 billion in gold and it had $40 billion in outstanding currency. That would mean the devaluation of the dollar against gold—in other words, an increase in the price of gold. But that would greatly undermine confidence internationally.

President Lyndon Johnson and Secretary of the Treasury Henry Fowler thought that if they removed the gold from behind the circulating greenbacks it would do two things. It would let them print unlimited currency; and it would shore up international confidence because they could make the whole $10 billion available to foreign central banks. With new gold available, the fears about the dollar would abate despite the fact that the United States owed three or four times as much as its total store of gold. So President Johnson urged the Congress to pass a law that would remove the gold backing from the paper currency inside the United States. At one time the paper currency had been a hundred percent backed by gold, later fifty percent, later thirty-three percent. Now even the twenty-five percent backing had to be abandoned.

What greater signal to the international monetary world that the dollar was sinking? Foreign treasuries were publicly uncritical; they didn't want to say anything to undermine the dollar because their own savings were almost wholly in dollars.

The demand for gold was cured only briefly. By March 1968 there was such a run on gold that the United States Treasury had to throw in the towel. All the markets of the world were closed while the heads of the central banks and finance ministers met in Washington to decide what to do. Unless the dollar was held to be convertible into gold, the Bretton Woods agreement was in ruins. Then what would they use for a monetary system? Then what would be the value of the stored dollars in the reserves of the various countries—their protection against a rainy day? It was to the interest of them all to support any move that seemed reasonable to preserve the status of the dollar. Therefore the invention of the two-tier gold system, whereby there was a set price for gold between governments, and a free market price (a people's price) for gold between people.

But a two-level price for anything is in direct contradiction of all natural law. A price is a level at which a commodity will trade back and forth — where the buyer is willing to pay the amount for which the seller will release the goods. There never can be two real prices. One must be an artificial or enforced price. It is, therefore, the weaker price because it is the unrealistic price. It will, therefore, sooner or later collapse. The two-tier gold system was a further signal of the desperate straits of the dollar.

But the countries hoped against hope that it would work so that their own reserves of dollars would be protected in their value. The gold-exchange standard had got them into this trap. There was no visible way out.

Their greatest wish was that the United States would cure its balance of payments problem. This may at first sound complicated, but it is extremely simple. The balance of payments is just like your bank account. If, at the end of a year, you have managed to save some money you have a balance in your bank account. If, at the end of a year, you have spent more than you have earned, your bank account has declined from last year's figure, or you have gone into debt and you have red ink.

Not since 1950, except for the year 1957, has the United States produced a more positive balance at the end of the year. It has always spent more. There was some defense for this: it was said that the United States was keeping armies in Europe for the protection of the European countries against communism; the United States was fighting Communism in Asia; the United States provided the nuclear umbrella, and so forth. Excuse after excuse was used as reason for the poor balance of payments showing.

Each and every year, from 1960, the U.S. Treasury officials had predicted that the following year would show a great improvement. Each new year would see the weaknesses of the past overcome and the turnabout would be at hand. The other nations wished desperately to believe this.

During the years 1967 to 1972 I was in Europe several times and talked to some of the authorities, particularly in Germany and Switzerland. It was obvious they were clinging to a wish that was being paraded as a belief. On each occasion they staunchly maintained that the United States was curing its balance of payments. The United States is the greatest industrial nation in the world. You see it has a good surplus of trade. That shows its essential health.

For many years it has been earning $5 billion in surplus trade.

Had I ventured to suggest to Mr. Pohl, Germany's deputy finance minister, that in two or three years even the trade balance would go into the red, I think Mr. Pohl would have frowned severely. But had I made the truly mad prognosis that the U.S. trade would be negative by $30 billion before the decade ended, I would probably have been tossed out on my head.

But 1970 was a year of horror. In that year trade barely balanced. And 1971 was a year of disaster. Trade went into the red and the United States bought $2 billion more than it sold in goods. The year 1972 was a cataclysm. The trade deficit increased to $6 billion. In 1973 there was a small surplus, but again in 1974 a trade deficit of nearly $6 billion.

Externally between trade deficit and other spending, the U.S. seemed to be on a course of about $12 billion a year deficit.

But even in 1975 most of the reserves of all of the countries in the world were in the form of U.S. dollars. Their savings were largely U.S. debts.

No wonder there was panic on the international monetary fronts.

In face of the true facts, Nixon's ravings against the speculators who were ruining the dollar was exposed as a weak and bare-faced lie. One might as well blame the undertaker for the patient's death as blame the speculators for the plight of the dollar.

But it is necessary to go back a step. The two-tier gold system of 1968, with Herculean cooperation by other nations, held the dollar for nearly three years. That was because the other nations agreed that even though they had the right, under Bretton Woods, to claim gold for the dollars in their treasuries, they would not claim it. They also agreed not even to buy any gold. They agreed further not to sell any gold. Among them they had *isolated* gold on the official monetary market in the vain hope that the free market price would fall to the artificial market price of $35 an ounce. If this could be accomplished, the theoretical value of their national reserves in their piggy banks could be maintained. If gold got away, Bretton Woods would be smashed and their reserves would shrink. For twenty or thirty years they had been counting on the stability of the U.S. dollar as a store of value.

In order to keep gold immobilized, gold had somehow to be discredited. The inventiveness of the U.S. Treasury was without limit.

Why not have an international reserve that had nothing to do with gold? Get the story around that this would be the new world money, and people would sell their gold. The Central Banks of course wouldn't sell an ounce, but the hope was that the foolish public would sell its gold. The idea was to get the public to think along these lines: If the banks won't pay anything for our gold—won't buy it all—we will find ourselves owning a dead horse. The price will go to next to nothing. What good is gold—really? Let's get out while we can!!

Thus the authorities, in the true spirit of the con men on the Mississippi River boats of old, would persuade the suckers into releasing the only enduring money they had, while the con men would pick it up for themselves later on—cheap.

Sometimes laymen are smarter than experts. The laymen of the world felt that if gold was cherished by the Central Banks to the point where they wouldn't part with any of their own, gold must be all right. Many said to themselves, "As long as it's good enough for the banks, it's good enough for me."

An example of the propaganda of those days was in a report by Pierre Rinfret* on November 28, 1969. As an instance of the type of economist who has been listened to by the masses — this is too good to miss:

> In 1967, I had lunch with a high official of the Bank of England. When I suggested that if gold were freed it might go to fifty dollars, the lofty official laughed. "You don't know anything about the price of gold! Give us two years and we'll smash the price to twenty-five dollars an ounce."

The Rinfret letter goes on:

> The luminary from the Bank of England explained: "The central banks will stop buying gold. The moment they do that, South Africa will have lost her market. Then there must be a free market. If the central banks refused to buy, South Africa will have to sell on the free market. Since she depends upon gold exports, she will have to sell it all there.

> "Now remember there is no floor anymore. People who bought at thirty-five dollars can't be sure they'll get thirty-five dollars. The central banks will then step in and with one billion dollars of gold will smash the price to twenty-five dollars. We're professional; we can beat the amateurs at their own game any day of the week. But here's the beautiful part. When we get the price down to twenty-five dollars an ounce, and all the gold that's been locked away comes out, we central bankers step in and buy at bargain prices.

> "We'll have taught the amateurs a lesson they won't forget. We will have stabilized the world monetary system. Just watch us. We're going to do it."

So much for this shallow-minded dreamer so high in the Bank of England. More importantly, what was Mr. Rinfret's considered judgment of this opinion?

"The truth is," he said in his letter of November 28, 1969, *"the central bankers now have control, and are having their own way. The first thing to realize is that they may drive the price down to twenty-five dollars an ounce."* One wonders what Mr. Rinfret's comments were on this point in late 1974 when gold sold for $200 an ounce.

Elliot Janeway† and Sylvia Porter‡ were also at the forefront of wrong headed economists who declared that gold was dead, thereby depriving their

---

* Pierre Andre Rinfret—Canadian-born American economist, b. 1924. Chairman, Chief Executive Officer of Rinfret-Boston Associates, New York City. Popular writer on economic subjects. Advisor to the Secretary of the Treasury, 1972-1973.

† Eliot Janeway — American economist, b. 1913. Publisher of Janeway Letter. Author, *Musings on Money* (1976) and other books.

‡ Sylvia Porter — New York writer on money management subjects. b. 1913.

millions of readers of the best money making opportunity in half a decade. They had lots of famous company.

The "Special Drawing Rights" or "paper gold" as it was called, was to be the magic formula for monetary reform. The authorities did not seem to be bothered by the fact that Special Drawing Rights were unadulterated hot air. S.D.R.'s were DECLARED to be money. We were back to the days of Kublai Khan.

But we have seen from our examination of the state of Freedonia that real money is a warehouse receipt, and as such is in itself wealth, and that the precious metals are only a *measurement* of that wealth. They were registering short weight on the beefsteak. So the authorities denounced the scale. The trouble, they said is not a shortage of beefsteak but the tyranny of this old-fashioned scale. Smash the scale. Demonetize gold!

Through the invention of, and as a result of, the gold-exchange standard, inflation was threatening to swamp the world. The only answer the authorities could come up with was more inflation — this time INTERNATIONAL inflation (S.D.R.'s) in addition to the national monetary inflation (the dollar).

13. SPECIAL DRAWING RIGHTS — THE ULTIMATE DELUSION

The name itself—paper gold—was a brazen admission that it was a fake. Soon it became the butt of jokes. In my newsletters I referred to it frequently in the same breath with glass diamonds, virgin prostitutes, etc. The authorities became rather sensitive about the derision being heaped on their latest monetary protege, and they began to restrict official reference to Special Drawing Rights rather than paper gold.

That at least sounded prestigious, and carried the implication that it was the brilliant creation of some very highly qualified monetary wizards.

Alas, even a cursory examination of this name showed it to be an accurate description of yet another farce. For Special Drawing Rights must certainly be *special rights* to draw—obviously special rights to *borrow*.

The new world money, then, was once again not money at all; it was a right to *borrow* money. But what money? It was nothing more than a right to create additional international debt. A new engine to be added to the era of inflation to blow the balloon bigger.

The common man shrugged his shoulders; slumbered on.

By 1972 nations had issued, in all, about $9 billion of these rights for countries to borrow, and these S.D.R.s were mixed in with all of the rest of the reserves in the Central Banks. They were rated to have exactly the same value in dollars as an ounce of gold. In other words, a thing called an S.D.R.—a goose egg—was *declared* to be worth one/thirty-fifth of an ounce of gold. If you had, as a Central Bank, 35 million of these goose eggs then you had a million ounces of gold. It was one and the same thing—based on the theory of Kublai Khan.

It was as if you had declared to your neighbor on the farm that three pieces of shavings were worth one egg; and as if you said to your neighbor, "I now give you thirty-six pieces of shavings, please give me one dozen eggs."

This is oversimplified but it is absolutely true, and the monetary authorities thought they could pull it off. Unbelievable!

By the end of 1972 several important countries were beginning to have reservations about the ability of the authorities to sustain this fantasy; and at the end of 1972 they refused to issue any further Special Drawing Rights. The curtain was beginning to descend on this the most nonsensical monetary idea ever conceived by man.

What had happened, to that point, was merely that the reserves of all of the Central Banks had been diluted a further $9 billion. More water in the whisky.

If the gold-exchange standard was an engine of inflation, the Special Drawing Rights were an inflationary engine with a four-barrel carburetor. To all sane men it must have foretold acceleration on the road to inflationary disaster — not for one country, but for the world.

By mid-1972, the concept was privately being recognized for what it was — a ridiculous farce. In the press it was still being occasionally touted as the magic new solution for world monetary reform. In the highest inner offices, however, sober bankers shook their heads, and began to see at last that, if there were an ultimate in the monetary land of delusion, surely S.D.R.s were it.

Delusion grows from illusion, and illusion grows from a wish. One pertinent thing about an illusion is that it is quite real as long as it persists. The difference between an illusion and reality is simple. The illusion, being unreal, always collapses; and reality, being real, survives forever. Sometimes it is hard to distinguish between illusion and reality, because, while illusion exists, it works just as well as reality.

The second pertinent thing about illusion is that it is an "all or nothing" deal. That is, it either exists completely, or it evaporates completely. When reality has been overrated there is something left. When illusion is exploded there is *nothing* left.

This makes mass illusion very dangerous. *When a whole nation or a group of nations come to believe in an illusion, the return to reality is so sharp, so abrupt, that it leaves no time for adjustment.* An exposed illusion wilts before your eyes.

Persistent illusions suffered by individuals are called "delusions." Delusions are the mark of insanity. They may be delusions of grandeur or of anything else that is not true—or not real. But to the victim the delusion is absolutely true—absolutely real; and given the premise of this delusion, all of the actions of the victim are logical. Take the premise away, and his actions are insane.

When an entire people get hung up on a persistent illusion, it becomes a delusion; and you have mass madness. Every so often the world goes mad. Common sense becomes nonsense. The crusades were utter madness. They had no real purpose, but they persisted through generations.

World War I was madness. Today no real reason can be found for it. The tulip mania in seventeenth-century Holland was wild economic madness. Fortunes were paid for a single tulip bulb. The delusion was that tulip bulbs were valuable and that they would continue to increase in value, no matter what. Finally someone came to his senses and asked himself just what is the real value of a tulip bulb except its blossom? — and that man sold!

The crowd was at last awakened, recognizing that there was after all no REAL value to tulip bulbs, except to a gardener. The crash that followed the tulip mania was the worst up to that point in history. There were numerous others.

During these periods of mass insanity the delusion works quite well. The danger of the delusion is not in staying in it, but coming out of it.

Western civilization has been operating under a mass credit delusion. It is the delusion that "NOTHING will substitute for SOMETHING" — "paper is as good as gold." The meaning is that a token is just as good as the real thing. The meaning is that a picture of you has as much reality as you. *Carry the delusion further and the madman declares that the picture is the real thing and you derive your existence only because of the existence of the picture.*

Expressed in terms of the deluded U.S. economists, it went this way: the dollar does not depend on gold or the value of gold. Gold only gets its value because the U.S. Treasury has been willing to pay $35 an ounce for it. Take away that willingness and gold is worth nothing. Gold derives its value by virtue of the reflection, take away the reflection (the dollar) and the gold presumably goes out of existence. Could you believe that in this twentieth century? I think witches and goblins have a closer reality.

Following this delusion, all backing having been removed from the U.S. domestic dollar and, finally, from the U.S. international dollar, the madness was expanded to embrace an international mechanism of S.D.R.s that were declared to have a gold value—although no one in the world would give any gold for an S.D.R.

Such a mechanism can work for a while. The tulips of yesteryear WERE VALUABLE as long as people had confidence in the value of the tulips, and believed that other people had the same confidence. The same mechanism worked for the dollar, even though the backing had been removed.

Here is a little satire I wrote about the S.D.R. at the time—on December 16, 1971.

DONUT HOLES
A One Act Play

Starring

Richard Nixon   Karl Schiller   Valery d'Estaing

Arthur Burns   John Connally

Nixon: Gentlemen, I have called this meeting because of a devastating crisis. As you know, we have run out of gold, and we have had to lay our bets on S.D.R.s. But the plain fact is, S.D.R.s are not catching on! Arthur Burns has come up with a new idea. Arthur—tell them.

Arthur Burns: The thinking is, gentlemen, that S.D.R.s are too vague. People can't imagine an S.D.R. You've got to have something they can visualize. At the same time it must be something which is nothing. Because if it is something, we shall be restricted in our creation of money. What I'm going to say may sound foolish at first. It did to me, when I read it in a Canadian financial letter. But don't laugh, gentlemen, I propose we rename S.D.R.s, and that from now on they be known officially throughout the world as DONUT HOLES.

Schiller: Whatever the Americans say is acceptable to the Germans. We have already upvalued twice to assist the U.S. Treasury at considerable sacrifice to our people. After all, we started the war, and we deserve to suffer—even if you get the donuts and we only get the holes.

Burns: Suffering will be unnecessary. Our international debts will be denominated in Donut Holes. Each Donut Hole is worth one thirty-fifth of an ounce of gold—exactly the same as an S.D.R. All S.D.R.s will be converted into Donut Holes. Now this has the advantage of giving people the illusion of reality. When you think of a Donut Hole, what do you think of? A donut, of course! Maybe even a cup of coffee. But an S.D.R. lacks this. I am suggesting that the world monetary system should operate on Donut Holes.

D'Estaing: France will go along with the idea only if you agree to use real donuts in order to get the holes.

Connally: The U.S. will not be crucified on a cross of donuts. We are going to de-emphasize the donuts and emphasize the holes. And we are going to use the holes, and that's the end of it! And that hole is worth one thirty-fifth of an ounce of gold—the same as an S.D.R. And that is what we *say* it is worth, so that is what it is worth. In the matter of international balances we will store all the Donut Holes in a single building. Each country will have his man in this building, with a rake, and as the balances change, the piles of Donut Holes will be raked into the bins of the respective countries.

Nixon: I got an idea on that. At the California White House we have these Japanese bamboo rakes. They're not very strong, but they would handle voluminous quantities of Donut Holes. Ha Ha!

Connally: Yes, but what about your quota on Jap rakes?

Nixon: I forgot that. By Jove!

Connally: There is no need to use Japanese products. In Texas we have ten-prong pitchforks. They have proved their worth in handling the products of Texas, and they can be washed off for use by the IMF.

Nixon: I agree, we should buy American. I will arrange tax rebates for factories producing these forks. This will create jobs, and we will sell the forks to the IMF for moving Donut Holes. Ha Ha!

Schiller: Germany agrees. Even if every German is out of work, I agree. Hitler started the war, and we deserve to pay. Let no one try to stop Germany from making its just retribution.

D'Estaing: France agrees that the Donut Hole is worth every bit as much as the S.D.R: We further agree that a Donut Hole is better than an S.D.R. because it gives the illusion of something real, while the S.D.R. concept could well return us to the middle ages, when the debate raged: "How many angels can dance on the point of a needle?" If we used S.D.R.s, our economists will surely begin to argue: "How many billion S.D.R.s can be stored in the eye of a needle?" But if we use Donut Holes, the question will not arise, because Donut Holes have a diameter of about one inch each. Nevertheless, France will never agree to just the holes—unless we also have the donuts.

Nixon: The perversity of France is obstructing monetary progress. I hereby declare that the United States recognizes Donut Holes as the sole international world currency. Each Donut Hole is worth one thirty-fifth of an ounce of gold and is instantly transferable into an S.D.R. And all dollars are convertible immediately into either S.D.R.s or Donut Holes. They all have the same value. Nobody can argue with that.

Connally (aside to Burns): Do you think it's going to work?

Burns: It better work! You see, Donut Holes are about the only thing the United States doesn't owe.

◦   ◦   ◦   ◦   ◦

Nevertheless the S.D.R. concept is not without value. The value lies in the concept of an international unit of money—a money against which *all* money would be measured. This would mean that no country in the world would ever again be in a position to dominate the monetary scene with its national currency. All national settlements would revolve around the *value* of this international currency.

If all countries rated their money in S.D.R.s, *and if S.D.R.s were given a gold value and were convertible into gold at a realistic price* in terms of the various currencies so related, then one could take an accurate reading on every monetary system in the world.

The S.D.R. could never be a true world money until it was redeemable for real goods or measured by a metal exchange. Thus the Special Drawing Right, as we understood it when it first came to be used, would turn out to be an entirely different animal. Its name would be obsolete. *The idea that a right to borrow money was tantamount to having money would have been exploded.* But the basic concept of an international money is something that may survive. It may be the cornerstone of a great advance for civilization—once we have come out of this "bad trip" of worldwide ethereal credit.

Here is some elementary substantiation that the S.D.R. concept was beginning to fall apart as early as the fall of 1972.

Karl Klassen, head of the German Central Bank, was asked if S.D.R.s ought to be based on gold. He replied:

"It would be premature to speculate as to whether or not S.D.R.s should be based on gold."

That was an immensely important statement from a central banker, because if S.D.R.s are to be based on gold, they are no longer Special Drawing Rights at all. They become real money. Not special, but universal. Not a drawing, but a deposit.

The ethereal becomes earthly. The spirit becomes a body. The ghost is banished.

So Mr. Klassen's answer amounted to this: It is too early to speculate that we ought to abandon the *concept* of reality as a backing for international currency.

That in itself was quite a blow to the whole "Alice in Wonderland" idea of imaginary money as a panacea for the monetary ills of the world.

France's D'Estaing had already said that S.D.R.s should be based on gold. When Klassen was asked to comment on this he thought that "D'Estaing had not over-emphasized the role of gold."

That was tantamount to an admission by two important countries that perhaps the S.D.R. as it was known should be scrapped and later changed into a different asset with a gold base. The U.S. press, either purposely or out of ignorance, quickly sluffed over these, the two most momentous statements about S.D.R.s since they had first been introduced.

In September 1972, I.M.F. chieftan, Pierre-Paul Schweitzer, had said that S.D.R.s should be kept but perhaps they should have a different name. But the name was already very descriptive—a highly accurate name. Could the head of the I.M.F. be implying that their nature should be changed?

For if the name were to be changed, wouldn't that be meant to reflect a change in the character of the S.D.R.?

In that case the new S.D.R., wouldn't be an S.D.R. at all. It would be a true international money backed by gold.

Following these statements by Klassen and others, the S.D.R. lost prestige throughout 1973, and by 1974 the term was seldom mentioned either by the monetarists or in the press. It would not be until the disturbing end of 1974, when the monetary authorities began to tremble in the face of a world recession, that they went back to the closet and again dragged out the S.D.R. for popular usage. However, it had been the subject of so much ridicule that it was allowed to lie undisturbed until the devastating crisis of 1978. Very quietly the World IMF Meeting in Washington talked of creating $15 billion dollars more. But then the subject was dropped. We heard no more.

Of course a world money such as the S.D.R. is possible, perhaps desirable. As an era of inflation ends, a new era may well be based on an international money convertible into gold, with the values of all currencies of the world described in terms of the international currency.

Because of the probable future enormous significance of the *concept*, a great deal of space has been taken up here with S.D.R.s. It is important for every man to understand just what the S.D.R. was originally and the monetary delusions on which it rested. As the mechanism of the S.D.R. may play a large role in our future, it is important to know what is being said as the news stories of the future refer to the "international currency"—whatever it may be called.

And whatever it may be called, remember this: the subject of money is quite simple. Only the gimmicks are complicated.

But don't you agree, after reading the above, that even the gimmicks, once they are exposed, are also as simple as a magician's trick—once you know how it is done?

14.
MULTINATIONAL
INFLATION
THREATENS YOU

Most of us are too nonchalant about what is going on in the world of money. We are inclined to take the attitude: "This is too complicated for me."

Not at all. Anyone with a tenth-grade education can understand it. It is the monetary authorities who make it APPEAR complicated. It is my purpose here to clear away that hocus pocus.

If you earn $10,000 a year and during the year you give out I. O. U's totaling $12,000, and do this every year for five years, you will find that your balance of payments is in deficit by $10,000. In other words, you owe $10,000 that you do not have. But this $10,000 is a claim on you and all your property. Your creditors are entitled to move in and sell your home, which is worth $20,000, and take their $10,000 and give you the balance — and then you must move into another house — probably smaller and much cheaper.

When the United States spends $30 billion a year in other parts of the world in excess of what it sells and collects from other parts of the world, it has a balance of payments deficit of $30 billion. And if this goes on for five years it has a balance of payments deficit of $150 billion.

In the spring of 1973, Paul Volker, Under-Secretary of the U.S. Treasury, admitted that there were some $70 to $80 billion in foreign Central Banks, and about $10 to $20 billion more in other hands.

Just like your IOU's, these dollars are IOU's of the United States. You may ask how can that be? Aren't our dollars good?

When the monetary system of the gold-exchange standard was working, those IOU's that the United States gave to other countries for goods and services, were returned to the United States Treasury—and the United States Treasury dished out the equivalent amount in gold—and the debt was paid! That was all right as long as the gold lasted.

Once again to relate this to yourself: when you spend $1,000 a year more than your income for five years, presuming you had a bank account of $5,000, you could have absorbed that from your savings. You would have given up all your savings. But when your savings were gone (the U.S. gold pile), your IOU's and your debts were irredeemable. It was no good for your creditors to come to your door with the IOU's; you didn't have anything to pay them with. You had to slam the door on their fingers.

In August 1971 when President Nixon announced that the United States was breaking with gold, he slammed the teller's window on his creditors' fingers, the same as you slammed your door. The United States refused to redeem its IOU's.

But some people felt that a U.S. dollar was still the mighty U.S. buck and it would still buy goods abroad, and so why should the foreigners be worried. The answer to this is also simple.

The normal reserves of Germany, for instance, were about $7 billion. About $4.5 billion of that had been gold and the other 2.5 billion was United States dollars that were "as good as gold" and redeemable for gold at the U.S. Treasury. By the spring of 1973 the German reserves were about $32 billion, and still only 4.5 billion was gold. The other $27-odd billion was sitting there. The question naturally arises—why not spend it somewhere else than in the U.S.A.?

Well, the reserves of Japan were normally about $5 billion. By the spring of 1973 the reserves of Japan were $25 billion, and 23 billion of that was U.S. dollars, with less than one billion in gold. And so it went around the world.

If Germany wanted to buy from Japan, Japan would be very happy to take French francs or Dutch guilders that could be traded for anything in any country of the world—or gold—that would buy any currency anywhere in the world—but Japan did not want to take U.S. dollars because already it could not spend the U.S. dollars it had. Just as all your creditors would be fed up to the teeth with all your IOU's that were no good to spend, so the national banks were chock full of dollars that no other national banks wanted.

But there is one point in all this that should be understood: When U.S. dollars went into Germany—for example, to buy goods or if U.S. citizens sent dollars into Germany to bank over there—those dollars had to be converted by the German Central Bank into German domestic currency. Look at the impact on the foreign country.

Germany's money supply was suddenly swollen to dangerous proportions that could break out in a ruinous wave of inflation. Try as they would to keep the extra funds in the Central Bank, those funds have a way of leaking out—and leaking out ever faster as they widen the hole in the dike. The countries of the world—banks and governments—were getting panicky. But what could they do to stop the dollars? If Volkswagen had sold half a million cars to the United States, the German authorities could hardly order Volkswagen not to pick up the payments in U.S. dollars and bring them home to convert into German marks to pay Volkswagen workers.

All kinds of foreign exchange controls were introduced, but they were no defense against the influx of dollars, as people around the world increasingly wanted to turn them in for some other currency. Huge U.S. corporations with operations in foreign countries scrambled to get rid of U.S. dollars so they would not lose their shareholders' money on an almost certain devaluation of the U.S. dollar.

President Nixon blamed the crises on the wicked speculators. Surely he knew better. He was well informed that confidence in the dollar—following his closure of the gold window—had crumbled.

But the point is that this outflow of dollars was spreading inflationary disease everywhere. Almost every country—including Switzerland—was now suffering an inflation greater than the United States as U.S. dollars swarmed in and were transformed into national currencies.

That is why you often heard the claim that the United States was *exporting* its inflation. While American authorities boasted that their inflation was less bad than elsewhere, U.S. dollars were causing the inflation in those other countries.

For example, if you get worried about the value of your U.S. dollars you may decide to convert them into Swiss francs and hold them in Switzerland. The Swiss try to stop you, as well as hordes of others.

If you had $5,000 in your bank account you felt would be safer in gold-backed Swiss francs, you would send this money to Zurich, where the Swiss bank would have to issue Swiss francs for your dollars. Multiply this to $5 billion and you can see why the Swiss government must issue the Swiss francs equivalent of $5 billion. If Switzerland had reserves of the equivalent $5 billion before, now it has $10 billion in the form of Swiss francs. How could the inflation invasion be stopped? The United States shrugged its shoulders and said, "That's your problem!"

This came to be known as dollar imperialism — later on a benign neglect.

And that is how the whole world, in the spring of 1973, found itself in the grips of an inflation that it did not know how to control.

By the spring of 1975 Switzerland was charging forty percent *negative* interest for the deposit of American money—mostly to no avail.

The reason is simple. Any central bank must issue its currency to another central bank. The Swiss sell Swiss watches. In order to use their money inside Switzerland they must have it in Swiss francs. Now, if France wants to buy watches from Switzerland, she would have to pay for these watches in Swiss francs. If the Central Bank of France offers French francs in Switzerland or on the money exchanges of the world, Switzerland must issue Swiss francs in exchange for the other currency—at the going rate—if it expects to sell anything. There is no way the Swiss national bank can avoid issuing a demand for francs.

All right—you want to change American dollars into Swiss francs. The Swiss say, "We will charge a forty-percent penalty per year for deposits in the form of Swiss francs in Switzerland." So you go to Amsterdam, or Vienna or some other place, and tell a bank you want to buy Swiss francs. The bank will order the Swiss francs from the Central Bank of Holland or Austria. Holland or Austria will present the dollars you have already changed into guilders or schillings and demand the Swiss francs from the Swiss government. Now you have a deposit of Swiss francs in Holland or Austria. The effort of the Swiss banks to block the transformation of American dollars into Swiss francs was futile.

And so every country in the world remains at the mercy of the inflowing dollars from the United States, which are acceptable on every exchange in the world at the going rate.

Therefore huge inflations in American dollars spread to other countries, which remained pretty much at the mercy of the Federal Reserve.*

By the spring of 1973 confidence in the U.S. dollar had been shot. Two devaluations, a small one in December 1971 and a ten-percenter in February 1973, had set the stage for yet another fall.

Now the Arab countries were asking for further guarantees for oil. Some were saying they would rather leave it in the ground, where they knew it would retain its value, than sell it for U.S. dollars, the value of which was certain to depreciate. If they were going to sell it at all, they would raise the price.

The home-grown inflation of the U.S., spreading to other countries of the world, was beginning to come home to roost.

Nickel, cocoa, copper, chrome, coffee, timber, paper; all that vast array of raw materials—all of it—was going up in price. These prices were not subject to any U.S.-imposed price controls.

So it did affect you. And it will affect you. Whatever happens on the monetary fronts of the world will affect you. As the prices of the imported raw material rise in terms of U.S. dollars (as the dollar is devalued) you pay more in heat, in gas, in power, etc.

---

* Federal Reserve Notes are printed by the Bureau of Printing and Engraving of the U.S. Treasury Department for the Federal Reserve System. They form the largest share of the liabilities of the Federal Reserve Banks. Until the Smithsonian Agreement broke down in 1973, these notes were 25 percent gold-backed. With gold officially pegged at $42.22 per ounce, Congress eliminated the gold backing, because it had reached the point where no more notes could be issued unless the price of gold were increased—which they refused to do. These notes' are now backed by paper assets of the U.S. governments.

The effect of all this is to reduce your standard of living—like it or not.

The results were becoming clear. By 1977 cars were smaller, homes were smaller; more Americans were settling for apartments, giving up the dream of a backyard and a white picket fence.

All of this is an outcome of very natural processes.

Let's look at some specifics.

15. THE ENERGY CRISIS AS PROJECTED— AND AS IT IS

Energy is by far the most vital component of our economic and monetary future. It is vitally important that the reader grasp the formidable impact of energy on his money, his lifestyle, and his very existence over the next ten years.

Let's go back to Freedonia. But first note the following facts: In the year 1972 the U.S. had to import oil and gas to the extent of $6 billion. By 1975 the cost of imported energy was over $15 billion. By 1977 it was running $40 billion, after the Arabs had increased the price fourfold to compensate for the declining value of the inflated dollar. The 1979 cost may hit $70 billion.

We are told that the balance of payments deficit must be cured. And the United States authorities are promising to cure it!

How will they cure it, and who is going to pay for $70 billion of purchases of foreign oil? Obviously the citizens of the United States will have to earn $70 billion from foreign trade to pay the bill. That means the United States will have to manufacture things pretty cheaply, and with an efficiency far beyond our present efficiency.

Now let's go back to Freedonia.

When we colonized the island of Freedonia we found a great supply of fresh water and several natural wells. Our prodigious industry, as we grew, required massive amounts of water. We used water—like water. We let the wells flow even when there was no one around to collect the water. We even let the water run into the ocean. We thought there would never be any end to the supply of water from those wells. Then one day a shepherd came from the far fields and said the well up there was running dry and there was hardly enough water for his sheep. So we said we will have to move the sheep to another pasture where the well is good.

One by one the wells began to run dry. And we woke up one day to find out that we were running into, of all things, a water crisis.

Our industry was faced with the prospect of cutting back, because our refiners could not run without a great deal of water, and our steam boilers required lots of water. Our people were used to using water—as if it were water.

Our leaders called a hurried council to decide what to do. All of the dowsers in Freedonia were called out to find new wells, but they could find amazingly few. Their report was that we had used up the best of the water supply, and while we would always find some new wells, there would not be nearly enough even to meet current demand, let alone the growing demand.

Our leaders were face to face with the grim fact that Freedonia would have to import water.

Now this meant using the productive efforts of men to build boats especially for water, and of manning these boats back and forth to a distant island, and of creating storage facilities for the water. It meant a steady stream of boats—so many that one water tanker would be unloading every twenty minutes day and night. Also, the islanders who supplied the water were going to charge us a fairly stiff price for their water.

Consider, for a moment, the amount of effort that we collectively must put into the business of bringing in water.

This is unproductive effort compared with our previous activities—just as our effort in the war was unproductive. We must divert the creative labor of a large segment of our population to provide our colony with water, whereas, before, this same amount of labor was able to contribute to our living standard — whether it was making wine to suit our taste or hammocks so we could spend our leisure time swinging in the sun.

Apart from the loss of this productive labor, we have to pay a bill for the water to the other islanders. We have to manufacture goods: shoes, pottery, or whatever; or we have to go out and grow more potatoes and corn (or else we have to eat less ourselves) to send over to those islanders to pay for the water.

Either our living standard is going to come down, or we are going to have to work many more hours a day (not less), or we are going to have to come up with some very smart inventions to increase our productivity.

And that is the position of the United States in the energy crisis.

But the U.S. energy problem is complicated by a factor we did not have to consider in Freedonia. That factor is international money.

If the producers of raw materials — oil, nickel, coffee, etc. — see that the U.S. dollar constantly deteriorates, they will constantly demand higher and higher prices in advance. It may even be that they will demand gold unless the monetary situation is stabilized. Up to now they have been demanding higher and higher prices.

As this happens the cost of gasoline goes up; the cost of heating homes goes up; the cost of industry, which is largely powered by oil and natural gas, goes up; and so all prices go up; and so we have an increased inflation. And there is a further erosion of confidence in our money.

Either inflation must be stopped or our suppliers are going to demand gold. If they do not demand gold outright, they will demand currencies of substance such as that of the European Monetary Union whose governments are backed by 500 million ounces of gold, by far the largest hoard in the world.

But some people claim this is scare talk. There is really plenty of energy in the United States. All we need to do is go out and develop it. Let's examine that point of view.

Is the energy shortage being exaggerated by the oil companies for their own purposes? Just how bad is this crisis? And what is the importance of energy in maintaining ourselves as a first-class power and having the world's highest living standard?

The cornerstone of man's existence on this earth is energy. It has been so from the beginning. First, a man had only his own energy. The most energetic could run the fastest and wield a club the hardest; and so he survived. The advance of civilization is the story of the increasing availability of energy through technology. Firstly, we enslaved the horse to get his energy.

Later came the lever, the wheel; and subsequently water power turned the wheel. Finally we used a combination of fire and water, which was steam.

We mastered coal, petroleum, natural gas, uranium. Advancing technology was able to harness and increase the efficiency of available energy; internal combustion, hydraulics, and the energy gathered from the force of water through the sophisticated use of electricity.

The United States became the world's strongest nation not without a great debt to her natural resources and the inventive ability that put them to use. The key to our power was cheap and abundant energy. Those days are over.

In July 1972 the air-conditioning drain in New York City proved to be too much for the available energy. There just wasn't enough electricity. Food began to spoil in freezers. Traffic lights quit working. A week of sustained heat would have caused a most critical situation.

Great attention should be paid promptly to such signals. Their message is tantamount to prophecy.

During World War II America was still so rich in energy that it could supply the fuel to drive all the navies and air forces of the Allies with some left over. But by 1972 all the oil wells in Texas were producing fullout. U.S. flow was 100-percent capacity. Imports for the year 1973 were almost seven million barrels a day, by 1979 nearly nine million barrels a day. Without that oil U.S. industry would have been hamstrung.

The Alaska pipeline began delivering a million barrels a day in 1978. It would eventually reach two million. But this wasn't going to help the balance of trade very much because, at the same time, the fall of production within the continental United States, because of exhaustion, would sooner or later offset the savings in consumption. The big import bill would have to continue, or millions would shiver in the winter and sweat in the summer.

The flow of money for oil will be concentrated toward the Middle East, and the Arab countries are to take in the lion's share.

This would make them the financial powerhouse of the world, with reserves almost equal to those of the rest of the world combined.

And there will be competition for this oil. The United States is expected to want twelve million barrels more each day; Europe twelve million barrels more; and Japan seven million barrels more.

Isn't there any way, one asks, that energy can be produced in the United States sufficient, at least, for our own needs? This is the core of our problem, the key to our independent existence, the basic factor in the quality of life in the U.S.A. It is the problem to which we will try to find some practical answers.

16. THE ENERGY SHORTAGE — MYTH OR STARK HORROR?

To know whether there is an oil shortage or not, we need to go back a long ways—like a few hundred million years—so let's go back.

At one time in geologic history the most notable feature about this planet was the massive carboniferous forests. Vegetation like you wouldn't believe. Massively thick; layer upon layer; millions of years. Then the sea came in, foot by foot; and mud and sand were built layer upon layer over the huge carboniferous deposits.

The second most notable feature in the history of this planet from the standpoint of energy was the quantity of sea life, so prolific that we can't even imagine it today. The organisms sank as they died tons upon millions of tons over millions of years. These died in the deeper ocean; also in relatively shallow waters where the corals built reef on reef.

And all of this was buried by layer upon layer; thousands of feet of layers of lime, sandstone, mud.

The most uneducated driller knows that the temperature of the earth increases foot by foot as the bit penetrates downward; in some cases to four miles. The very heat generated because of miles of overburden in the trillions of tons "*stewed*" these organic materials into a potent brew. Where there was *not too much heat*, such as volcanic activity, the brew became petroleum and its gases. But at this depth the pressure is so great that the gases are compressed within the petroleum; and often it is a homogenous substance—only to separate when pressure is relieved by the puncture of the bit.

In certain areas huge subterranean lava movements generated another kind of heat, and when this heat was strong enough, the compressed carboniferous forests were transformed into coal. The greater the heat the more of the foreign elements were driven off, and the nearer we came to pure carbon. Thus we have anthracite—very concentrated coal. At the other end we have soft lignite coal—where the transforming heat was not so great.

We will never find oil adjacent to coal because the heat would have fatally damaged our brewing process. We will never find oil in an igneous area such as the great Canadian Shield covering more than half of Canada; never in the high volcanic mountains.

We are limited in our search for oil to *the sedimentary formations*, and particularly the huge sedimentary basins.

THE BASINS

Now when you say basin you imply differential elevations. Think of a shallow washbasin. If it were 3,000 miles across, the lowest layer would curve toward the surface on all sides. Imagine a basin 20,000 feet thick at its center, with the sides sloping gently upward for hundreds of miles. Now these are laminated sides, but the laminations are sedimentary formations each of which may be hundreds to thousands of feet thick.

One other matter we must consider is that nature abhors a vacuum. But these limestones, and most of these compressed sandstones are full of interstitial space, tiny little pores. And always these pores are chuck full. Mostly they are full of salt water. Now these sediments are the source of petroleum and natural gas—and *nothing else is the source*. These sediments are more than ninety-nine percent full of salt water. Then how do you find the oil?

Again a very natural fact accounts for that. Oil is lighter than water. If you were to fill a sponge mixed full of an emulsion of oil and water and if you could seal it all around and leave it overnight, you would find the next morning that the oil had risen to the top of the sponge as far as it could to where it was sealed off. If there were equal parts of oil and water, the interface would be halfway down the sponge.

Now remember, these massive sediments are on a slope—as a result of the movements of the earth. Once they were flat, but practically none of the very old sediments are flat today. So isn't it therefore quite natural that in the slanted sediments through the hundreds of millions of years the oil has gradually moved through the pores seeking the top. Where the top is exposed to the surface, the oil has oozed out, as in the case of the tar sands of Alberta. There simply was no seal here, and so we have a very heavy bitumen, the tar-like residue of petroleum. The lighter ends have evaporated. All of the precious natural gas has escaped. What is left is a thick, bituminous muck.

But during geologic times the ages of the uplifts of the sedimentary beds were usually followed by another incursion of the sea which laid *flatbeds on top of the now tilted beds.* Where such a bed is mud, it later through metamorphosis became shale, and became the *perfect seal.* This means that oil gradually working its way up along the slanted beds eventually hit the shale sealer on top, and stopped there. As the oil moved forward and upward throughout the millions of years, it gradually rose toward the seal. If the beds are only mildly slanted—and if there was a massive amount of source material in the first place—you get a hugh oilfield in *area,* and a thick oilfield in *depth;* then you have fields like *Texas.* These fields are normally called stratigraphic traps; and probably most of the oil in the world comes from stratigraphic traps.

THE ANTICLINES
But there are other kinds of fields; and these are sometimes more prolific; being smaller in area. Think of the hump on a camel's back. Imagine that there is oil in the skin of a camel, through his neck, his shoulders, and along his trunk. The oil would gradually rise through time to fill the top of the hump. The more oil there was, the more of the hump would be full of oil. The camel's hump is really an anticline. Coral reefs are anticlines, and sometimes sediments have been arched to form anticlines.

Now imagine all of this covered over by the sea and buried under thousands of feet of subsequent sediments. Man comes along, and starts to look for these humps. The geologist and the geophysicist know that it is absolutely stupid just to go drilling anywhere in the sedimentary basin for oil. Ninety-nine plus percent of the sediments are only full of salt water. You have to find the right place.

There was great excitement in Alberta in the early days following the Leduc discovery, because this oil was found in the Devonian formation, and the Devonian was known to underlie most of Western Canada. What a bonanza! they cried. But of course a geologist knew that the oil would not be in all of this Devonian. It would only be in the very high peaks of the Devonian, in the anticlines—if the Devonian had anticlines; or where the Devonian sediments rising toward the surface were covered over by an impervious seal. In the case of the Devonian, it turned out that all of the oil was anticlinal oil. You had to find the anticlines—the camel humps. They were 3,000 to 5,000 feet below the present surface. The first one was Leduc; the second was Redwater. There were various—and many—smaller humps. But the bulk has been found. There isn't any question left about that. Seismologists have combed the country. Some pimples undoubtedly remain to be found. By chance we may make a few substantial discoveries, but the best is surely behind us.

SIZE OF OILFIELDS
What has been said above applies to the oilfields of the Middle East and to all of the oilfields of the world. Generally speaking, that is their genesis. How much oil is in a field depends on how much source material nature offered in

the first place. It also depends on the massiveness of the sediments which are rising toward the surface at the point of the oilfield. If they go back thousands of miles under the sea, and if they were very rich in the first place—you have the Middle East. For remember that the oil that you get in Saudi Arabia and Kuwait originated a long, long ways off, and it has traveled a long, long ways to reach its *destiny* in a trap beneath the Arabian sand.

There are two more elements that are vitally important from the standpoint of *recovery* of oil. One of them is the amount of pore space in the sediments. Obviously if the pore space is scanty, the reservoir can contain less oil than where the pore space is prolific—as it is in coral reefs.

Then there is still another element. The *connections* between the pore spaces. The pore space is known as porosity. The *connection* is known as permeability. If these pores are not adequately connected, the flow of oil through the rock is very slow. So you may have an oilfield that contains huge reserves, but the wells produce only at a slow rate. Also, if the pore space is scanty, the *ultimate recovery* may be relatively small. Sometimes there is lots of oil left in the formation, it can never reach the surface, because the pore space connections are poor.

Where a lot of gas has been generated by the transformation of animal and sea life into petroleum, the gas rises faster than the oil. Just as the oil is lighter than the water, so is the gas lighter than the oil. In this case in the top of the hump of the camel you have what is knows as " *the gas cap.*" Now as you puncture this hump by a drill hole below the *interface* of the gas and the oil, the enormous pressure of the gas pushing down on the oil pushes the oil up the drill hole at an enormous rate. Here you have the GUSHERS. It is very important not to drill out the gas cap, because you rob the oilfield of the driving force to recover the petroleum.

And so even at the top of a stratigraphic trap, you may have an upper layer of gas which should not be drilled. But even where there is no gas cap, the enormous pressure of the gas *in the oil* drives the liquid to the surface through the drill hole.

In some reservoirs there is not much of such pressure, and the oil must be pumped. In all reservoirs—as they reach exhaustion—the gas pressure becomes exhausted—and the gushers eventually become pumpers.

THE OIL IN THE U.S.A.

Oil exploration is a highly developed science. Anticlines can be found by the seismologists. They can also be found by geological deduction. So many hundreds of thousands of wells have been drilled that the contours of the underlying strata of the continent are very well known and even mapped. Not every little hump is known; but all the *major* humps are known. It can be taken for granted—and *absolutely without qualification*—that the major oilfields of the continental U.S. have been tapped; have reached maturity; and in total are now on the way downhill. We will never find such oilfields again. Some may still be hiding, but that will have very little effect on the overall picture.

Nevertheless there is much oil still to be produced in the States. But this will be from the leaner, deeper areas—where there is less gas pressure—where there is less porosity; less permeability. The *PROLIFIC* days are a thing of the past.

There will be stripper wells for years to come. The U.S. will still be producing oil in 2050, and probably still some oil in the year 2100. But it will be lean. Ever milk a cow? When the bag is full, you can get a cupful in a matter of seconds. When you come to strip the cow—you never get the last drop. The last halfcup full can take you as long as a pail full if you insist on getting the last drop. So it is with an oilfield. So it is with the U.S. We have taken the bulk of the milk off the bag.

THE OIL IN THE WORLD

All of the major sedimentary basins of the world are known to the geologists. All have been mapped. All of the prospective territories in broad outline are known. This is not to say that all the anticlines have been found; that all the stratigraphic traps have been found. They certainly have not. By and large the best have been found. There are prospects of enormous oilfields in the far North; oil formed in semi-tropical climates that migrated through the underground sediments which are hot at depth, despite the surface cold of the Arctic. Or there will be other traps in sedimentary basins that approach the continental shelves; but not probably far out to sea. Most of this oil will have migrated upward to the continental shelves. The North Sea oil is an example of oil that has migrated from rising bands of sediments. The North Sea is very shallow. At one time it was not covered by water at all. The offshore areas of the world offer considerable prospecting opportunity; but not probably anywhere near the opportunities that exist on the high portions of the land which are the continents above the water line.

So the great prospecting areas of the world are known. The Venezuelan Basin has been tapped, and heavily milked. It is on its way downhill, and has been for some years. Production dropped from 3.7 million b/d in 1973 to 2.3 million b/d in 1979. Of a massive reserve of 48 billion bbls. in Maracibo Basin, 34 billion have been withdrawn — to the point where the surface has sunk in some places as much as 18 feet! With 14 billion bbls. left, Venezuela worries that by 1987, the oil bonanza will be over and the fields exhausted a few years later.

The Arabian penninsula has been tapped and is in its flush flow. In a matter of ten years, at the present rate of production, it too will certainly be on its way downhill.

Mexico is new and highly promising, but it has only a percentage of the Arab oil reserves, and is no solution for us. Certainly not during our most critical period, in the next five years. We simply shall not find fields as rich (or as frequently) as we have found in the past.

Nature provided only so much of this distilled Aladdin's power. It is finite. When it is gone, it can only be replaced by the decay of further carboniferous forests and the decay of prolific sea life in the oceans, which in these days is not nearly prolific enough, and which would take some billions of years anyway.

So when some self-appointed expert tells you the oil scare is a hoax — go back to the genesis of oil and look at the history of the production.

U.S. ZENITH — 1970
*Million Barrels Per Day**

Year	Imports	U.S. Crude Oil Production	Total Consumed	Imports as % of supply
1967	2.54	8.81	11.35	22.3
1968	2.84	8.66	11.50	24.7
1969	3.17	8.78	11.95	26.5
1970	3.42	9.18	12.60	27.1
1971	3.93	9.03	12.96	30.3
1972	4.74	9.00	13.74	34.5
1973	6.26	8.78	15.04	41.6
1974	6.11	8.38	14.49	42.1
1975	6.06	8.01	14.07	43.1
1976	7.31	7.78	15.09	48.4
1977	8.81	7.88	16.69	52.8
1978	8.19	8.67	16.86	48.6

*(Dept. of Energy Annual Report to Congress, Vol. II, 1978).

No keen sense of discernment is needed to see that the U.S. production, going full out, is on its way downhill. It rose to a peak of 9.18 barrels per day in 1970 and thereafter began to drop off. The great effort in 1978 brought production up once more, but only to well below the 1970 peak.

Nevertheless, the use of oil has been increasing and the table of imports as a percentage of supply shows that in 1967 we were importing only one-fifth of the oil we needed, but by 1977 the figure had reached more than half. As the result of a major production effort in 1978, the percentage receded only to the 1976 level.

Who can look at these figures and say that the oil shortage is a hoax? Going back further—as far back as 1945—I remember writing oil news for the *Calgary Herald* at the time of the oil discovery in Western Canada, and making the outrageous statement that the U.S. would become a net importer of oil. At that time, it was the greatest oil exporter in the world. It had not only looked after its World War II needs, but it had looked after the needs of nearly all the allies. The Middle East was then only an infant. Sure enough in the late

1950's the U.S. began to be a net importer. By 1960 it was importing between five and ten percent; and by 1967 one-fifth of its oil; now a half.

The U.S. in 1977 was using 17.8 million barrels per day; importing 8.3 million barrels per day; and almost 9 million barrels per day in 1978. Where does the U.S.A. get this oil?

It gets eighty-seven percent of the half which it doesn't produce from the OPEC countries. So if there is an embargo by OPEC, the U.S. would be virtually crippled.

Would Arabs embargo oil again, as they did in 1973, as a weapon to control U.S. diplomacy? Our vulnerability is certain.

What I have tried to do above is to bring out the *TRUTH* of the world oil situation and the *VULNERABILITY* of the U.S. to the political developments in the Middle East.

ASSUMING NO EMBARGO

Here's what gets to you. Just assume there is no embargo at all. Assume that the Middle East countries will go on producing as they are. Then what is the picture up to 1985 and even to the year 2000? First of all some present statistics.

The oil bill for the U.S. in 1976 was *$36 billion*. The total agricultural exports of the U.S. ran about *$15 billion*. The greatest agricultural exporting country in the world couldn't sell half enough to pay for the oil. Now the oil bill approaches double the 1978 bill.

17. OIL: THE SUMMARY

If you believe in fairytales, you can believe that massive quantities of oil remain to be discovered in the U.S. Up to the time of the near catastrophe at the Three Mile Island nuclear power plant in April, 1979, you could fancy that nuclear power by itself might rescue us. (I shall deal with that in Chapter 18.) You could even dream that large offshore gas deposits would see us through. You can follow the previous line of reasoning promoted by the major oil companies which says that the OPEC's will desperately need money and so they will reduce the price of oil and flood the market. You can dream all that.

MOST MASSIVE CHANGE IN HISTORY'S SWEEP

What we are faced with today represents the most massive change in the way humanity lives on this planet that has ever taken place. Moreover, it will be in the shortest time. Actually in terms of history, this change will take place like a flash of lightning—over the course of five, ten or fifteen years. Certainly we feel the flash approaching even now.

The industrial revolution took a hundred years or more. The automobile changed the face of America over the course of seventy years. The age of aviation is fifty years old. The age of television is twenty-five years old. Here we are facing something many times as great as any one of these changes in a period of one or two decades. It will be a shock. The question is: can our modern, social institutions; and our democratic way of life sustain this shock?

How are we going to meet it? How are our governments going to deal with it? And indeed, is it possible? I think it is, but there's one thing I know: if it's possible at all, it's going to take the fastest footwork ever seen in the U.S.A. since World War II.

The energy squeeze is absolutely real. It will continue to tighten like a vise even with the best cooperation of the Middle East oil producers.

So America will have to find its own answer for self-sufficiency. In opposition, you will hear the following arguments:

1. There is lots of undiscovered oil at depth. *Answer:* There is some, but because oil naturally presses ever upwards, and because the earth has been fractured and refractured countless times, most of the oil in deep reservoirs

has had ample chance to migrate into closed traps nearer the surface, which have already been found.

2. There is lots of oil offshore. *Answer:* True, but to keep up with depletion, we need to find at least one *giant* field a year (one billion barrels) such as Prudhoe Bay. We have only found one such field in the last ten years.

3. Mexico is another Middle East. *Answer:* Mexico is extremely promising, but to rate it alongside the Middle East, is irresponsible. Even if Mexico becomes capable of supplying a large part of U.S. needs, it's not very likely to come as a gift. The cost to the U.S. will be the world price whether the source is Iran, Canada or Mexico.

In short, there is plenty of oil in the world to meet oil needs to the end of the Century, but that doesn't help the U.S. living standard. As we proceed toward the year 2000, oil will become increasingly hard to find, thus increasingly costly.

The free-wheeling days of Freedonia, when water gushed unrestrainedly from the surface, are gone.

We have entered a *NEW ERA* in energy.

❈   ❈   ❈   ❈   ❈   ❈

"We can easily be slipping into an unimaginable catastrophe. To be blunt, I am not ruling out the very real possibility of social upheaval and revolution." — Dr. Arthur M. Bueche, Vice President - Research & Development, General Electric Company; March 1977.

The U.S. oil crisis was clearly predictable in 1962 and has been advancing exactly on a predictable schedule. This tendency cannot be reversed, simply because the resources do not exist. Regardless of discoveries elsewhere, the U.S. has lost its advantage of cheap and abundant energy. The living standard will, therefore, continue to fall as our resources are required to buy energy abroad.

The following facts and conclusions were presented to high Washington officials back in 1962.

Subsequent events would indicate that the warnings were not taken very seriously.

It is a shocking revelation of the bankruptcy, cowardice and head-in-the-sand psychology of American political leadership.

The graphs shown on Pages 102 and 103 are probably the most convincing evidence that the U.S. was on a downhill road. *No matter how many feet of exploratory footage was drilled, the results were becoming increasingly small.* Clearly this showed that we had picked the best of our berry patch. The pickings were becoming slimmer and slimmer. All the lush oilfields had been found and it was getting more and more expensive to find a barrel of oil. The conclusion was clear. The U.S. would become enormously dependent on oil imports or it would have to pay a huge price for the energy it found at home.

This would surely mean a decline in exploration activity at home because of the cheapness of foreign imports.

What happened was to be expected. Cheap oil continued to flow in. Wildcat drilling activity in the U.S. continued to decline. It just didn't pay because the oilfields that were discovered were too small, and the depths were too great. At that time I well remember it was costing a dollar a barrel to find new oil in Canada. It was costing $2 a barrel in the U.S.A. It was costing $.05 a barrel in the Middle East; and $.25 a barrel in Venezuela.

The U.S. was running into an energy disaster.

All that was absolutely clear 15 years ago.

Too clear, maybe. When facts are so clear the danger is that people become numb to them. When all these forces finally reach a climactic stage—nobody is ready. When we got the four-fold Arab price increase in 1973, nobody was ready.

Here in a nutshell is the pragmatic truth as it has emerged year by year for the last twenty-five years.

Year	Footage Drilled	Total Wells	Wildcats
1953	49,279	198,839,104	11,062
1954	53,930	218,986,112	11,280
1955	56,682	226,270,000	12,271
1956	58,160	233,902,000	13,034
1957	55,024	223,087,055	11,739
1958	50,039	198,224,092	9,588
1959	51,764	209,231,416	10,073
1960	46,751	190,702,672	9,635
1961	46,962	192,116,114	9,191
1962	46,179	198,558,641	9,003
1963	43,653	184,357,230	8,607
1964	45,236	189,921,870	9,258
1965	41,423	181,427,015	8,265
1966	37,881	166,025,335	10,313
1967	33,558	144,234,721	8,886
1968	32,914	149,287,860	8,879
1969	34,053	160,949,360	9,701
1970	29,467	142,431,468	7,693
1971	27,300	128,355,404	6,922
1972	28,755	138,285,876	7,539
1973	27,602	138,937,944	7,466
1974	32,893	153,164,191	8,619
1975	39,097	178,505,570	9,214
1976	41,455	185,344,695	9,234
1977	46,479	215,010,591	9,961
1978*	48,161	229,149,000	10,720

*Estimated

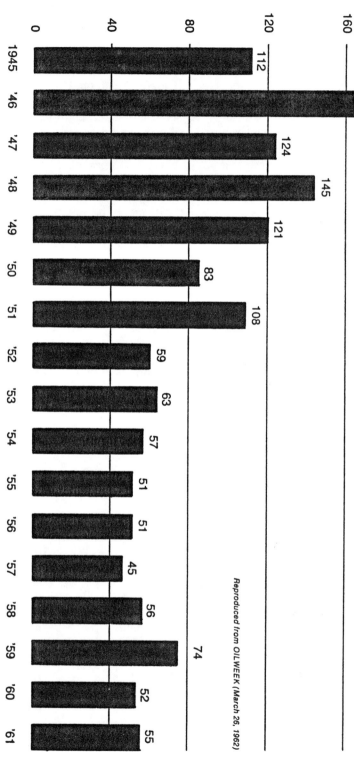

GROSS NEW U.S. CRUDE RESERVES PER EXPLORATORY FOOT DRILLED. New U.S. oil reserves amounted to 163 barrels per exploratory foot drilled in 1946, but only 55 barrels per foot in 1961.

Reproduced from OILWEEK (March 26, 1962)

Year	Value
1945	112
'46	163
'47	124
'48	145
'49	121
'50	83
'51	108
'52	59
'53	63
'54	57
'55	51
'56	51
'57	45
'58	56
'59	74
'60	52
'61	55

This graph reproduced from OILWEEK 3/26/62

U.S. EXPLORATION DRILLING FOOTAGE, 1945-1961 (in millions of feet). **As** fields became less lush, as the discovery ratio fell, as price stayed stable because of cheap foreign oil, drilling activity went into a nosedive in 1956. Washington was unconcerned. Exploratory drilling footage in the U.S. reached a peak of 58.5 million feet in 1956, but only 40 million feet in 1961. (These graphs suggest a decline in the discovery of oil reserves in the U.S. They suggest that the present price of oil is not enough to keep the U.S. oil industry looking hard enough to maintain a healthy reserves/production ratio. If this is so, the graphs suggest declining reserves for every foot drilled, an oil industry that is going downhill.)

ENERGY AND NATIONAL SURVIVAL

A publication called *Commanders Digest* is distributed by the Department of Defense to the commanders of the U.S. Armed Forces and other key personnel. The issue of May 12, 1977 carries an article by Secretary of Defense Harold Brown that we quote here in full.

"There is no clearer or more serious threat to the long-term security of the United States and to its Allies than that which stems from the growing deficiency of secure and assured energy resources.

"A high rate of energy consumption is the hallmark of industrialized societies as we know them today. Even with severe and mandatory conservation to reduce consumption this will continue to be so in the future. The standard of living that now exists in the more developed nations, and to which the developing nations of the world aspire, is a very recent phenomenon. It first appeared in the United States about fifty years ago, and in the other parts of the world where it exists at all, only since the end of World War II. At present it rests on fossil fuels.

"More specifically it is dependent on oil and natural gas, which accounts for 75 per cent of U.S. energy consumption.

"The enormous economic development which the world has seen in the Twentieth Century and particularly since World War II, including the phenomenal German and Japanese economic resurgence, has been almost entirely based on the fact that unrestricted and inexpensive energy was available from oil and natural gas, with oil by far predominant. It follows therefore that a cutoff or deep reduction of oil and gas supply would result in the destruction or at least the crippling of the advanced free-market economies within a relatively short span of time. In 1973-1974 the world had a very brief and very small sample of what an oil shortage can do. There is now, I believe, a general awareness of the fragile nature of the world's economic balance and its critical dependence on an unrestricted and expanding supply of oil. That awareness gives added credence to the potential for political, economic or military pressure on us by those who have, or are perceived to have, the ability to halt or at least substantially reduce the global distribution of oil. Steps which reduce this dependence — by conservation, substitution of coal, or development of new, renewable sources, are therefore vital.

"We are fortunate in the U.S. that such measures can substantially reduce our dependence on outside sources, if we take the necessary steps, to the point where we can accumulate a stockpile equal to six-months of imports. In the foreseeable future, our European and Japanese allies do not have such a prospect.

"The threat to national security, the economy and our way of life which arises from the energy crisis is not yet fully recognized by all. Some refuse to accept the fact that the energy crisis is real, and that its solution will require the development of a national policy and purpose commanding the dedication of the Nation, its resources and its people over many years. Ultimately, the only alternative is disaster.

"We are familiar with the continuing risk of oil supply interruptions and upward pressures on prices from politically motivated embargoes such as we experienced four years ago. Much less attention has been given to the potential for a much more serious interruption of oil supply by hostile forces in time of war. In the event of some future confrontation the Soviet Union might be able to restrict access of the Western world to its essential oil supplies to a degree of severity and duration greater than any embargo by the oil producers. The USSR might attempt to deny access to the oil of the Persian Gulf by direct attack on the facilities of the major oil loading ports which lie near to Soviet territory. Simultaneous action to interdict on the high seas tanker movement of oil from other exporting nations could vastly exacerbate the oil supply situation for the United States and its Allies.

"The military, political and economic risks of oil interruption are very real, and are steadily increasing as dependence on imported oil continues to grow. We must do what we can to mitigate those risks during the years which must pass before the United States can again develop an acceptable degree of energy self-sufficiency.

"The potential adverse impacts on national security can and must be eased by adoption of the President's energy proposals, particularly those concerning the reduction of oil import dependence through energy conservation, the encouragement of domestic oil and gas production, substitution of coal and nuclear energy for oil and gas in electricity generation, and the development of a strategic petroleum reserve as insurance against periods of supply interruption.

"There is a third and greater energy threat to the Nation which has until recently received all too little popular attention, but which, as the President has said, should be the foremost consideration in development of national energy policy. The third threat is neither military nor political. It is, quite simply, resource depletion. A finite world supply of oil and gas will soon repeat the cycle so long evident in the United States. Growth in producible reserves will slow, halt and then go into decline as the remaining undiscovered resources grow smaller and the rate of discovery diminishes in the face of steadily increasing demand. The annual expansion in worldwide production which has been the foundation of twentieth century world economic growth will level off and begin to decline.

"Arguments that much greater hydrocarbon reserves remain to be discovered miss the point. A growing consumption rate assures that even if so, they too will be quickly consumed. There is every indication that these turning points loom in the very near future. The time remaining to us to rectify the situation is very short. If the United States and the rest of the developed and developing world do not soon move strongly to reduce oil demand and increase supplies of energy from alternate sources, economic growth will cease also and the free-world economy will go into long-term stagnation and decline. The consequences for free world security are all too apparent.

"Inevitably U.S. and allied needs for hydrocarbon imports constrain our foreign policy and create potential risks of confrontation and military conflict. DoD interest focuses primarily on maintaining the United States defense posture by avoiding disruptions or the threat of disruptions of energy supplies to the Armed Services and the industrial mobilization base. In the broader context of United States national security, DoD also wishes to avoid any policy which would adversely impact United States allies and thereby indirectly weaken the United States. Furthermore, the Department of Defense is crucially aware of the prospect for the depletion of world liquid petroleum reserves and the need to begin now to conserve energy resources.

"We in Defense believe that:

●The United States needs to minimize its dependence on Persian Gulf oil and develop alternative sources of supply preferably in the Western Hemisphere;

● The United States should secure a billion barrel petroleum stockpile as quickly as possible;

● The United States should develop alternative supplies of energy, both conventional and non-conventional to reduce demand on a depleting world oil resource base.

I believe there is comparatively little time for the United States to respond to the President's call and move toward reducing its dependence on imported oil."

* * * * *

In all of the world there simply is no alternative source to the Middle East. The United States has 38 billion barrels in reserve. Canada has 11 billion barrels. The Middle East has 300 billion barrels, and Saudi Arabia alone has half of that. This Middle East oil is already found, proven, and in the process of vigorous development.

Can't we use electricity? Well, electricity comes from water power or from plants operating on oil or coal. It is also wasteful of energy content, wasting two-thirds in the conversion from fossil fuel to electricity.

Seventy-five percent of all the energy consumed in the United States is from oil and natural gas. Industry uses almost one-third of all the energy in the United States. Transportation and utilities each use about one-quarter and private homes use 14 percent, leaving less than 5 percent for other smaller uses.

In the event of a serious energy shortage, industry would be hit first. That means a cutback in production and employment.

Making the energy picture worse is the fact that U.S. oil production has already peaked out and will now go into decline. As consumption rises by seven million barrels a day in the eighties, production is expected to fall three or four million barrels a day.

What is more, the current costs of obtaining oil are disruptive to normal economic patterns of the industrial world.

The chief executive for the Continental Oil Company, John G. McLean, laid it on the line in January 1973. He said:

"Our growing purchases, coupled with those of Western Europe and Japan, will create major new centers of financial power. By 1985, the oil producing countries of Africa and the Middle East could be collecting oil revenues at an annual rate of almost fifty billion. Most of these countries are not yet ready to use new funds of this magnitude internally. And so large portions of the oil tax revenue will move into the money markets of the free world with impacts which are difficult to predict. One clear possibility is that these countries could become large equity holders in the financial institutions and industrial companies of the United States, Western Europe, and Japan."

Mr. McLean goes on to ask a most pertinent question: *"In order to get the money to pay for this oil what shall we sell and to whom shall we sell it? We cannot look to the industrialized countries of Western Europe and Japan because they will be struggling to increase their own net exports to pay for growing fuel imports.*

"Ultimately the situation can come to equilibrium worldwide only when the oil exporting countries are able to absorb greatly increased imports from us and from other oil importing countries.

"But they do not have the population, markets, and economic infra-structures to accept large imports from us."

Mr. McLean appears to leave us without an answer. He points out that Russia will be the only major power self-sufficient in energy.

It is apparent that, in any military contest between the United States and Russia, Russia would immediately seize the Middle East oil fields. If there were to be a military contest for control of those fields, the Russians could blow them up—if the Arabs did not.

Historically, powerful nations never themselves suffered sharp depriva-tions by weaker nations simply as a matter of principle or out of respect for private property. Powerful nations have no notable reputations as good sports. Complicating the situation further is the competition among the powerful nations for the world's store of energy centered in the Arabian Peninsula. If one goes in to take the energy by force, will the others stand by? Will thief fall upon thief?

The Arabs are not altogether without their defenses. They may be likened to a blind Samson with his hands on the pillars supporting the palace. Arabs could mine oil wells, pipelines, installations of all kinds. They could be prepared to blow up—like a hijacker on a plane—harbor installations and refineries. It is not conceivable that any large country could use military might to seize these energy supplies without the ensuing result of world conflict.

The situation will develop into one of three alternatives:

a. Bargaining with the Arabs by various countries individually, and paying them off in hard, cold, redeemable money;

b. Bargaining with the Arabs collectively by the Western nations, and paying them off in cold, hard money that they would then be willing to reinvest, because they would know that this money would hold its value;

c. The introduction of armed force, where the world's strongest country will simply seize the energy—if there is any left when the smoke clears away.

The first alternative requires that the United States pay for the oil in warehouse receipts—hard money—gold or its equivalent. This will mean an enormous reduction in the living standard in the United States.

The second alternative is the most pleasant of the three, but may be the most unlikely. International cooperation is universally commendable, but rarely—when the chips are down—functional. Each country can find reasons why it ought to have a larger share. The Arabs—in view of their conflict with Israel—can find reasons why they ought to allot more of the energy to one power or another, depending on who is on their side against Israel.

If the third alternative should develop, the result would be so disastrous that there is no point even trying to imagine what we should do.

The reader may think that all of this is rather an alarmist reaction to the facts. Let me assure you there are numerous serious students of the situation who are no less concerned. Professor Nevil Brown, British professor and an international oil authority, prophetically warned a European-American conference in Amsterdam, in 1973, of the possibility of an Arab embargo of oil shipments because of the struggle with Israel. He said:

> . . . In the event of such an embargo the West may face the choice of capitulating or going in physically to get the oil.

> About the only other practical answer has come from Walter J. Levy, New York consultant to the U.S. government. Mr. Levy recommends an international agreement, virtually a worldwide rationing system of oil supplies. It would amount to a program of "equitably sharing import availabilities during an emergency." This would involve a program of stockpiling and a standing system of rationing.

If we look on the bright side of the situation we have to come up with the conclusion that the best solution is for the United States to pay for its oil in real, hard money. That is to say, it will have to reduce its living standard just as Freedonia had to reduce its living standard when it woke to discover that its wells had gone dry.

I must warn you here that a serious reduction of the United States living standard means a depression and the collapse of credit money. That may result in widespread violence bordering on, or developing into, revolution.

Many people believe that none of this need happen, and that the answer to our problem lies with nuclear energy. Let's examine that.

18. NUCLEAR POWER

Even before the accident at Three Mile Island in April 1979, nuclear contracts had nosedived. Here is a chart on nuclear reactor orders (*London Financial Times*). Already the experts had begun to realize (but weren't saying much about) the danger of accumulating nuclear waste, the lack of any solution, and the still great challenge of what to do with nuclear corpses.

Nuclear energy, once the great hope, has four well-publicized but perhaps not-too-well understood disadvantages:

1. the cost and increasing amount of time needed for construction;
2. the danger of meltdown;
3. the problem of disposal of nuclear wastes;
4. the problem of disposing of the worn-out nuclear plants.

Of these, the most dramatic is meltdown. Just precisely what is it?

"Meltdown could be disaster". That's as much as our press coverage, the government, and the Nuclear Regulatory Commission have told us. The real meaning of meltdown is beyond anyone's visualization. To understand as much as possible we need to consider the volcano.

The volcano erupts as a result of heat rising from below. The meltdown eruption would result from heat *sinking*.

Simply described, volcanoes happen when molten rock at temperature of 1800 to 2700 degrees, rises surfaceward encountering water in sub-surface formations. Phenomenal pressures (8000 lbs. psi) build as the molten magma rises. Super heated steam produces the explosion that propels the earth's crust skyward. The gaping hole which results, then becomes a funnel for the magma which bursts above the surface of the earth, sometimes in great waves. As it solidifies when falling, it may build a cone or mountain, as the excess lava flows down the sides.

This of course all follows the steam. The huge avalanche of clouds is comprised of the volcanic gases, which are however about ninety-eight percent water. Nevertheless they carry with them, in the case of a volcano fantastic amounts of solid material reduced to ash. (In 1902 such a cloud traveling at an enormous speed covered the French island of St. Pierre; it wiped out 30,000 souls in a matter of seconds. This ash naturally carried no radioactivity).

To keep ourselves rational, we ought to recognize that this was unusual; the greatest steam phenomenon in history. I use it to *illustrate* the principle of how a volcano operates. A great deal depends on the amount of ground water which the rising magma encounters, and at what depth such water is encountered.

Meltdown reverses the volcanic process and its results are therefore largely conjectural. However there are a number of certainties. None of them are nice.

The meltdown means that the nuclear heat which was to have been drawn off in the course of thirty years, to satisfy needs for electric power is suddenly concentrated in an uncontrolable mass sinking into the earth, like a red hot coal sinks into a snow drift.

The faster this core sinks into the water table the more water rushes from the sides into the hole, falling downward to encounter the rising super-heated steam, being flung hundreds of feet into the atmosphere. All of this steam carrying the radioactivity from the sinking nuclear core.

Try to imagine a hole—for example, ten feet in diameter—descending into the earth, unstoppable. The water table extends for endless miles on all sides of the hole, and the deeper the hole gets, the more water rushes into the hole because of the increasing length of the bore hole admitting it.

The supply of water to make steam is all but infinite. The only limiting factor is the final exhaustion of the nuclear core. How deep would it go? How big would those clouds be? How far would they extend? No one can remotely guess.

My knowledge of geology, ground water and waterbearing formations to 20,000 feet leave me to conclude that billions of gallons of water would be converted into a continuously increasing jet of steam, decreasing only as the core finally became overwhelmed with descending or ascending water. I have no way even to guess the mass of such clouds. But the rising cloud of steam would never stop until the core was dead and could heat no more.

The rising steam would unavoidably—under such great pressure—pick up some of the earth's crust, (in the manner of a volcano) as it erupted and drop these materials indiscriminately as the clouds of steam moved on.

No one can really know how much solid radioactive material would thus be scattered over the countryside, rivers, cities, oceans. But even if no solid material erupted with the steam, the steam itself would become condensed and would descend in droplets over hundreds or perhaps thousands of miles.

Much would depend on the nature of the geologic formations below the plant, a thick and porous and therefore profuse water table, or a thin water table, and whether near the surface or deep. In Spokane, Washington the whole city is supplied by wells at depths of over 1000 feet. Palm Springs, California is supplied by wells of even greater depth.

But the surface water does not limit the conversion of the meltdown core into steam. There is no vacuum in nature. Sedimentary beds are all porous, some more than others. When oil wells are called dry, they are not really dry. They are dry as far as oil is concerned. But when they are tested they often flow salt water.

The earth's temperature increases about 2 degrees per hundred feet. So at 1000 feet it increases 20 degrees, at 10,000 feet—200 degrees. The increase in the temperature is less important than the increase in the pressure. When the melted hole reaches two, three or 20,000 feet, as it certainly would unless it had been exhausted at shallower depths—it would be sure somewhere to encounter the salt water of the deep sediments.

The deeper the hole got the more water would rush in, to be expelled violently through the flume upwards to the surface made by the descent of the melting core.

The point I make is that one should not in such an event be comforted by assurances from authorities that the ground water table was thin, and that the danger would soon be over. The melting core could not be exhausted until its heat had been spent.

We are told by government, the utility companies, and zealous nuclear scientists—"What the hell—you have to take *some* chances!"

Yes, but you don't have to take this kind of chance.

Maybe you live next door to a gas plant, or to an oil-fired boiler, or to a refinery. You take *some* chance. There could be an accident, or fire. When we talk about a meltdown in nuclear plant, chance is hardly the word. We are talking about an unimaginable disaster—if it should ever happen.

No one can stop a volcano. No combination of experts could stop the descent of the core. Nothing in God's world could stop the resulting steam— nor the primordial power of its thrust.

In the United States we now have seventy-two nuclear plants and ninety in the planning or early construction procedures. All over the world they are building new nuclear plants. In early May we began to hear of dangerous deficiencies in the safety system of the Chalk River Plant in Ontario. Sure—no accidents happened. No accident may ever happen. But if you get enough nuclear plants—and we now know such an accident CAN happen—then we may conclude for certain that sooner or later there's going to be a meltdown somewhere. *Then the world public would demand the closure of all plants— at a time when our dependence on them would have become fatal.*

It narrows down to this—we are not taking a chance, we are taking a certainty. Ultimately, that certainty may not affect us directly. It may reflect on us indirectly, remotely, instantly, or not at all. We do know we are tempting fate. When fate is tempted enough it will respond. Ten years, ten months, ten days. *It will happen!*

The nuclear champions have hinted that Three Mile Island may have been sabotage by the anti-nuclear group to fuel their campaign dramatically.

This is no defense at all. It is the scariest thing I have heard. If the anti-nuclear group could bring about conditions threatening a meltdown, then why couldn't any other saboteur? *What these people are really saying is that nuclear plants are subject to sabotage and to terrorists.*

Who wants to take the responsibility for the lives of perhaps an entire city by the comforting assurance that *sabotage is difficult and "most unlikely"!* Yet that's the best assurance we can get.

The fact to remember is this: for a time the Three Mile Island reactor was completely out of control. Technicians were baffled, dumbfounded and helpless.

Now the nuclear proponents are asking *"What are you kicking about — it didn't happen!"*

That's Russian roulette. How often can you win?

Recently, I came across the following newspaper story:

"(AP) — The FBI is investigating what might be the first case of attempted sabotage at a U.S. Nuclear Power Plant an official of Virginia Electric Power Company said Tuesday.

"Inspectors discovered on Monday that a caustic white crystalline substance had been dumped into 62 of 64 new, non-radioactive fuel elements stored for use later." Luckily the fuel elements were not damaged, but we have to conclude that was more the result of the naivete of the possible saboteurs than of good management.

The Company's vice-president said:

We are told we have the best security system of any nuclear plant in the country."

For the best — this isn't much comfort.

Implicit in the existence of all nuclear plants is their vulnerability to sabotage, mechanical failure, human error and outright negligence. The more plants there are, the sooner the first accident will happen. Then what do you do with the existing plants when the world public rebels? How do you get rid of them, when to destroy them is in itself dangerous?

NUCLEAR PLANTS WEAR OUT

Nuclear power plants wear out. When worn out they have to be disposed of. The first nuclear plant built near Los Angeles in the early '50's has now expired. Its curse is projected into the centuries as demolition squads labor to take it apart—and don't know what to do with it.

This is the smallest plant. Here is what it's like, according to the Los Angeles Times:

"It's like a tall silo, 30 ft. high, buried in the ground. Its walls are 5 in. of steel and around this steel is 5 ft. of concrete. The inside of this silo is so radioactive that if a man were to jump in, he would be burned to death in seconds. So it is filled with water.

But it has to be dismantled. It cost $13 million to build in the 1950's. It will take $6 million and two years to get rid of it only *temporarily*.

A huge machine has bared the upper portions of the silo and by remote control with a powerful torch, it is cutting out pieces of steel about 4 ft. square. No one dare approach the demolition. Even the crane that is being used by remote control will have to be cut up into pieces and disposed of like the nuclear reactor itself. The temporary expedient will be to immerse every piece in a lot of water and then take the water away. The water can later be evaporated, but then no one is quite sure where to bury the deadly remains. The radioactivity will last for thousands of years."

This will be the fate of every worn-out nuclear plant in the U.S.A. This first plant is relatively tiny. Now there are 72 plants. The plants are far bigger. All the plants will wear out. Each one of them carries with it a death sentence reaching into the centuries.

Moreover, it's not even known if the big nuclear plants today could be disposed of at all. They are a hundred times larger than the pygmy which is now causing so much trouble near Los Angeles. As a consequence of their size, their walls are so thick and so high that there is no technology known to man which could adequately cut them into chunks for disinterment—*even if a burial ground existed.*

One suggestion is simply to weld the whole thing shut with heavy steel and put guards around it for a hundred years until some of the radioactivity has worn off. Actually, that's no answer at all. Another suggested answer is to bury the whole thing. But nobody knows how this could be done. It had been a possibility until recently, for it had been thought after a few hundred years the plant would be safe enough if buried. But now there is reason to believe that it would not be safe for several thousand years, and radioactivity would continue to seep out of the earth into the atmosphere. One isotope, Nickel-59, which is produced in the reactors, would require 100,000 years to decay. Carbon-14 would require 65,000 years.

NEW NUCLEAR COST

It seems no one has bothered to add the dismantlement cost to the construction cost to find the power cost of a nuclear plant. Probably that is for two reasons. Firstly, they don't know how to do it. Secondly, how can you then evaluate a cost?

But we have been told that Three Mile Island may never operate again, and it might cost $1 billion to wrap it up if it doesn't.

Without reckoning burial or destruction costs (methods unknown), the

London Financial Times gives this scale in reckoning electric power generation costs:

Uranium 15   Coal 20   Oil 40

But even in ignorance of these hidden costs, growing uncertainty about waste disposal has begun to paralyze the industry. Since 1974, orders for nearly 200 nuclear stations have been cancelled or postponed. In 1978 only two new orders were announced. This graph from the London Financial Times in early 1979 shows the collapse of reactor orders.

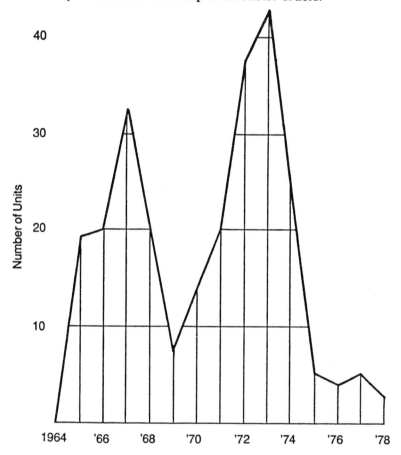

U.S. REACTOR ORDERS (Source: U.S. Atomic Industrial Forum)

Worldwide, twenty-two nations have installed them, and one hundred thirty-nine such stations are under construction.

The U.S. has seventy-two plants in operation and ninety in process.

It's hard to believe that people, who are not insane, could go on with this without having a remote idea as to how to handle the Frankenstein when it's all over.

It's kind of like a cat starting up a 100 foot pole. Not knowing how to get down, he keeps on climbing. If at the top no one rescues him, he's a dead cat. As we build more plants, we climb higher on the nuclear pole. We assume, in each case, that in thirty years someone will know how to rescue us.

But the atom is the stuff of CREATION, and when it is split, man may never be able to destroy the results.

Still our government leaders urge us up the pole.

From the London Financial Times: "The French Government has said unequivocally that the accident will not impede its own plans to continue ordering 5,000 MW of PWR capacity a year, to apply one half of its electricity by 1985."

In the U.S., James Schlesinger said: "We have no alternative if we are going to maintain energy production . . . Jimmy Carter still figures the nuclear power supply of fourteen percent today will grow to twenty-five percent of U.S. electric energy by year 2000. About eight percent of total U.S. energy today.

DISGUISED BLESSING

The Three Mile Island accident may prove to be a blessing. It has alerted and alarmed the public of the world. What now will emerge is a fuller TRUTH. Final disposition of nuclear corpses had never been a subject of public discussion before. With all the reading I do, I was totally unaware of this, the worst problem of all, until November 1977.

Until you realize the enormity of it by reading what it takes to temporarily get rid of a tiny nuclear toy of 1950, you are apt to give credence to some of the far-out schemes now being put forward.

THE OVERALL PROBLEM OF WASTE

The following is from the *South African Weekly*, March 1979: HIGH FLYING RUBBISH — *"A West German engineer has come up with a high-flying idea to get rid of nuclear waste. He says dangerous atomic rubbish should be rocketed into space.*

"Dietrich Koelle, of the giant arms firm Messerschmitt—Boelkow—Blohm, in Munich, says that by 1990 West German nuclear power plants will be producing 4500 m³ of highly radio active waste each year.

"Because no one wants a nuclear "tip" near his home, regardless of stringent safety measures, the best way to dispose of the stuff would be to shoot it right out of our solar system.

"Koelle is currently working on a study that foresees returnable, re-usable transporters unloading smaller, waste-packed rockets in space and then turning for home.

"The small rockets would carry lead-sealed containers each holding up to 30 tons of waste to a point close to the planet Jupiter before unloading them in turn and 'boomeranging' back for a soft landing on earth.

"Jupiter would then take over and boost the containers out of our solar system into free space on a journey that would last several thousand years before they hit anything.

"'But by then the waste would have lost its radioactivity,' says Koelle. 'The containers would be no more dangerous than meteorites of the same size.'"

GLASS ENCASEMENT SCHEME

I have had a great deal of criticism for my stand against nuclear power. Recently someone wrote me that it had all been solved by encasing the waste in a new type of glass that soaks up surrounding water like a sponge. Well, we can wisely bring a little geology into that, too.

Nuclear burial grounds are most apt to be tucked away far from populations, if for no other reason than that populations won't stand for them. The result is the burials are most likely to take place in remote mountains, *which are exactly the most prone to earth movements.* Glass may not let the poisonous fluid out, but earth movements can crush the glass with impuntiy.

For the glass method to work, the cemeteries would have to be in areas of known quiescence. We would have to be confident that these areas would remain quiescent for tens of thousands of years. Only there could we dump our glass enclosed wastes and glass enclosed chunks of concrete lead and diced automatic cranes which had been used to cut these plants in pieces. Deep, deep ocean is suggested. There again we're uncertain. The whole world is uncomfortable with that.

THE GOLD ENCASEMENT SCHEME

A scientist of considerable stature comes up with the following solution:

"Nuclear wastes can be stored safely by only one method. *Canisters buried 600 feet enclosed in steel and encased in gold.*

"Goesta Wranglen, foremost corrosion expert in Sweden, Professor at the Royal Institute of Technology, Stockholm, President of the International Society of Electro-chemistry, categorically states that the most intricate plan yet devised to hold nuclear wastes is unsafe. The plan is this. Solidification of the nuclear wastes in glass; the glass encased in a welded steel cylinder; the steel enclosed in copper. The canisters to be buried in a hole to be dug 500 feet deep. The Commission admits that the radio-activity would begin to escape in 100,000 years. Wranglen says: *'No good.'*

"Even though the ground water is stagnant at that level under normal conditions, the radiation emanating from the canister would heat the ground water to a temperature of around 100 to 150 degrees C. This would cause it to rise to ground level. Radiation would increase the oxygen content much higher than ordinary hot water. Localized corrosion under these conditions can easily occur in even stagnant water—possibly even in a few months. Wranglen warns that the radiation would begin to arise to the earth's surface at the very best in 100 years—might even become very dangerous in 10 years. The answer?

"Gold is the only material which will withstand the attack of radiolysis in

surrounding water over thousands of years, resisting all corrosion.

"It may seem drastic, says Wranglen to recommend encapsulating the canisters in pure gold—but only the best in this case is good enough. He readily admitted great quantities of gold would be required. If a gold shortage occurred, it will apparently not be possible to allow use of gold for jewelry or other such purposes."

THE NAKED TRUTH — NO KNOWN ANSWER

As recently as mid-April 1979, *Time* magazine reported:

"Still unsettled—and unsettling—is the question of how the U.S. can safely dispose of garbage from nuclear operations. Spent fuel and other wastes remain radioactive for thousands of years. At present a lot of such waste is stored under water in 'swimming pools' at plant sites, but nuclear plants are running out of pool space. Some may have to be shut down as early as 1983 unless a more permanent method of disposal is found." (Nuclear plants are built to operate for about 30-35 years.)

The people of Washington State were chilled to read the following in the *Spokane Spokesman Review* and other Washington papers mid-1978. It was news to them.

"The problem of what to do with nuclear waste remains unsolved, much to the consternation of the people in Eastern Washington where seventy percent of the nation's nuclear garbage is stored. A news dispatch from Olympia, Washington says that 47 million gallons of high-level radioactive wastes are stored in a 570 square mile reservation at Hanford, Washington.

"They are staying there and accumulating there because first of all no one knows where to move them. Secondly, no one knows how to move them.

"Frank Standerfer, U.S. Dept. of Energy, said officials are not sure it will be feasible to move the wastes. The extracting, processing and shipping will cost billions of dollars. The crews could be exposed to the radioactivity, and some of it might be released into the environment. He says the decisions will be postponed at least until the mid-1980's.

Meanwhile the greatest concern is the storage tanks. In 1973 one of the tanks began leaking and the dangerous waste seeped 90 feet underground, within 115 feet of the water table. Had it reached the water table, the results could have been disastrous in many areas. After that they started making double steel-wall tanks encased in jackets of concrete."

So far no one has made an application to Washington, D.C. to play host. So it appears Hanford may be stuck.

CARTER MIGHT HANDLE IT

President Carter in 1977 suggested the U.S. might store other countries' nuclear waste along with our own. The following is reprinted from MFE November 4, 1977.

"While the plants are in operation, they discharge rods of spent fuel. These spent rods contain plutonium. As a waste product they are absolute dynamite.

"At a Congressional Hearing in mid-October, it was revealed that there is even now *"a tremendous backlog of spent fuel."* The utilities are starting to run out of storage space for the discharged fuel from some sixty-seven operating nuclear reactors. What they are doing now is removing the spent rods and simply dumping them in water. That, of course, is the most temporary end solution. Congress learned that there was some 3,000 tons of this highly potent garbage at the end of 1976. *It is estimated that by the end of 1983 there will be 13,000 tons of virtual black death.* Nobody has yet dared figure out what there will be by the year 2000.

"Now President Carter has suggested that the Government take over nuclear garbage. Taxpayers will become the custodians—*not only for the U.S. garbage, but for nuclear plants all around the world.*

"There are no volunteers among the communities of the various 48 states to be host to the waste. The best they've come up with is that the spent fuel will be buried in underground geologic formations. That makes it a little fancier when you say "geologic formations." Of course it's geologic formations. What else is at depth underground?

"James Schlesinger says that probably all of this fuel will have to be '*reprocessed*' to solve the problem of waste. The only thing is no one knows just how to reprocess.

"*The atom is the stuff of the creation of the universe. We have broken the atoms apart. The spent remains are not apt to disappear harmlessly.*"

There is always the happy possibility that we will someday develop clean nuclear energy, or learn how to effectively harness the power of the sun. These are a long time away, and will only be possible then with an enormous commitment of money for research. For the present, the Three Mile Island accident may prove to be the blessing of the nuclear age. It has alerted and alarmed the public of the world. Yet the world's politicians take these inexplicable positions — that construction of nuclear plants must go on, no matter what.

It will take a while for nuclear wishes to die. It will take a while for this realization to become clear to our leaders — but nuclear is essentially finished.

Nuclear plants already in existence will probably have to keep going. To stop the nuclear plants around Chicago would cut off half the electricity. Much the same applies to New England and parts of the south-east U.S. A city like Chicago would cease to exist as an organized community.

Nevertheless the brakes will be put on the nuclear industry throughout the U.S. That is going to mean a greatly reduced economy. Yet there *is* a solution to the energy problem, and it lies right at our feet.

Our only real and practical salvation lies in coal. The critical period— whether we live or die—is the next five years. Only coal affords us the chance for independent survival. Are we prepared to spend what it costs to do it now?

19. COAL

Consider the following

1. The Western World could be forced into war or submission this year by a military eruption in the Middle East.

2. Deprived of half its daily oil supply, the U.S. would be economically and militarily impotent in ninety days.

3. Japan could be completely choked off in sixty days.

4. Western Europe would lose three-fourths of its potency in two or three months.

5. An explosion of the Arab-Israeli Peace could force choice between war or energy suffocation.

(6) This is the result of negligence that borders on TREASON.

The U.S. had its warning in no uncertain terms in 1973. Had the Arab oil embargo lasted another sixty days, the Western economies would have faced a shut down.

Transportation is the bloodstream of the American Nation. It nurtures the whole economic body. Cut the flow of blood by one half; nay one third; nay even one-quarter; and the country is crippled on the land, on the sea, and in the air.

What did our leaders do?

1. They increased nuclear power, but now don't know how to handle it or its waste.

2. They increased our oil dependency from 6.5 million b/d to 9 million b/d, by nearly forty percent.

3. They increased our coal production by one percent.

They allowed a coal reserve adequate for our needs for 500 years to be bound by chains of red tape. R. E. Samples, Chief Executive of the Consolidation

Financial Times Saturday April 7, 1979

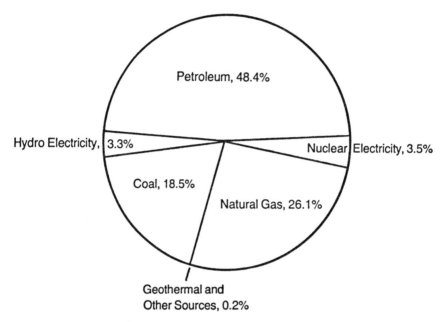

ENERGY CONSUMPTION, 1977. Total: 76.299 quadrillion (million billion) BTU's.

Source: US DEPARTMENT OF ENERGY

Coal Co. says, "We are sitting on billions of tons of coal reserves that we can neither dig nor burn because of a tangled mass of bureaucratic red tape," and thus our leaders have lost six valuable years. Worse, they have knowingly allowed our vulnerability to accelerate dangerously for seventeen years.

The potential danger of energy strangulation of the most powerful nation in the world was easily foreseeable. Just to keep even in the U.S.A., we would have to find a new Alaska North Slope every sixteen months; and for the world, a new Saudi Arabia every eight years. Red lights were flashing and the bells were ringing in 1973, but nothing was done.

Is anything being done now? Not much.

Consider the total inadequacy of the Carter plan in view of the mortal danger to which the nation is exposed.

In 1977 the U. S. satisfied eighteen percent of its energy with coal (which constitutes eighty percent of its reserves) and satisfied seventy-five percent of its needs by oil (half imported), which amounts to seven percent of its energy reserves.

Does it plan a crash program for coal to match the Synthetic Rubber Blitz so technologically successful during the war? Not at all. It proposes a modest fifty percent increase in coal by 1985. How does it expect to survive?

Obviously on the shaky assumption that the Middle East oil will continue its uninterrupted flow at manageable prices—even as the Moslem World grows increasingly antagonistic towards the Christian West.

The target should be a minimum 500% increase in coal's use by 1985. A Technological Blitz of unprecedented proportion. Self-sufficiency in energy by 1990.

Is this goal unrealistic?

Under the present leadership it probably is.

For example, in early March 1979 our planners based our energy future (1985) on these oil prices—$13 per bbl., low range; $15 per bbl., medium range; $20 per bbl., high range. Well within 6 months—fall 1979—oil had reached the 1985 projection of $20 a barrel.

And what do our planners see for oil in 1990—$13 low; $20 medium; $30 high?

Is there an argument in favor of nuclear power? YES. Edison Electric Institute estimates that present atomic plants produce at a cost of $1.71 per kwh, versus $1.74 to $2.08 for coal—some argument!

That does not include the cost of disposing of the nuclear monstrosities when they die. Which could easily double the price—if it could be done at all.

In the light of our problems, it is interesting to observe what has been happening in South Africa.

Here is a country with no oil—but vast reserves of coal. Farsighted leaders did not wait for the Middle East hurricane to arrive. Long ago, starting with some pages out of the German book (Germany kept its war machine going on oil from coal.), it began a coal to oil conversion technology.

Here is a quote from the *South African Digest.*

"*South Africa will be the most self-sufficient nation in the world in two years, according to the ACSA Foundation of Arizona.*

"*South Africa now produces about seventy-five per cent of its energy needs, far more than most Western nations, said the Foundation in a report in The . Citizen.*

"*Within two years South Africa would be the most energy sufficient nation in the West, thanks to Sasol and huge coal reserves. It would have a more varied and practical energy technology than any other country in the world.*

"*South Africa is playing an increasing role as exporter of coal, uranium, oil-from-coal and nuclear technology. It is self-sufficient in strategic mineral resources and food and nearly self-sufficient in manufactured goods, arms and energy, according to the foundation.*"

Additionally, South Africa is said to have accumulated a two or three year supply of oil in its expansive mine shafts. Also, more oil tankers are said to be unloading at S.A. ports than before. South Africa can pay in gold. Gold will buy anything—even your life in case of a pinch.

This former stockpiling of oil may explain why S.A. balance of payments were in the red and have now turned suddenly positive, with the financial rand rising dramatically.

The bottom line these days is self-sufficiency. And the bottom line of that these days is energy and gold.

Notice that while South Africa is vastly rich in uranium, it utilizes coal for its own energy generation, while it exports the uranium for others to use.

* * * * *

BRITAIN AND COAL

"LONDON (UPI) — When the Middle East and North Sea oil wells pump no more—and sooner or later that is going to happen—Britain plans to run its cars, power its factories and produce its petrochemicals with the fuel that first made it an industrial giant: coal.

"Not ordinary, but coal turned into crude oil.

"'Coal is not just a lump of black stuff you throw on the fire,' said Keith Beeston, spokesman for the British National Coal Board.

"'You can either look at coal as solid oil or oil as liquid coal.'

"After coal is in liquid form, said Beeston, 'you can make virtually everything from it that you can make from oil with the existing oil refining techniques.'

"By the 1990s, experts expect oil to be very expensive and very scarce. Britain's North Sea reserves will be on the decline and it will have to limit petroleum to premium uses like motor transport.

"'The oil companies are investing in coal as fast as they can,' said Beeston. 'They see the writing on the wall.'

"Britain is looking at two methods for turning coal to oil.

"Using the 'liquid solvent extraction' technique, a hot chemical solvent is poured over coal, dissolving it into a tarry liquid. Hydrogen is added—oil contains twice as much hydrogen as coal—and it is then refined. The end product, researchers say, is ideally suited for refining into transport and aviation fuels.

"In the 'gas solvent extraction' method, coal is dissolved by exposing it to a very hot compressed gas. Various stages of processing produce a tar-like solution which is hydrogenated and refined. This method is particularly effective for producing petrochemicals used in the manufacture of plastics, resins, rubbers, artificial fibers and paints.

The only major drawback with both methods is the price. A major coal refinery would cost about $3 billion to build. Coal Board officials estimate a barrel of oil from such a refinery would cost about $26, compared with the OPEC price—constantly rising—often exceeding $26.00 on the spot market.

"'It sounds like a lot of money,' says Irving Oldfield, an official with the NCB. 'But energy is a lot of money.'

"Price does not concern Alex Eadie. If Britain is going to remain a leading industrial power, he said, it is going to require a petrochemicals industry. And the only way to be sure of a continuing supply is by exploiting the coal lying beneath the British Isles.

"Britain, with its estimated 300 years worth of coal reserves, will be in a very strong position to sustain itself."

❂   ❂   ❂   ❂   ❂

When the above article was written OPEC oil was $13 per bbl. Who knows what price by 1988-1990—short of war.

Also, improved technology with experience and volume is bound to bring down the cost of coal energy.

In the case of the U.S.A. there is no alternative—expensive energy from coal — *but all you want* — or maybe no energy at all from the outside world.

WHAT STOPS COAL IN THE U.S.?

Since the 1973 oil embargo, coal production in the U.S. has increased one percent—even as we sit on billions of tons. We have the technology, the manpower, and the reserves. Then we have the bureaucratic red tape. Among the laws and systems coal producers must buck are these:

> The Surface Mining and Control Act (1977), The Federal Safety and Health Act (1977), The Surface Mining Control and Reclamation Act (1977), The Federal Land Policy and Management Act (1976), The National Forest Management Act (1976), The Alaska Claims Settlement Act (1971).

> The Federal Coal Leasing Amendments Act (1976), The Mining in the Parks Act, The Clean Air Act and Clean Air Act Amendment (1977), The Federal Coal Mine Health and Safety Act (1969), and the Community Health and Environment Surveillance System.

Known and recoverable reserves are 218 billion tons—70 years supply of total energy.

The known or indicated deposits recoverable with present technology are 440 billion tons—enough for 140 years. Ultimately recoverable reserves are estimated at 1000 billion tons (enough for 300 years) to 1800 billion tons (enough for over 500 years). *And more than ninety percent of existing industrial boilers can't burn coal.*

OIL AT $6.00 BBL.

Since 1973 about ten percent of the mine forces of 200,000 have been laid off. Regulations are causing plants to switch from coal to oil. Utilities have to install million dollar scrubbers to remove sulphur even for coal that has no sulphur. Because some need them *all* have to use them.

A ton of coal equalling four barrels of crude oil sells at $25 (as of Mid 1979) — approximate equivalent of $6 a barrel compared with $18 for Mid-East crude. That doesn't, of course, include transportation. But pipeline transportation for coal exists. Government gives little or no thought to tax incentives for that.

Coal reserves of the U.S. absolutely known and recoverable right now (218 billion tons) equals almost *900 billion* barrels of oil. Saudi Arabia's oil reserves are *165 billion barrels.*

Yet, with a technology in use in South Africa and ready to go, we BEG the Saudis and the Lybians, etc. to stay friendly.

Have we made any plans to change over? Or will we just sit and go the way of the ancient dinosaurs, who simply died off because of their ponderous immobility?

It is interesting to note that there are indeed plans. With oil hopelessly inadequate, coal unlimited, unbounded, and a technology that is almost ready for the asking, our leaders plan to double coal's seventeen percent contribution by 1985.

TECHNOLOGY EXISTS

Fluor Corporation is presently building the biggest coal gasification plant in the world in South Africa. When finished, S.A. will become the first country in the world that can thumb its nose at the oil producing states.

Coal conversion takes two forms: gasification and liquefaction. When coal is converted to gas, the product can be picked up by gathering systems and distributed nationwide in natural gas pipelines.

In liquefaction coal comes out as the product of any oil refinery. Over half the raw liquid coming off coal is almost ready to be trucked out as fuel oil to utility plants and homes.

Right now technologists are placing the cost of coal energy, including motor gasoline at $30 per bbl., oil equivalent.

One always finds that as these things progress and as volume increases, technology improves, and unit costs recede. Even without that — we would not have a $30 per bbl. ceiling on all the oil we could use, at least until 2000.

If we only had gone to work seven year ago!

Even if we had turned the oil companies loose at the world oil prices in 1973, we could probably have significantly more indigenous energy today.

TECHNOLOGY EXPLAINED

One of the very best articles on technology appeared in *Financial World*, February 15th 1979. I draw freely on it here, but the more serious student should get a copy.

"In addition, the giant oil companies have the coal, the technology and the distribution and marketing capabilities to develop a fully integrated coal liquefaction industry—provided the Justice Department lets them keep their coal holdings . . ."

"The three major processes are Exxon's donor-solvent system; Gulf Oil's solvent-refined coal; and Dynalectron's H-coal. All three are at the pilot plant stage right now. If these plants prove successful, the next step is to build commercial-scale liquefactories at around $1 billion or so each . . ."

"The Exxon process is flexible," says Lawrence E. Swabb Jr., of Exxon Research and Engineering. "It can handle a range of coal feeds, but the coal quality affects yield. The process also has the flexibility to vary the product slate. The naphtha yield can be as low as twenty-five percent, for example, or as high as fifty-five percent of total liquid product." That last point is important, for naphtha is the liquid that would be blended into automobile fuels . . ."

"The Gulf process, developed by its Pittsburg & Midway Coal Mining subsidiary, is a technological spin-off of efforts to develop cleaner-burning solid fuel. Under this technique, pulverized coal is mixed with a solvent. The resulting slurry is mixed with hydrogen and converted under heat into liquid hydrocarbons. Sulfur is removed in the process, reprocessed and sold. Also produced are pipeline gas, liquefied gas, naphtha and fuel oil.
"The special appeal is that the Gulf process can convert high-sulfur coal into clean-burning liquid fuel for utilities, thus eliminating the need for expensive pollution control equipment. High-sulfur coal is more abundant than other types.
"The Department of Energy is wasting no time deciding the fate of the Gulf project; it has already reached an agreement with the West German Government to share the cost of the demonstration plant for the solvent-refinement process. The participation of West Germany is somewhat ironic; Germany was something of a pioneer in the use of coal liquids. Hitler's war machine, in fact, used coal liquids on a massive scale, but price and pollution were not considerations at the time."

"*Magnetohydrodynamics.* This technology is actually a coal spinoff, but is still in its infancy. It works like this: When combustion gases from burning powdered coal are passed through a narrow channel surrounded by a powerful magnet, a direct current is generated. In addition, the hot gases can be used to heat steam boilers, thus significantly improving the efficiency of the generating plant. Combustion Engineering is probably farther along in developing magnetohydrodynamics than anyone. It has collaborated with Avco Everett Research Laboratory Inc. in designing a 100-megawatt MHD plant and plans to bid on another project with General Electric."

"Gasification faces a number of nontechnological problems that are likely to hinder its growth. A major one is that gas companies are regulated as utilities and thus face price and other restrictions on both the Federal and local levels. Furthermore, electric utilities, who are major buyers of gas, are also regulated. A key question is whether the electric utilities will be permitted to buy synthetic gas at the premium prices that will be required to make coal gasification feasible."

OIL USAGE

	Uses	Imports	Produces
U.S.A.	19 m/b/d	9 m/b/d	9 m/b/d
Western Europe	14 m/b/d	12 m/b/d	2 m/b/d
Japan	8 m/b/d	5 m/b/d	0 m/b/d
Totals	41 m/b/d	26 m/b/d	11 m/b/d

Saudi Arabia boosted production from 8.5 m/b/d to 10 m/b/d, but has now cut back to 8.5 m/b/d. Iran is exporting perhaps 2 m/b/d. Africa exports 5 m/b/d and other Mideast nations 6 m/b/d. Canada produces 2 m/b/d and uses 2 m/b/d. Mexico approaches 1.5 m/b/d and uses it. Russia produces 11 m/b/d and uses it in the East.

Principle oil using and producing countries use 50 m/b/d and produce 45. Shortage is about 5 m/b/d, but would be only 3 m/b/d if Iran produced 2 m/b/d more.

Entire world must cut back at least 5%.

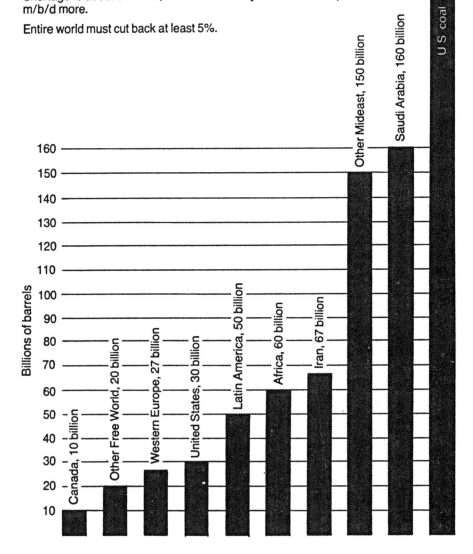

Also in the field are such companies as Dynalectron (working on a special liquefaction process using an easily available catalyst to enhance conversion of the H-coal process), Dravo Corporation, a specialist in coal gasification, Foster Wheeler, Ralph M. Parsons, Dupont, Fluor and others.

Russia, nowhere near the danger of the U.S.A., has three underground coal gasification plants; one near Moscow, one in Central Soviet Asia, one in Siberia. They produce 145 billion cubic feet a day.

The Russians say the gas is not good quality. They suggest laser or electronic guns.

But the Russians—even though they don't need it—are not sleeping.

To sum up (as of Fall, 1979):

1. With 220 billion tons coal underfoot and ready, the U.S. is the Saudi Arabia of coal.
2. The technology is ready or nearly ready.
3. 1 ton of coal equals energy in 4 bbls. of oil.
4. 1 ton of coal costs $25. Four bbls. oil will soon cost $80.
5. Since 1973 scare, U.S. increased coal production one percent.
6. Since 1973 scare, U.S. increased oil dependency over thirty-five percent.
    (The figures on the opposite page are as of Jan. 1979.)

20. OTHER ENERGY

Apart from coal, are there other answers? People hopefully mention oil sands, oil shale, solar, wind, alcohol, geothermal. Might one of these give us the BIG ANSWER? To be able to assess that we must comprehend just how BIG the answer is. The figures are of a magnitude beyond our ken. How big a tank would we have to fill each evening to last us to the next evening?

A barrel occupies 5.5 cubic feet. Let's call it 5. We use 20 million barrels a day. Each evening we'd have to fill a 100 million cubic foot tank.

If we built a tank a city block square (650 feet) how high would we have to make it - 50 feet - 100 feet - 500 feet?

The answer is 250 feet.

If we are going to fill our tank between 8:00 P.M. and 6:00 A.M. we have to fill at the rate of 2 million barrels an hour, 330,000 barrels a minute, 5,500 barrels a second. That requires a BIG hose - *190,000 gallons a second*. It takes a lot of oil wells to produce a flow like that.

U.S. oil wells average 16 barrels a day—that's because most are old strippers. We need 1.25 million oilwells. For our 220 million people we need one oilwell for every fifteen people.

❁   ❁   ❁   ❁   ❁

That's how big oil is. When we look for an alternative to oil, small or modest answers are NO answers. Outside of coal are there *any* with this potential? Let's look.

CANADA OIL SANDS

A lot of oil here; 220 billion barrels classed as available, more than Saudi Arabia. Including deposits at depth—a trillion barrels or more.

The product, though, is a heavy tar-like substance. Actually the oil sands can be considered a mineral deposit; eighty-five percent sand by volume, ninety percent sand by weight.

We must mine about two tons of residue for every barrel of oil.

To get one million barrels of oil a day we must dredge, heat and treat two million tons of sand. And we have an additional problem:

The treated sand takes up more space than the compacted sand we mined. Where are we going to put this extra sand as time goes on, and as we mine billions of tons of sand? The disposal problem in itself is incredible.

Also imagine the number of bulldozers it will take to mine two-million tons—100,000—tons every hour of a twenty-hour day. How long would it take and how much would it cost to make the machinery? That's for one million barrels of oil daily. If the U.S. were to continue to supply half its petroleum needs (which it won't) we still need to mine enough for ten million barrels of oil a day—or nearly one million tons of sand every hour—17,000 tons of sand a minute.

A nine-company effort now in the planning stage will produce 140,000 barrels daily by 1986 and cost $5 billion, no doubt underestimated. Always add a couple of years to a project like this and we are coming very close to 1990 before we get a measly 140,000 barrels daily. The Alaska Pipeline alone delivers over a million barrels a day—five percent of U.S. needs.

(If these oil sands mineral beds which dip below the surface 2—3,000 feet could be injected with a solvent to free the oil and bring it up, we'd be looking at a brighter hope. Scientists are working on this, but the solution is a long way off.)

The U.S. is going to stand or fall on its energy solution in the next ten years; the oil sands of Athabasca offer no quick answer. Neither do the huge oil sands deposits of Venezuela or Russia or anywhere else; or the oil shales of Colorado. *It will be too late for us.*

Compared to coal, oil sands are a poor source. When you mine a ton of coal, you get a ton (less ash) of concentrated energy. The sulphur can be scrubbed out and even sold. The carbon dioxide gas can be piped into existing but badly depleted oil fields to raise gas pressure to raise more oil to the surface; or it can be injected into countless exhausted natural gas reservoirs.

When you mine a ton of oil sands, you get *one-tenth* of a ton of energy. Do we have any choice?

ALCOHOL

Here again the crucial consideration is *volume.* How many tons of wood, wheat, or garbage to make a ton of oil?

What we are speaking of is vegetation — *current vegetation.* That is, the required tonnage must be produced each year.

We reach desperately for new ideas. Alcohol is an excellent fuel. It can be made efficiently from wood, grain, or almost any organic matter. Agreed. But how much?

Alcohol proponents say we could get 61 gallons per acre of wheat. That is 1½ barrels with a value of about $30. But if that land produced 30 bushels of wheat, the wheat would be worth about $90, or three times as much as the alcohol, and we haven't started to think about the cost of processing the wheat.

I have heard it said that artichokes will yield four times as much oil per acre. I wonder how much artichoke acreage we have, because at six barrels per acre we would need 150,000 acres of artichokes for a million barrels a day. And what are the world's people going to eat when we convert huge land masses into growing vegetation to be turned into oil?

Another study claims that 19 billion cubic feet of wood residues in Canada would produce 800 million barrels of fuel alcohol. I wonder how we are going to gather, load, transport and handle 19 billion cubic feet of supplies and residues. Add those costs and the processing costs; the 800 million barrels of fuel alcohol, even if the claim is true—recedes into dreamland.

Once again when you introduce the concept of *volume* your answer disappears.

A help, sure — an answer, no.

Think of the genesis of coal and oil.

The alcohol proponents rely on one year's vegetation for one year's supply. But coal and oil are the result of hundreds of millions of years of accumulated vegetable and animal matter—that is to say sea life—dead and buried by nature and stewed into petroleum with the escaping gases becoming the natural gas of today, trapped in impervious geological formations overlaying the porous sedimentary reservoirs.

Our coal is decayed vegetation of an abundance unimaginable on earth today. The dense forests of the Carboniferous era of some 500 million years, grew, decayed, and fell one upon the other. Then nature, by piling thousands of feet of rock overburden deposited by the sea, compressed the vegetation like no pressure we could ever produce, heated it, aged it and bequeathed it to our modern world, where the vegetation of the land mass is mainly consumed as food in the form of small plants. Only a small percentage of our land mass is in forests which are needed to produce our shelter.

And we suppose that year by year we can use *current* vegetable growth to match nature's hoard?

We forget that we are drawing from a bank which nature took hundreds of millions of years to produce, and in less than a hundred years we have nearly exhausted the full essence arising from the most prolific sealife imaginable.

Alcohol — yes. It will produce energy and quite a bit — *if you are thinking in limited terms*. But in terms of a percentage of our needs — as an answer — alcohol is no answer at all.

SOLAR POWER

I believe the point is made. I shall not try to calculate the hundreds or thousands of acres of photoelectric cells needed to even approach a significant fraction of our needs.

Solar power will heat swimming pools, will heat homes in the sunny states. It will help and as it helps it will lessen the shortage. In the twenty-first century solar contributions may be very significant. But for the next five to ten years, which is our critical period—our live or die period — forget it. Yet Carter has just announced a very expensive program to pursue solar power.

WIND POWER

Windy areas could become virtually self-sufficient. But constantly windy areas are a very small percentage of our total area, and because of the wind, sparsely populated.

U.S. Windpower Incorporated of Massachusetts will build the biggest wind energy system so far at Pacheco Pass, about 100 miles south of San Francisco.

The $75 million project will produce enough power for 1,000 people—the equivalent of 175,000 barrels of oil a year. It will consist of twenty-three bladed windmills each with three—45 foot whirling blades sitting on towers 150 feet high. Each tower would have three generators.

The state will buy power from the company at going rates. The company says the rising price of oil has made the windmill project economically feasible.

If successful, the company will set up several hundred more windmills in the west where the winds blow constantly around 20 - 30 miles an hour.

A quick calculation tells me that if it requires 75 million dollars to serve 1,000 people, it ought to cost 75 billion dollars for only 1 million people.

Again, the answer is the same. The wind can be a helper, but not an answer.

NUCLEAR FUSION

Very promising for the next century. Fusion may very well solve humanity's energy problem forever. No radioactivity as in fission (atomic splitting). The U.S. is spending $500 million on two fusion projects and a group of countries including Russia plan cooperation to produce a $25 billion project to actually begin producing energy some time in the 1990's.

While fusion may be mankind's eternal answer, it is over the next ten years that we face the crucial test of our survival.

SHALE OIL

Like the oil sands, this is a mining venture. One ton yields about 2 barrels of oil. There are two catches too — *volume, production.*

1. Each barrel of oil produced requires two barrels of water for processing. So, even 1 million barrels of oil a day would require 2 million barrels of water. This possibility is non-existent in dry Colorado, Utah and Wyoming.

2. Like the oil sands the resulting volume of shale is larger than the volume mined, creating a huge disposal problem when you start talking about excess shale from one-half to one million tons every 24 hours.

The idea of cooking the oil out of the shale *in place* is undeveloped and may well be impractical. Certainly it amounts to no answer at all over our critical period, the next ten years. And why we would go to all this trouble when we can mine a ton of coal and get nearly a ton of instantly available energy, is hard to answer.

21. ONE THOUSAND DOLLAR GOLD

Coal can be our salvation; we would be wise to move quickly. And if we don't?

Some of the points that follow have been made before, but they are worth repeating. For they point up one enormously important fact—the inseparable relationship between energy (in this case, oil) and gold, and the desperate need to get our financial house in order.

For seventy-five years America has used petroleum as if it flowed without limit from deep and infinite artesian sources. We have lived as though infinite sources were securely based beneath the Continental U.S.A.

The general public hasn't yet got the message, although U.S. oil production began falling from its peak of 10 million b/d in 1970. Since then it has declined to about 8 b/d despite the scores of thousands of wells drilled.

The public is sort of like a de-stallionized stallion. For six months or so after the operation he continues to behave like a stallion prancing and pawing in the presence of seasoned mares, sometimes becoming even unruly. The common expression is, "He hasn't got the message yet."

The U.S. public continued to use petroleum through the Seventies exactly as they had used it before.

Here is the message.

1. We now have to buy half our consumption from foreign sources who set their own price.

2. The cost of energy from foreigners has risen from about $3.7 billion in 1970 to $45 billion in 1977 — and rising prices may make that $60 to $70 billion in 1979-80.

3. In 1978 it cost every man, woman and child neary $200 for imported energy.

4. We paid for this by running a deficit—in other words, we haven't paid. Simply printed up dollars and gave them in exchange for the oil. Not real currency. Just figures for books.

5. It is really not very plausible that we can keep on getting half our oil, 8 to 10 million b/d, by this easy method.

6. Our national security is jeopardized. As per the following:

    a. It is calculated by the Ford Foundation that by 1995 the U.S. would be seventy-five percent dependent on foreign petroleum.

    b. Our 1973 imports were twenty-two percent supplied by volatile Arab countries; last year forty-three percent of our oil imports came from this source.

    c. This oil comes through an artery. As the aorta serves the heart, the Straits of Hormuz out of the Gulf of Aden feed the energy to the Western World.

    d. At the moment, not only the blood supply itself out of Saudi Arabia, Kuwait, etc. is wholly beyond our control, but "passage" at Hormuz is out of our control.

7. We could be blackmailed into choosing between a *nuclear* war and energy strangulation within a few months.

8. The energy lifeline of the West can be punctured at any moment. You might say it's unlikely. It's unlikely you will *kill* someone with your car tomorrow, but only a fool would drive without public liability insurance. Do you?

Now what are the chances that the oil supply will keep flowing? We must look at the two largest oil sources in the world, Iran and Saudi Arabia.

IRAN

It hasn't been put in these words by anyone yet, but here it is. *The principal reason for the fall of the Shah was that he produced too much oil.*

Iran was the lynchpin of the Middle East, Military policemen, Military deputy of the U.S.A.

In order to become and remain a military guardian, the Shah had to spend billions. To do that, he drew and sold from Iranian reservoirs 5 million b/d of oil. That was nearly $70 million a day. About 1 million b/d more was used in Iran. The bulk of the rest of it was used to make the Shah the *guardian of the* Middle East.

For whom did he have to guard it? For the sake of the Iranian people? Not at all. *For the sake of the rich Western Countries.*

In this context, it is basically true that the Shah was a puppet of the West, principally the U.S.A., and the Iranian oil production was used for the benefit of the West.

The new regime will be relieved of the billions of military expenditures. If it produces 3 to 4 million b/d, that will be all it can sensibly use as it goes. To produce more would be to convert the oil wealth, which is becoming evermore valuable into paper money, which is becoming ever less valuable.

We must conclude, therefore, that even under a stable regime, (the best we can hope), this world will be 2 million b/d short.

So we must face it. *The energy artery to the West has been irretrievably and seriously contracted by Iran.*

SAUDI ARABIA

Five million people in Saudi Arabia are simply incapable of using the proceeds of 10 million b/d. Even at the now obsolete price of $12 a barrel, Saudi Arabia had accumulated $60 billion in shrinking paper currency. Had that oil been left in the ground, it would probably be worth $100 billion at the end of 1979. And what will these accumulated dollars be worth 10 years down the line?

Saudi Arabia cannot possibly and sensibly use the proceeds from more than 4 million b/d according to reliable economic studies.

To serve whose purpose does it produce the balance?

Regard yourself as a rancher with a large but depletable artesian well. You already have great wealth. In the lowlands they have very little water. They have been buying from you with IOU's on their produce. They want you to produce your artesian well at maximum flow to satisfy their irrigation needs. Aren't you apt to say, "Whey should I? Whenever I need your IOU's either for your produce or to spend elsewhere, I will sell enough water to amply satisfy all my wants.

"Water is becoming more valuable. I shall husband the supplies I don't need for my children and their children. Over-production simply accomodates you. It does not accomodate me.

"If I received from you money that would hold its value, I might invest those proceeds, and open my well up. But since I see a poor future for your IOU's, I will only sell as I go, according to my needs."

Saudi Arabia, at production of 9.5 million b/d, is producing more than twice as much as it can use. Its huge fortune is being used mainly to finance the U.S. deficits, both internationally and nationally. The Saudi Treasury bills and C.D.'s were the foundation under the 1979 internal Treasury deficit. So our money went out. The oil came back. Then our money came back too. Good deal!

At new higher prices, it will be exchanging its oil wealth to a ridiculous degree for the benefit of the West, and in order that Americans can drive as many miles as they like in cars as big as they like.

Saudi Arabia will have producing capacity of 13 million b/d by 1980. What can we offer them to produce it? Stable currency? No, rotting currency.

The look for the immediate future is that Saudi Arabia will be impelled to cut back.

It seems to me the Western World and Japan are facing an oil shortage of about 4 million b/d. That is 7% of the 60 million b/d used. That's a lot.

Other Arab countries may follow suit, increasing the shortage. Saudi Arabia produces eighteen percent to twenty percent of U.S. imports. Overall, we rely on the volatile Arab-oriented States for forty-two percent of our needs.

In line with the projections of some of our economists, we will need to increase imports from 10 million b/d to 12 million b/d in the next few years.

A dream!

Production will at best fail to increase. More likely it will shrink by 3 to 4 million b/d. At worst, it could be totally cut off. (As a point of reference, the Alaska pipeline brings us 1.2 million b/d.)

Assuming the best, we can stay as we are with a 3 to 5 million b/d shortage and mandatory gasoline rationing. *Even this is predicted on a stable currency.*

If we do not have a stable currency, we face two alternatives, both eventually disastrous.

1. If we print more money to offset rising oil prices, we shall have still higher prices to compensate for watered down money, causing the manufacture of still more money. Obviously, this can't go on. The producers have had enough of it. They will demand gold or other currencies, and the *strain will split the world monetary structure asunder.*

2. The producing countries will cut back on their production, putting a painful squeeze on the industrial countries catapulting them into a depression.

In the case of either 1 or 2 above, we are only one step away from force and probably war.

So it seems to me the only solution will be to put stability behind the dollar, which is the World money. *No tricks* will do.

That means a 180 degree reversal in U.S. monetary posture. It means the U.S. will have to pay in real money (store of value money).

I don't know of any answer to that except to make the dollar convertible into gold. *There just isn't any other answer.*

The last eight years prove the case conclusively. Since Nixon closed the gold window, U.S. dollars around the world have increased by the hundreds of billions, because the Fed. and the *country* were released from all *restraint* in manufacturing dollars.

It isn't that gold is so magic. It is that *restraint* is magic. Limited reserves of gold at a *set* price prohibit the undisciplined expansion of the money supply, and will mean the U.S. will no longer enjoy a free ride on the money machine. So it will have to live on its real production, its effort and its resources.

Anyone should know that has to mean a very large downward adjustment in the living standard—because until now we have been enjoying the produce and efforts of others—just for promises.

So I believe that we will see the dollar back on gold. *Either that or the use of force to seize* oil supplies—world war. And this is not likely yet.

That opens up two questions:

1. What will be the price of gold?
2. Will you be allowed to own it?

$1000 GOLD

If we look at the industrial world as one, which in respect to money it really is, we can see a big picture clearly.

The reserves of the central banks are comprised mainly of two assets; U.S. dollars and gold. World claims in U.S. dollars in central banks are around $175 billion. Then there is the massive Eurodollar afloat, outside the banking system, but free to enter it at any moment. We don't know how much, but $600 billion would probably look after it.

So. we are talking about $720, maybe $750 billion.

·So, if we look at it as one big picture, we see 500 million ounces gold in Europe, and 250 million assayed gold in the U.S. (40 million more in unassayed gold).

Roughly, take it at 750 million ounces. At $1,000 an ounce, that is $750 billion dollars. About the amount of outstanding bogus currency in the world.

A startling case came to court in mid-March 1979. The Justice Department filed a $62 million civil suit against Firestone Tire for allegedly acquiring $31 million of gold in 1973 and 1974 in violation of the Federal Gold Reserve Act of 1934. This Act restricted U.S. citizens or corporations from owning gold.

The frightening thing about this case is that it seems to have a *purpose for the future.* It's common knowledge that hundreds of cases of violation of this law were known to the Justice and Treasury Departments. Most people believed the law was unconstitutional—and the government seemed to be afraid to test the law. They lost one such prosecution and backed away from taking it any further, and closed their eyes to hundreds of violations. Most U.S. citizens believed the Act was a flagrant violation of rights under the U.S. Constitution.

Gold ownership was legalized December 31, 1974. *It's quite significant to see a test case at this late date. It's not reasonable to believe that the purpose is to set right the wrongs of the past;* or for that matter the money that could be recovered, even if the case is won.

It has, in my opinion, a much greater purpose—*a purpose for the future.*

The $1,000 an ounce price for gold *is only feasible for international convertibility.* If we take into consideration some $3 trillion of internal debt, there is no way gold convertiblity could be implemented within the U.S.

To implement nonconvertibility at home, you must prohibit the citizens from owning gold.

The purpose of a law prohibiting gold ownership is not the amount of gold the government would acquire from the citizenry. Rather it is to prohibit and forbid any loophole whereby paper dollars internally could be a demand on gold. If convertibility is practised internationally, it only makes sense that it will also hold true within the country *unless* there is some *other law* that would prohibit *ownership* of gold at all.

My interpretation of the Justice Department suit against Firestone is as follows:

The government has by now recognized the disaster facing the U.S. Monetary Policy. It has come to be seen in high places that the present policy is heading toward virtual suffocation of energy supplies unless these policies are reversed. It has no answer to a stable world monetary system, except international convertibility which we had until 1971—and it sees this limited return of goldbacked money in the new European Currency Union* of January 1, 1979, of which gold is the lynchpin.

But it's just wild to conceive of U.S. internal debt becoming convertible to gold. Gold would have to be an absolutely fantastic and totally unrealistic price.

Before making any move on the international monetary front, the government wants to know for sure that it can prohibit gold ownership by U.S. citizens and corporations. *Gold would only be used internationally for settlement of debts between countries.*

The government does not believe that this time the public would accept the new law unless it was ratified by the Supreme Court.

I expect the Firestone case to go to the Supreme Court.

I very much doubt there will be other prosecutions, because the purpose is neither (a) the recovery of gold; (b) or the punishment of those who had it. The purpose is to *establish a guideline* and a foundation on which to build a gold-based international monetary order.

There really hasn't been enough gold bought in the U.S. to make, in itself, much difference. A few million ounces in Krugerrads and a much lesser amount in bullion would be insignificant to the 280 million ounces claimed to be in stock. So it's quite possible coin collections (old coins) would not be called in. Not certain, but quite possible. Bullion would be a no-no for sure.

The U.S. is getting ready and now sees it must get ready to make a 180 degree reversal in monetary policy and military policy. The first is an absolute *must* if any kind of international order is to survive. The second is a *must* if energy supplies for the Western World are to be assured.

The second is contingent upon the successful implementation of the first. These steps are not avoidable unless our western social order is to sink.

---

*European Currency Union—Monetary system formed March 1979 including West Germany, France, Netherlands, Belgium, Denmark, Italy, Ireland. It envisions a European Currency Union (ECU) to be used as a currency sometime in the future. Its reserves, prominently made up of gold at the time of its formation in March, were approximately $30 billion. Size of the fund has increased along with the rising gold price.

So the whole thing goes back to stable money—and this goes back to gold as the only possible balance wheel for order in the monetary world.

That is why I now expect 1000 dollars an ounce for gold.

THRUST OF EMS TO COME

The monetary world still seems not to have awakened to the momentous development of March 17th when the European Monetary System went into effect.

In short, the U.S. ten-year effort to demonetize gold has collapsed.

Time magazine says, you can "look for action soon" and quotes a "discouraged" Treasury official:

"The drive to demonetize gold has clearly suffered a major reversal. In just one year the weakness of the dollar has wiped out all the progress that we made in two decades."

If that is so, we must view seriously the 700 odd billion out in the world. This should confirm to you the validity of our foregoing arguments, and must bring to mind the bogus money of France when a reissue of 400 million bogus assignats multiplied to 50 billion. That is just over 100 fold — *but gold jumped 600 fold!* Projecting gold to $1000 amounts to only an increase of *35 fold* over $35 an ounce. The $1000 price may at first glance bring smiles, but at second glance becomes reasonable.

If gold has won, the *750 billion* from dollars must be gold related — and if they are, there is your price.

In this context, the U.S. sale of 750,000 ounces a month, producing a measly *$3 billion* in 10 months becomes ludicrous as a last ditch effort to beat gold.

The EMS will issue the European Currency Unit, common to the member countries. To understand how specifically gold based it is, we have reprinted the box that appeared in MFE December 22, 1978 (with revised point corrections) on the next page.

Of course, gold was nearly $400 per ounce September 1979, so 400 million ounces was worth $160 billion, and dollar reserves have declined somewhat,

Therefore, the overpowering element in the European Fund is gold. It goes without saying, the dollars find themselves related to gold, not the other way around.

At first the ECU will be used only between the banks of the EMC; but later it is expected ECU's will be spent by people in stores.

From here on out it becomes of vital interest to the EMS to keep the price of gold from falling. This is easily done because so little gold is on the market, and the central banks have $68 billion paper dollars to draw on. Gold purchases would hardly make a dent in that.

The question mark is the ceiling. They are not able to control the ceiling.

In January 1979 the members agreed the price of gold would be set at the average price for the last six months. The price will be revised every three months.

So the U.S. has worked itself into a hole by starting the 1.5 million ounce monthly gold sales. Then the treasury backed off to 750,000 ounces. If they keep on selling, they deplete this nucleus of national wealth for the benefit of others. If they stop, they admit they have lost the battle and gold skyrockets.

Remember that when the U.S. quits selling in the face of EMS, it admits the dollar has become a subsidiary to gold. Then, like it or not, a numerical relationship takes place between gold and dollars.

Incidentally, the greatest endorsement of the European Currency Union I've seen yet was an article emphasizing the *disapproval* of virtually all economists as expressed in an article by the National Institute of Economic Research, London, and quoted in the *London Financial Times*:

> "The article notes that the most striking feature of last July's Bremen proposals for a new EMS was the scepticism, and in many cases hostility, with which they were received by *professional economists* of all major schools of opinion — orthodox, monetarist and international monetarist."

	Millions of Ounces	Gold at $200	Total Monetary Reserves
Germany	118.4	236.8	39,900
France	101.8	203.6	7,522
Netherlands	54.6	109.2	3,530
Belgium	42.5	85.	2,611
Denmark	1.9	3.8	2,636
Italy	82.9	165.8	9,446
Ireland	.5	1.	2,372
TOTAL	402.6	805.2	68,017

Additionally,

Switzerland	83.3	million ounces
U.S.A.	267	million ounces
Canada	22	million ounces
Japan	23.7	million ounces
U.K.	22.7	million ounces
TOTAL	418.7	million ounces

Total central bank reserves exceed 820 million ounces. IMF reserves in excess of 200 million ounces bring total free world gold to over 1 billion ounces.

To update monetary reserves, multiply ounces by gold price.

22. LAST DAYS OF DOLLAR IMPERIALISM

We have already spoken of dollar imperialism; but in view of the three foregoing chapters, let's examine it briefly again. If the United States can print money and refuse to redeem it, and the recipient countries cannot use it at its face value in buying goods from other countries, then it follows that United States citizens are receiving oil, cocoa, steel, lumber, etc., at the expense of other people. By imposing a lower living standard on other countries, they are helping to support a nation that maintains a much higher living standard.

The Japanese worker in an auto plant who receives each week only one-third of the purchasing value of an American worker is not going to be very happy with his government when that government revalues the yen upward. It means that fewer Japanese cars can be sold abroad, and foreign-made cars from the United States are more easily available for rich Japanese to buy. So the jobs of the Japanese are being squeezed. If the upward revaluating process continues, as it is now doing under the system of floating exchange rates, it puts more and more of the weight of the high living standard of the United States onto its trading partners.

When the U.S. Federal Reserve System printed bogus money, and this money found its way out into the domestic economy in the form of social benefits and subsidies, this money eventually became a part of the surplus that is spent abroad. With this money American corporations were able to buy foreign corporations. To the extent that this money was not redeemable back in the United States, they had obtained the foreign corporations for nothing.

Meanwhile Americans had been living high on the hog.

The current policies of the United States cannot continue to survive. They call for others to give alms to the United States—*for others voluntarily to sacrifice a part of their labor for the benefit of Americans.*

That is the only way the high living standard has been maintained. Any administration that tries to reduce that standard will be thrown out. Yet that was really what President Carter was aiming at in his anti-inflation policy of late 1978. Had he stuck to his guns, it would have been the kiss of death for 1980. If he hadn't—and he didn't—the U.S. dollar would be headed for another crisis—perhaps its last. Carter was in an impossible spot because dollar imperialism had been a deliberately established policy of the American Government. That was obvious when the U.S. passed the Full Employment Law of 1946. This law means that regardless of the U.S. balance of payments or trade, internal conditions will be prosperous; employment will be full.

In effect, it says: "I am the head of my household and my family and my family is going to live as well as the Joneses or better; and that is my first consideration regardless of my balance of payments—regardless of whether I go into debt to others." Certainly if you go into debt far enough you can never pay them back, but that is a secondary consideration. Arrogant? Certainly. Foolish? Not if you were strong enough to enforce your debt on your neighbours.

All of this means that when other countries refuse to go along with the U.S. any longer, the U.S. will have to pay its full way every year. To cut back $30 to $40 billion a year (the trade deficit) means that much of a reduction in benefits.

Up to now the American answer has been this:

The dollars are still good: you can buy American goods with them; you can buy American cars and washers and radios. We have no natural resources to sell you, but we have all kinds of manufactured products.

But the workers in the Volkswagen factory in Germany reply: "If we German people buy your cars, we have no jobs in the Volkswagen plant. Or if we are able to sell any Volkswagens to you we will have to work for lower wages to keep the price low. But already your workers in General Motors get more purchasing power for every hour worked than we do."

And so the German or Janpanese or French or any other government is traitorous to its people if it continues to support and accept into its country this international counterfeit money that is used to buy real services and goods. *This a fundamental position of the United States dollar throughout the world—as long as it remains officially unredeemable at the U.S. Treasury.*

It is a fundamental fact that one group of people will refuse to subsidize another group except through the use of force. Dollar imperialism must come to an end, and inflation will have to collapse, *unless it is strictly limited to internal inflation.*

If such limitation were practicable, a country could use an internal scrip that would not be acceptable abroad. How could such money be used practically unless the country were encircled with the most vicious type of foreign exchange controls?

Remember that whenever you take a dollar out of the country to buy some chocolate bars in Holland made by a Dutch candy maker, that dollar becomes a claim on your country. Even if it circulates to ten other countries first, there is always a last man on the end of the line who is going to send it back to your country and ask for value received. As an American you have received value in the chocolate bar, but somebody in the course of that chain is stuck if your treasury, ultimately, will not give anything for it.

In that case, the Dutch candy maker who "sold" you that chocolate bar actually *gave* it to you. If he didn't give it to you, then the last man who ended up with that dollar for equivalent services rendered is the one who is finally stuck with the buck. Right now, the rest of the world is stuck with our funny money.

The total bucks they are stuck with well exceeds $500 billion unredeemed U.S. dollars around the world. That is several times the combined reserves of all of the central banks in the world.

Today the United States is called the richest country in the world. It is like the man who lives in the big house on the hill and drives a Cadillac. He is called the richest man in the neighborhood, but if he owes a hundred thousand dollars more than he is worth, he is not as rich as the man in a three-bedroom paid-up bungalow. And the big man's collapse will surely come.

Money among countries on the international scene is the same as money among families within the national scene. If you go into debt you have to pay it. If you don't, then someone else has worked without compensation solely for your benefit.

On the national scene, the manufacture of excess purchasing power by government is exactly the same as the manufacture of currency by counterfeiters. One is legal. The other isn't. But the results are identical.

On the international scene, the manufacture of money by one member who refuses to redeem his money is international counterfeiting. Collectively, the people of that country are enjoying the results of the manufacture of international counterfeit at the expense of all those who take it.

And that is how international money excesses strike at the living standard of all of the families within all of the nations.

When other countries refuse to endure this practice any longer, we shall have come to a very critical juncture in the way of life in the United States, and in the world. We are very close to that today.

Sooner or later dollar imperialism was bound to meet its Waterloo.

The European Monetary Union threatens to trigger a confrontation. It means we approach the end of the age of inflation. It means that we are coming off the drunk. The joyride is over.

23. BACK TO EARTH

If raising the price of gold and making the dollar redeemable in gold is so essential to monetary stability, why does the United States resist it with might and main? Why not just go ahead and do it?

That question is widely asked.

The answer is: It would mean coming back down to earth.

Why doesn't the drunk who has been on a two-week binge and who has spent money until he is broke and caroused until he is in trouble — why doesn't he voluntarily drink two or three quarts of coffee and come back to earth? The answer is the shock is too terrible to contemplate, and so he just takes another drink—and another—as long as he can get it.

The damage to the American position, created during an era of inflation begun thirty years ago, is so horrible; the overspending has been so great; the debts so huge; the bankruptcy so complete that going back to real money will be a shock that will shake the nation to the very roots of its social structure.

Why doesn't John Smith who lives in the mansion on the hill and drives the Cadillac, and who is in debt up to his eyebrows—why doesn't he quit borrowing money that he knows he will never pay back to his unfortunate creditors, and come right out and face the truth? Because he *can't* face it, and he goes on, desperately hoping that somehow he will come out of it. He will just go on taking money from people until he can get no more.

That is why the United States virtually stopped gold redemption of the dollar by the Washington agreement of 1968, but continued to *pretend* that convertibility existed. That is why, as bankruptcy loomed, President Nixon formally closed the window on convertibility in August 1971. With a store of only $10 billion in gold, and even at that time with $60 or $70 billion against it, and with redeemability claims mounting like fury, the United States simply was *unable* to meet the claims. Had the United States paid out this last store of gold, it would have burned its last bridge behind it. Then even devaluation wouldn't have done any good.

If its creditors—the countries from whom it bought oil, cocoa, and lumber—ever refused to deliver on new orders, the United States would need gold; and if the United States had used up all its gold, it wouldn't be able even to get any oil—except on charity.

When Nixon closed the gold window it was not an act of considered policy. It was an unavoidable notice of bankruptcy.

In 1973, with redeemability out of the question, the lack of confidence in the dollar grew so great that hordes of dollar holders wanted to change them into other currencies. That precipitated the crisis of February 15 that culminated in a two-and-a-half-week suspension of the money markets of the world in March.

Such a thing had not happened before in the history of world commerce.

The shock of the bankruptcy of the world's richest nation left the other countries stunned. There was no way they could foreclose. There was nothing to foreclose on. For the time being they continued in a trance. Their first groggy reaction was to stop paying the agreed price for U.S. funds coming into their countries. First a few, and then all, of the nations allowed the dollar to find its own value against their currencies; that is to say, floating (free market) exchange rates. But as the heretofore unbelievably U.S. deficits of $50 to $60 billion began to register in early 1975, the U.S. dollar broke to new lows in nearly all markets. The dollar fell so badly that, once again, Central Banks had to agree to go in and support it. (That is, to buy dollars with francs in Switzerland, with marks in Germany, with yen in Japan, etc. The dollar even fell against the bankrupt lira.) Other nations had to try to support the dollar, because the lower the dollar went the higher went the mark or the yen in comparison to dollars; the more expensive became the Volkswagen and the Toyota on the big American market; the more the sales would shrink; and the more unemployment would grow in Germany and Japan, already beginning to suffer recession. So it was with most countries of the world.

The floating exchange rates of 1973, which really represented a breakdown of the Bretton Woods agreement, proved to be slim protection for the other countries against the massive influx of the continuously created dollars of the United States.

A half-hearted effort, increasing the price of gold from $35 to $42 per ounce, hadn't helped one bit toward restoring confidence in the dollar. It meant that the U.S. gold stock increased from approximately $10 billion to $11 billion — a change of no consequence.

It is of vital importance to understand what will happen when the United States is required to pay its way as it goes.

If the dollar were to be made redeemable in gold at about ten times the $42 price of gold, the United States would have reserves of $110 billion. It is very doubtful that creditors then would bother to change their dollars for gold —

just as the people in Freedonia did not care about asking for gold as long as they knew it was there, and could get it if they wanted to.

But the multiplication by ten would make a gold price of $420 an ounce. That would mean that the German Treasury with its $4.5 billion of gold would then have $45 billion in gold, plus the 30-odd billion in U.S. dollars it already holds, for a total in excess of $75 billion in reserves. Normal reserves, as I have said, until a few years ago were $7 billion. Such a tremendous inflationary landslide could imperil the strongest currency in the world, more: Such a global explosion of money would threaten to destroy our civilization.

There is good reason to believe that the other countries, realizing that they have extended credit much too long, have discussed the funding of much of the U.S. debt. That is to say, they would agree to put off their claims for gold on a certain portion of the U.S. debt. I use the following figures as examples:

Assume the nations said to the United States: "You owe our Central Banks $100 billion. We shall set aside $50 billion of that for twenty years. In other words we will lend this to you for twenty years at only two-percent interest. You will not be called upon to redeem this $50 billion for twenty years.

"However, to do that we shall require that you make your money redeemable from now on. We know you only have $20 billion in gold, and you still owe $400 billion over and above what we will fund. We will all of us make the gold price $210 per ounce. That will give you over $50 billion in gold, which is equivalent to the call we have on you for the next twenty years. It will make you fully solvent and in a position to redeem your dollars if you are asked.

"This will once more make the dollar as good as gold, and a hard and dependable currency. Stability will be returned to the monetary world, and we can all get on with our business of progress. In other words, you are back on your feet. But from now on we expect you to make good. From now on you must pay your own way as you go.

"What is more, you will have to earn enough surplus by the sale of your goods and the efforts of your people in the next twenty years to save up enough foreign exhange to pay off your bill of $50 billion that we have extended as your credit line. You won't be able to consume what you produce. You will have to produce $50 billion worth more than you consume in the next twenty years—and that includes your energy imports.

However this does not include the Eurodollar overhang — see chapter 21, "Thousand dollar gold!"

This is sober reality. In the year 1978 the United States ran a balance of trade deficit with other nations of $30 billion. If, on convertibility, it should run the same deficit, it would have to pay out of its gold stock $30 billion, reducing its total from $50 billion to $20 billion, and leaving it again suspect. That couldn't be allowed to happen. The cutbacks might be in the military (the international might), the monetary (international investment), and in freedom (the right of a U.S. citizen to spend abroad).

While the American public slumbers—because it has been ill-informed by the press—this is the somber game being played out behind closed doors.

Convertibility would mean that the balance of payments must be in equilibrium. It would mean that if the United States spends money on troops in foreign lands, it would have to have a surplus in trade to meet that bill.

The redeemability of the American dollar would mean that the United States, like all other nations in the world, could not consume any more than its total population collectively produced. It would at last become a choice of guns or butter. Up to now it has not been a choice—it has been guns *and* butter, even if the cost is borne by someone else absorbing bogus dollars. Under the new era of reality and of redeemability, U.S. industry would have to be more competitive. Which takes us back to the *real* wages paid to the workers in the various countries. In order not to suffer a trade deficit, U.S. cars or washers or dresses, or whatever, would have to sell at lower prices in order to get a share of the world market. That would mean U.S. workers would have to take less *real* money, and buy fewer cars, washers, and steaks for themselves.

Their take-home pay could only be maintained if the U.S. Government were willing to take less in taxes. Or give a tax rebate.

The 1978 tax rebate of $16 to $20 billion was designed to keep the living standard where it was, and to allow the United States to continue to consume far more than it produced.

In common sense, it must be admitted that this tax rebate is a reduction from government income. A sane financier would say, "We've just got to cut down on expenses if we don't have the income. There is no other way. Either we must cut down on our airplanes and navies around the world, or we must reduce our social benefits at home."

The American people do not recognize natural law. The defense budget must be kept where it is if the United States is to be strong. The social benefits must not slacken. The taxes must be reduced so that the economy can be stimulated.

Unless natural law is only a joke, it must be apparent that we are approaching a tremendous comeuppance; and that this comeuppance—when it occurs—will come home to roost on every hearth in the land.

That comeuppance is really the "*collapse of inflation*" or, in other words, the "coming storm."

The most dangerous aspect about the collapse of inflation is the probable unwillingness of American workers to take less pay, even though they already enjoy two and three times the living standard of comparable workers in other countries. U.S. workers do not know that the country has been on a binge. They do not understand that the enormous deficits are having a shattering effect on peoples of other countries, because the bogus dollars that are the deficit to a large extent are buying up goods and services in other lands, *and these bogus dollars will never be redeemed.*

They do not understand that there is a basic connection between their jobs and jobs in Japan, Germany, France, and elsewhere.

U.S. workers have not understood that it is a question of the collective population of each and every country consuming only what they themselves collectively produce, and that, if they consume more, other people in the world are the involuntary victims.

The likely result of such a program of harsh realism would be the collapse of labor unions, and if you care to project that into demonstrations and riots, you can arrive at your own conclusion about the results of the collapse of inflation.

If the workers, on the other hand, were to decide to take less and to put themselves more nearly on a par with workers in other countries, they would be able to *buy* less. So instead of two cars in the family, there would be one. The Japanese worker wonders why there should be two cars in the garage of his American counterpart while he rides a bicycle or a Honda.

But as soon as workers begin to buy fewer cars and fewer washers, and go to fewer restaurants, the jobs in the restaurants and in the automobile factories begin to shrink, and so unemployment begins to mount.

That is what began to happen in late 1974 and into 1975. And that should have been the tip-off that the era of inflation was ending. A long period of deflation was being foretold.

Under the strain of unemployment a worker could not pay the installments on his automobile and his house. Remember, the upshot of this thirty years of inflation and credit has been the erection of a trembling structure of debt. The graph on page 67 shows the growth of public debt; private debt follows the same pattern.

When a worker could not pay his debts, foreclosures would result. The mortgage companies and the savings-and-loan-associations, who have lent out the savings of people to other people to build houses, would not be able to collect their monthly installments, and savings institutions would suffer a loss of confidence. The proposition is not very different for the banks.

Under such conditions the production of large industrial companies would shrink. We all know that profit appears in the topmost production figures: let's say the top twenty-five percent. With a quarter less volume there may be no profit at all. The result of this would be shrinking dividends—an outlook for much lower earnings. The result of that would be a nosedive in the prices of those companies' shares on the stock market. Then margins would be called right and left, which would produce air pockets in stock market prices, which would bring them down further.

The next step after all of this—unemployment and the need for money— would be the sale by the public of their mutual fund investments. Mutual funds would be forced to sell the stocks they hold. Buyers would be scarce and sellers plentiful, and more huge pockets would develop.

There is absolutely no question that, in the conditions arising from convertibility of the dollar, there would be bankruptcies across the land. There would be bankruptcies among huge corporations, which would reflect back on the banks that have lent them millions of dollars and hundreds of millions of dollars. Banks would go under.

People's savings would be uncollectible.

A fury of indignation, as unreasoning and as violent as the fury of the French Revolution, could sweep the country.

The only answer the government would have to such a situation would be a massive new printing of money, so that debt requirements and margins could be met. The meaning of that is abundantly clear. If someone owed a thousand dollars, he would still pay a thousand dollars, but in order to make this possible the government would have doubled, tripled, or quadrupled the money supply, and you would only realize $250 in purchasing power. So three-quarters of what you had lent the man would have been taken away from you. All creditors would find themselves suckers; all debtors would find themselves fully paid up, although only having paid, literally, a portion of the debt.

But this is no remedy either. Not one crust of bread has been created by doubling the money supply. Not one market has been opened to one American automobile in other parts of the world. The only way that market can be opened—under dollar covertibility—is for the American nation to produce as cheaply as the other nations. It's a hard answer, but there isn't any other.

This was not always necessary, because America had a technology and an ingenuity far ahead of any other country in the world. Also it had the mass market to exploit this technology and ingenuity, and other countries did not. So it became the richest nation.

Today other countries also have similar technology. The Common Market also has a vast market area of more than 200 million people.

Dollar redeemability means coming back to reality. Coming back to reality means competing with all of the rest of the world. Competing means lower wages. Lower wages means the scenario above. That means repudiation, because there is nothing in the treasury or elsewhere to back this debt.

If anybody can show me a flaw in this logic, or a substitute form of logic, I would dearly love to see it. In all my years of study I am unable to discern any other scenario.

But that is not totally the end of the story. If this had happened twenty years ago it wouldn't have been nearly as bad—even five years ago, when it should have happened. Now the energy crisis has struck the United States. Now it will be necessary to pay *real* money to obtain energy to run factories. It is already evident, although it may not yet have come about, that the rest of the world is going to go on hard money. That is, money that is represented by goods and services, as in the land of Freedonia. There will be much competition for oil, since Japan and Europe will require huge increases. *Hard money* will buy the oil. Unless the United States can produce hard money it will not be able to get its supply—without a world war.

How then will the United States purchase oil, nickel, copper, cocoa? The purchase will have to be made with goods of equal value, or with gold, which is exchangeable into goods of equal value. It comes down to gold. If the

United States could find an enormous quantity of gold within its boundaries, that would bolster the national treasury and could buy any product anywhere in the world at any time.

Lacking the gold, the United States must earn the equivalent in commodities by the sale of its manufactured products at a competitive price.

When we come to convertibility we have come eyeball to eyeball with reality. Coming back to earth is painful, but it is inevitable—because that is where we live. It is not a question of *if*; it's a queston of *when*.

WAGE AND PRICE CONTROLS

As confidence in the dollar nosedived around the world, the price of commodities began to rise. It took more dollars to import copper. The energy bill loomed large. The price of gasoline and, therefore, transportation and, therefore, of living was going up. The price of food was going up. Housewives went on strike because of the cost of meat. They forgot that the cost of maturing a critter is mainly due to the the grain he eats. They hadn't noticed that the cost of grain had exploded as U.S. warehouses were emptied for huge shipments to Russia and China. Everyone was looking for a scapegoat.

There really was no scapegoat. The man producing chickens, pork, or beef had found that his costs were suddenly higher. The packer paid more for the critter. The butcher paid more for the carcass. The supermarket passed on the cost to the housewife.

The villain was far, far back along the line. The villain was inflation, and it was the age-old story. Prices of commodities were not rising nearly so much as the value of money was declining.

Always, when this happens, there is a clamor for wage and price controls. That's because people confuse price with value. Erroneously equating price with value, they believe that since the real value of a pound of beef has not gone up, the price should not have gone up. There must be a dirty profiteer somewhere.

But is there? Or is it just a question of the immutability of value? I made an analysis of this in the "Quiet Corner" of *Myers' Finance & Energy*, October 19, 1972:

Can Value Be Controlled?

Value, says the dictionary, is "a fair or proper equivalent in money or commodities." And what is the meaning of fair? Fair means impartial or unprejudiced.

So value is an impartial, unprejudiced, equivalent of goods or services.

But a control is "arbitrary exercise of authority."

Usually authority and impartiality are enemies. So to control a value is not only contradictory; it is impossible. A value cannot be controlled. *A value is.* You can *say* that a value is less or more, but true value remains proudly independent of pronouncement.

You can control a price. You can say I don't care what the value is—this is the *price.* You shall buy and sell at this price. But the moment you say it, you have destroyed the *price mechanism,* which is a function of *value.*

The price mechanism is a fundamental wheel in the economic engine because it shows what is happening to *relative* values in the market place, and is a reflection of supply and demand—as well as a reflection of the value of money. Monkey with this mechanism and you are inviting a major *mechanical failure.*

Price controls *do not recognize* changes in value. Therefore every time a value changes, the inflexible price mechanism gets a little further out of line. A man will not sell at less than value unless he is forced to sell. A man will not buy at what he considers more than value at all.

Fundamentally inherent in price controls is a distortion of value—as values change. This means an inevitable dislocation of the economic process.

That's why although price controls appear to work in the beginning, the cure never lasts.

As each month passes, certain values inevitably change. These accumulating dislocations lead to black markets which skirt the price controls; *so it is a hundred percent predictable that the longer the price controls remain in force, the greater the dislocations are; and the more shocking the adjustment when they are removed.*

At that moment all inflationary forces previously suppressed break out. Because they were suppressed, their breakout is dramatic; not only is the economy brought back to where it would have been anyway at the same point in time, but it has been further harmed by the shock of the breakout.

There is no way that a wage and price control can stop inflation; because *value* cannot be controlled; and value always *bosses* price. The commodities taken in total are not changing in value. It is the *money* which is changing its value.

Thus an attempt to contest prices is an attempt to control value. But value as we have seen is beyond and immune to control, so any attempt to control prices is a futility to start with.

How did the relationship between money and value ever get so badly out of whack? In our state of Freedonia, where money was itself wealth because it was the equivalent of a warehouse receipt, there was no way that a dislocation between money and value could occur.

How then did this drastic divorce occur? It occurred because money was changed by the economic authorities into a gimmick.

The divorce of money and value is forcefully demonstrated by the Federal Reserve Note.

24. THE FEDERAL RESERVE

The amount of information available about the Federal Reserve is staggering. But what is even more staggering is the curious lack of *vital* data—essential facts that remain shrouded in darkness even today, more than a half-century after the Federal Reserve's founding. And the little known may be more important than the well-known.

Here are the main shockers about the Federal Reserve, each of which will be substantiated in turn.

1. Although the Federal Reserve has virtually dictatorial powers over the money and credit of the U.S., and although it operates at the taxpayer's cost, *it has never been subject to a public audit.*

2. The U.S. government does not own the Federal Reserve.

3. The banks do not own the Federal Reserve.

4. No one has ever succeeded in identifying the ultimate owners of the Federal Reserve.

Dealing with the first statement above, I refer you to the 739-page book published by the U.S. Government Printing Office, Washington, 1975, entitled, *Audit of the Federal Reserve — Hearings Before the Subcommittee on Domestic Monetary Policy.*

I refer you to page 147.

> Chairman Patman: "Considering the importance of this agency (the Fed) to the Federal Government and the day-to-day lives of every citizen, it is amazing that so much controversy ... is still existing about this simple suggestion that Government auditors should be able to get inside the Federal Reserve. ...
>
> "The portfolio of the Federal Open Market Committee contains almost $87 billion of Government securities. ... The Federal Reserve draws between $5 and $6 billion annually in interest on these bonds. It is out of this huge slush fund

that the Federal Reserve finances its operations without coming to the Congress for appropriations or appropriations review, despite the fact that the Constitution of the United States says; and I am quoting the Constitution of the United States:

'*No money shall be drawn from the Treasury; but in consequence of appropriations made by law.*' ...

"For too long the Congress has been satisfied to accept the Federal Reserve's own idea of what should be known about the Federal Reserve. ... "

It is well known that even the State Department and the Defense Department are subject to exhaustive audits by the General Accounting Office, despite the highly secret aspects of much of their operation.

Should you think that there are really no mysteries to be discovered, please refer to the *Congressional Record*—House, June 16, 1975. Herein Mr. Patman is given permission to extend his remarks. He inserts into the record a letter from a U.S. citizen, (page H 5570):

Re. Federal Reserve Audit Bill,

Hon. Wright Patman,
House of Representatives
Washington, D.C.

Chardon, Ohio,
June 13, 1975

Dear Mr. Patman: ...

What right has the Federal Reserve Board to refuse to consent to an audit?

Who owns the bonds and other securities held by the Federal Reserve? Who reaps the enormous profits resulting from the vast operations of the Federal Reserve System?

I think it is high time that the Federal Reserve becomes accountable to Congress and to the public.

Will your Committee kindly consider this Audit Bill in the near futre?

Thank you.
Respectfully,
Mrs. Marie Miller.

Mr. Patman then inserts his reply to Mrs. Miller, and it is a very interesting reply. It is quoted here in part:

House of Representatives,
Washington, D.C., June 16, 1975.

Dear Mrs. Miller: ...

Certainly I agree with you that the Federal Reserve has no right to refuse to consent to an audit, but the Chairman of the Federal Reserve Board, Dr. Arthur Burns, has refused and has stopped the audit.

You ask who owns the bonds and other securities held by the Federal Reserve. You doubtless refer to the portfolio bonds accumulated by the Federal Reserve banks, amounting to $93 billion. These bonds have been paid for once with good American currency and should have been canceled, but the Federal Reserve did not cancel them when they were bought, and now as the interest becomes due, the interest is paid by the U.S. Treasury and when the bonds become due, they will be paid again although they have been paid for once.

So I agree with you — it is high time that the Federal Reserve becomes accountable to Congress and to the public ...

Sincerely yours,
Wright Patman.

One wonders why such important news never reaches the ear of the public. In 1959, Mr. Patman complained:

"Our exposes are scandalous and shocking but they are only printed in the daily Congressional Record which is read by few people ..." (Page 219 — *The Federal Reserve Bank).*

In all of the many thousands of newspaper and periodical articles I have read I have never yet come across a comprehensive report, or even an uncomprehensive report, of what is going on with the Federal Reserve. The CIA, yes. The FBI, yes. The SEC, yes. The Federal Reserve, no.

Take, for example, the following, I don't know why one wouldn't see this in *The Wall Street Journal.* I think it's very exciting, and terribly important. (Page 369 from the aforementioned 739-page book, *Audit of the Federal Reserve,* Chairman Patman is questioning Governor Mitchell of the Federal Reserve Board of Governors.)

Chairman Patman: "You know, every important agency of the U.S. Government ... has been audited except the Federal Reserve.

"Now the Federal Reserve, of course, has been able to get around that. The Federal Reserve does not even have to obtain its funds through congressional appropriations.

"They thought about going to Congress for appropriations and they said, well, we do not want Congress to interrogate our people. We have to stay away from that. Then they thought they would get the banks to put up the money for the organization of the 12 Federal Reserve banks. But the banks would not do it because a large number of them were not for the Federal Reserve.

"And then they figured out a way — and I think it is very clever — to get around this provision in the Constitution. That is, to try to divert the money some way so it would not be in violation of the Constitution. So they devised this very clever way by which they had the power to manufacture money, to create money, just like commercial banks have, except the commercial banks do it on a reserve basis. The Federal Reserve can create money on no basis at all — just create the money.

"Now they have created $93.4 billion to buy Government bonds. They could do the same thing and buy the entire national debt right now, and get $35 billion a year interest, instead of $6 billion a year interest they are now receiving. They could do that; there is no question about it.

"So we have to get to these things as we learn about them. I believe ... you said 'the auditors do not audit the Federal Open Market Committee.'"

Governor Mitchell: "External auditors. That is correct ... The outside auditors do not."

Chairman Patman: "Do you not have them audited by the General Auditor?"

Governor Mitchell: "The New York operations of the desk are audited internally by the New York Bank, and they are also audited by Federal Reserve Board employees. But that is all. The private firm does not audit those accounts."

Chairman Patman: "The private firm does not audit them. . . . Now there are a few questions I just must ask you ...

"How big is the System's Open Market Account? ..."

Governor Mitchell: "It is in the order of $90 billion."

Chairman Patman: "And how is that used? Is that used by the System, by the 12 banks?"

Governor Mitchell: "Well, it is owned by the 12 banks, and the interest goes into our gross earnings. And, as I indicated $5.5 billion went back to the treasury last year."

Chairman Patman: "Yes; but the Federal Reserve does the taxpayer a gross injustice because that money is spent by the Federal Reserve without ever really having to account for it to anyone.

"Furthermore, William MacChesney Martin, who was Chairman of the Federal Reserve Board longer than anybody else, said that the bonds held in the Federal Reserve had been paid for once. Well, if they were canceled, as they should have been when you paid your debts, you would not have this portfolio. If you need money you can create it on the books of the Federal Reserve without reserves of any kind. That is what is done now. So you do not need this $93 billion portfolio from which you are receiving over $6 billion a year in interest. That is a terrible thing; to pay debts and then continue to make the taxpayers pay $6 billion-a-year interest on those bonds after they have been paid for. That is awful.

"*So when you talk about turning back into the Treasury, you are turning back money that you took away from taxpayers that you should not have taken in the first place.*"

Governor Mitchell: "I think, Mr. Chairman, that I would describe the operation this way. That when we buy a Government security, we pay for it with a check."

> Chairman Patman: "In other words, created money."
> Governor Mitchell: "That is right."

I would have to think that, after two decades on the Banking Committee, Patman knows what he is talking about. *Why are 200 million American people so uninformed of this situation?*

The lack of reporting on the Federal Reserve is shocking. Let's deal with the three other points in short order.

Most people believe the Federal Reserve is part of the government of the United States. It is not. It has nothing to do with the government. It is a central bank, like central banks in other countries. Its money power is absolute. And no one in government controls it.

This last point was brought out in *The Congressional Record* of August 1962. When Congressman Patman asked former Fed chairman Eccles, "Does the Federal Reserve have more power than the President and Congress of the United States? The chairman of the Fed replied:

"In matters of money and credit—yes."

The term "Federal," as we shall see, was deliberately selected to fool people into thinking that they, the people, somehow controlled the money managers.

The banks are commonly thought to own the Federal Reserve. It is even taught in college textbooks that the many banks together comprise the Federal Reserve. But when chairman of the Fed MacChesney Martin was asked (1956), "Do the banks own the Federal Reserve," his reply was "No".

Here is part of the exchange:

> Chairman Patman: "All right. No. 2 is that the banks own the Federal Reserve Banking System, and it is run by the bankers; it is operated for their benefit. That is a fallacy, is it not?"
>
> Mr. Martin: "That is a fallacy."
>
> Chairman Patman: "That stock, or that word 'stock' is a misnomer, is it not?"
>
> Mr. Martin: "If you are talking about stock in terms of proprietorship, ownership — yes.... You and I are in agreement that it is not proprietary interest."
>
> Chairman Patman: "Yes. Therefore, this does not convey any proprietary interest at all, and the word 'stock' is a misnomer. It is not a correct word at all. It is just an involuntary assessment that has been made on the banks as long as they are members. Therefore, the statement that the banks own the Federal Reserve System is not a correct statement, is it?"
>
> Mr. Martin: "The banks do not own the Federal Reserve System."

The facts are that the banks' so-called "stock" (a) carries no proprietary interest — is unlike any other stock in a corporation; (b) cannot be sold or pledged — so does not represent an ownership claim; (c) does not carry any voting rights.

Nobody knows who owns the Federal Reserve. Ownership identity has never been published or revealed.

How did the Federal Reserve come about? One most interesting version appeared in an issue of *Frank Leslie's Magazine,* 1916.

According to this feature article, several of this country's most powerful men, including Senator Nelson Aldrich, international banker Paul Warburg, representatives of the Rockefellers and many other financiers, met in 1910 on Jekyll Island, the private Georgia estate of J.P. Morgan.

For nine days, according to the article, these men worked out the "Aldrich Plan," which, with few modifications, finally became the Federal Reserve System.

Aldrich, a partner of the Rockefellers in the rubber and tobacco trusts, had headed up the national monetary commission whose job it was to tour Europe and learn about money — a subject we realized we knew very little about after the money panic of 1907 had resulted in a wide cry for monetary reform.

But the Aldrich Plan was initially doomed, because of the senator's connection with the powerful banking interests. Putting up Aldrich to recommend a safe system of monetary control was like appointing the fox to safeguard the chicken coop.

The attempt to sell the plan to Congress was made again — in 1913. This time the concept had a label calculated to assuage the fears of concerned legislators and voters.

Obviously it was necessary to avoid any hint of private interests or private banks or even the idea of a European-style central bank. What could be more democratic, more American, than the word "federal"? What could be safer than a "reserve"? And what could be fairer than a "system"?

So the Aldrich Plan for a Central Bank of the United States became the Federal Reserve System. A clever repackaging of the same old ingredients sold the scheme.

The Federal Reserve System issues federal reserve notes. When the government of the United States needs money over and above what it collects in taxes, it must borrow from the Federal Reserve. Where does the Federal Reserve get the money? It creates it out of nothing and charges the government interest to boot.

At one time, the Federal Reserve could only create money to the extent of our gold holdings. When the gold backing, first nationally, then internationally, was abolished, it was free to create without limit — and that is how it comes into our story as a feature player in "The Age of Inflation."

In our country of Freedonia the money was issued by the state. It all represented goods and services and it could be expanded according to the amount of goods and services. It was a money economy. Originally the U.S. economy was also a money economy. But when the Federal Reserve System was allowed to *create* money, then debt was issued in the form of money, and ours became a debt economy. *Your assets were someone else's debt. Someone else's debt became your assets.*

The Federal Reserve System issued money on the credit of the United

States, and all of the people of the United States were responsible for the payment of those debts. Remember, at the same time, that the people of the United States have no control over the Federal Reserve System.

The power of the Fed was not recognized by many. It is still not recognized by most. A few did recognize it. A prominent maverick banker, Leslie Shaw, stated then:

"When you have hooked the banks together, they can have the biggest political influence of anything in this country...."

One of the most outspoken critics of the Federal Reserve, attorney Alfred Crozier of Cleveland, told the Senate Committee:

"The so-called administration currency bill grasps just what Wall Street and the big banks for twenty-five years have been striving for. That is private instead of public control of currency.

"*This robs the government and the people of all effective control over the public's money, invests in the banks exclusively the dangerous power....It puts this power in one central bank.*"

Thomas Jefferson had said long ago: "A private central bank issuing the public currency is a greater menace to the liberties of the people than a standing army."

On December 17, 1913, five days before the Fed bill was enacted, Henry Cabot Lodge wrote:

"The bill as it stands seems to me to open the way to a vast inflation of currency ... I do not like to think that any law can be passed which will make it possible to submerge the gold standard in a flood of irredeemable paper currency."

In 1971 that projection came into full flower.

Was he right? Only sixty years later, in 1978, no amount of interest seemed able to coax gold back to the United States. In fact the U.S. was selling a million and a half ounces a month from the precious remaining pile it had. Much money fleeing the U.S. would rather earn no interest in a stronger currency (Swiss franc) than to return and risk further deterioration. The money hemorrhage of 1974 began to reoccur and by October 1978 we were bleeding badly. The damage was halted temporarily. Very few believed the emergency rescue operation would last. The reason lay in the fact that $30 billion of borrowed currencies were the sole defense against 600 billion nervous Eurodollars scattered throughout the world.

The statesman Elihu Root called the Federal Reserve bill an outrage on our liberties and he prophetically said: "Long before we wake up from our dreams of prosperity through an inflated currency, our gold, which alone could have kept us from catastrophe, will have vanished and no rate of interest will tempt it to return."

The sixty-year-old Fed had been sired by Messrs. Morgan, Aldrich, Warburg, et al. and delivered by President Wilson. The squalling voice of the child was muffled so the public wouldn't know that he was born.

Woodrow Wilson was a university professor. He knew about as much on the subject of money as any other university professor. His backers, however, knew what the people wanted and he was swept into office on a promise that he would give the people of the United States a law on money and credit that would be free from Wall Street influence. *Wilson was the candidate of monetary reform.*

And thus materialized the fear expressed in the prophecy of Abraham Lincoln shortly before he was assassinated:

> "I see in the near future a crisis approaching that unnerves me and causes me to tremble for the safety of my country; corporations have been enthroned, an era of corruption in High Places will follow, and the Money Power of the Country will endeavor to prolong its reign by working upon the prejudicies of the People, until the wealth is aggregated in a few hands, and the Republic destroyed."

Wilson gained office on the promise to put through the "monetary reform" that he genuinely believed to be a *reform*. But within three years of the passage of the Federal Reserve Act, Wilson, too late, saw the light. He said:

> "A great industrial nation is controlled by its system of credit. Our system of credit is concentrated. The growth of the nation, therefore, and all our activities are in the hands of a few men ... we have come to be one of the worst ruled, one of the most completely controlled and dominated governments in the civilized world — no longer a government by free opinion, no longer a government by conviction and the vote of the majority, but a government by the opinion and duress of small groups of dominant men."

In sixty years there have been no basic changes. The baby grew into a giant; the giant has become a Frankenstein monster; and the monster is inflation, whose hands now clutch the throat of Western civilization.

In the land of Freedonia the money was issued by the elected representatives in an amount equivalent to the goods and services for sale, or at least on their way to market. In the first instance they had no gold or silver.

Representative Wright Patman, among others, sincerely believes that gold and silver are unnecessary so long as the elected representatives are in charge of the money and credit. But we saw that even in Freedonia politicians soon realized that those who promised the most would be elected, and so the Promisers began, before long, to control the government—and therefore the money.

In *absolute terms* Mr. Patman is right. It is human nature that destroys Mr. Patman's theory. Only when man is bound and limited by a Scale—like the one that keeps the butcher honest—can he be restrained from his proclivity to aggrandize himself by means of subterfuge and methods that are not immediately discernible; that is to say—inflation.

Admittedly it is much better that Congress should create and control the money than that an agency of special interests should have this power— infinitely better. But it is better still if these representatives are forced to weigh the meat on a scale with the needle visible to the customer. Gold and silver are that scale.

There can be no honesty in government, no enduring republic, until the elected representatives of the people are in control of the money and the credit, and until they also are controlled by the discipline of exhaustible commodities beyond which they dare not go in the creation of the money and credit.

Here is what Chairman Patman of the House Committee on Banking and Currency sees for the future. (Page 177, *Audit of the Federal Reserve*).

"The Federal Reserve is allowed to manufacture money. It does not cost them a penny.

"I asked Dr. Burns a question in a hearing not so long ago before this subcommittee. I said, Mr. Chairman, who owns the title to the $70 billion of bonds (at that time) in the open market portfolio that have been purchased on credit initiative? Dr. Burns said the $70 billion (at that time) on the books of the Federal Reserve banks are owned by the Federal Reserve banks.

"Now that looks to me like that is a complete departure from our monetary system, if we are going to let the Federal Reserve own those bonds....

"I asked Dr. Burns who owns them, and he said the Federal Reserve banks own them, as distinguished from the Government. So I think it is a serious queston here. If we let the Federal Reserve continue to do that, they will not only have squatters' rights, as we say in the West, on land titles, but a precedent set as to what they can do in the future.

"If they can take the money that they create without any reserves of any kind behind money and buy bonds that are interest bearing and do not cancel them when they are bought, why they have a privilege there that no other financial institution on Earth ever had, to my knowledge. A counterfeiter is fined heavily if he is caught doing what the Federal Reserve is doing....

"If this is carried to its logical end, the Federal Reserve will not quit with just ... its (present) portfolio. It has been increasing the portfolio by the billions every year in the last few years. They will go ahead and they will buy the entire national debt if they want to in exactly the same way. There would be no restriction against them doing it. *And then, after they own the entire national debt and get about $35 billion a year interest on it, none of which cost them anything, they will then commence to acquire private bonds or the bonds of States, counties, and cities and other political subdivisions. There will be nothing to stop them.*

"*It looks to me like if we do not settle this question and settle it now, we are in for a lot of questions involving the solvency and security of this Nation.*

"Would you like to comment on that?"

"Mr. Staats: Well, I do not believe I have any general comment to make, Mr. Chairman."

Without the control of the money in the hands of the elected representatives of the people, our country of Freedonia was transformed, like the United States, into a country subservient to monetary imposters.

25. A SWAP FOR A SWAP FOR A SWAP

The United States Treasury has admitted that Federal Reserve notes are not in themselves lawful money.

This may seem a strong statement but you can check it if you happen to have in your possession Federal Reserve notes of older vintage. You will see that until a few years ago they all carried this inscription:

"This note is legal tender for all debts, public and private, and is redeemable in lawful money at the United States Treasury, or at any Federal Reserve Bank."

This inscription appeared on all Federal Reserve notes. The one photographed below was signed by Henry H. Fowler in 1950.

The natural conclusion is that if this note is redeemable in lawful money, it certainly cannot in itself be lawful money.

The confrontation between the promise and its fulfillment is not without a touch of humor, as demonstrated by the correspondence between Mr. A.F. Davis and the U.S. Treasury herewith reproduced:

A.F. DAVIS
12818 Coit Road
Cleveland 1, Ohio

December 9, 1947

Honorable John W. Snyder,
Secretary of the Treasury,
Washington, D.C.

Dear Sir:

I am sending you herewith via Registered Mail one ten dollar Federal Reserve note.

On this note is inscribed the following: "This note is legal tender for all debts, public and private, and is redeemable in lawful money at the United States Treasury or at any Federal Reserve Bank."

In accordance with this statement, will you send to me $10.00 in lawful money.

Very truly yours,
(Signed) A.F. Davis

TREASURY DEPARTMENT
FISCAL SERVICE
Washington 25

December 11, 1947

Mr. A.F. Davis,
12818 Coit Road,
Cleveland 1, Ohio.

Dear Mr. Davis:

Receipt is acknowledged of your letter of December 9th with enclosure of one ten dollar ($10.) Federal Reserve Note.

In compliance with your request, two five dollar United States notes are transmitted herewith.

Very truly yours,
(Signed) M.E. Slindee, Acting Treasurer

A.F. DAVIS
12818 Coit Road
Cleveland 1, Ohio

December 23. 1947

Mr. M.E. Slindee,
Acting Treasurer,
Treasury Department,
Fiscal Service,
Washington 25, D.C.

Dear Sir:

Receipt is hereby acknowledged of two $5.00 United States notes, which we interpret from your letter are to be considered as lawful money.

Are we to infer from this that the Federal Reserve notes are not lawful money?

I am enclosing one of the $5.00 notes which you sent to me. I note that it states on the face, "The United States of America will pay to the bearer on demand five dollars."

I am hereby demanding five dollars.

Very truly yours,
(Signed) A.F. Davis

TREASURY DEPARTMENT
FISCAL SERVICE
Washington 25

December 29, 1947

Mr. A.F. Davis,
12818 Coit Road,
Cleveland 1, Ohio.

Dear Mr. Davis:

Receipt is acknowledged of your letter of December 23rd, transmitting one $5. United States Note with a demand for payment of five dollars.

You are advised that the term "lawful money" has not been defined in federal legislation. . .

The $5. United States note received with your letter of December 23rd is returned herewith.

Very truly yours,
(Signed) M.E. Slindee, Acting Treasurer

I wondered whether there might have been some change in the Treasury reaction to the redemption of its promise in the twenty-three years since 1947 when Mr. Davis wrote his letters; so on April 14, 1970, I wrote to Treasury Secretary David Kennedy as reproduced below:

April 14, 1970

Mr. David Kennedy,
Secretary of the Treasury,
U.S. Treasury Department,
Washington, D.C. USA

Dear Sir:

I am enclosing two $100 Federal Reserve notes inscribed . . . "Redeemable in lawful money at the United States Treasury, or at any Federal Reserve Bank", one signed by Henry Morgenthau, Jr. (1934); one signed by Henry H. Fowler (1950), both Secretaries of the Treasury.

Webster defines redeemable "to pay of (mortgage or note) . . ." — "to convert (paper money) into coin" — "to fulfill a a promise."

That is what I ask for here.

The reason I approach you directly is that Federal Reserve branches have in the past failed to make good on this pledge of the U.S. Treasury. Instead they have claimed that the note is in itself lawful money. This is unacceptable: *For to make a promise, and in the next breath to say that the promise is its own fulfillment is patently absurd.*

To maintain that the promise can be fulfilled by repetition of the promise (another Federal Reserve note) is likewise patently absurd. To point to subsequent legislation nullifying the promise (as Fed branches have done) is patently a repudiation of the promise.

I do not think that you will repudiate on the written pledge of a U.S. Secretary of the Treasury.

I confront you here with the solemn guarantee of the richest nation in the world, and I am asking that the promise be fulfilled. I do not know what you will send me as lawful money but you must know what the U.S. Treasurers called lawful money in 1934 and in 1950, when they wrote these promises. I do know you have silver dollars in the Treasury and I will be satisfied with them.

Thanking you in advance.

Yours very truly,
MYERS' FINANCE REVIEW
(Signed) C.V. Myers

P.S. Since I have several thousand dollars in these pledges, this is no academic exercise, but a matter of considerable material importance.

Here is the reply from the U.S. Treasury.

THE DEPARTMENT OF THE TREASURY
FISCAL SERVICE
Washington, D.C. 20220

May 12, 1970

Mr. C. V. Myers
Myers' Finance Review
903 Lancaster Building
Calgary 2, Alberta

Dear Mr. Myers:

Your letter of April 14, 1970, addressed to the Secretary, has been referred to me for reply.

As you have been informed, the two $100. Federal Reserve Notes which you forwarded with your letter are lawful money. United States notes and coin of the United States are also lawful money.

Silver dollars have not been issued since March 25, 1964, when the Secretary exercised the option granted him by section 2 of the Act of June 4, 1963 (31 U.S.C. 1964 ed., 405 a-1) and determined that silver certificates were thereafter exchangeable only for silver bullion. Prior to March 25, 1964, only the holders of silver certificates had an absolute right to exchange them for silver dollars.

Your two $100 Federal Reserve Notes are returned herewith.

> Very truly yours,
> (Signed) J.P. Purall
> Special Assistant Treasurer

Enclosures: 2

My commentary then was, and remains, as follows:

The U.S. promise to redeem mountains of Federal Reserve notes in world Central Banks is worth no more than their discredited promise to me. How severely can we censure Kosygin when he said, in a different context (Cambodia):

"What is the value of international agreements, which the United States is or intends to be a party to, if it so unceremoniously violates its obligations?"

I say that the violation of a solemn understanding — whether it is related to a sovereign boundary, or a promissory note — proves a mentality of *lawlessness*. That the U.S. bureaucracy and executive branch — having trampled their Constitution — have raped all *law* — and that the lawlessness of the population did not begin at the bottom. It began long ago at the top — and *remains alive today* at the *top*.

I couldn't know then how prophetic that commentary would be. It was not until August 1971 that President Nixon officially repudiated the claims of Foreign Central Banks for the lawful money of the United States, which of course had always been convertible into gold.

26. THE TRANSFORMATION

During 1973 the printing presses of the United States added so very much to world money that in three years the world's Central Banks had accumulated reserves greater than the sum of all the past cumulative reserves of all the Central Banks in world history.

The Central Banks were trying desperately to keep the dollars locked in their treasuries. When the dollars came into Germany, for example, the German government had to issue German marks to absorb those dollars. In a few years, since 1968, Germany's reserves had risen from the normal figure of $7 billion to more than $30 billion. Japan's reserves have risen from $5 billion to more than $25 billion.

The recipient governments were frightened to death that all those marks in Germany and those yen in Japan would get into circulation and start a runaway inflation. They were between the devil and the deep blue sea. If they took in the dollars, they were risking the ruin of their currencies. If they refused to buy the dollars, it meant that the dollar depreciated against their currencies because huge offerings would not be taken up. When there is a greater supply than a demand in any marketplace, the price of the offering goes down. But if the dollar went at too big a discount, then these countries were at a terrible trade disadvantage with the United States. Their products would be high-priced in the United States and American Buicks would be low-priced in their own countries. This would mean unemployment in these other countries.

The unrestrained flow of American money and credit caused a growing resentment and mounting international complaints. The U.S. Treasury merely replied, "What are you going to do about it?"

In Europe this became known as dollar imperialism. But the question was a good one. What were they going to do about it?

There was an answer, but it was a most unappetizing answer. These countries could go on the gold standard, let the dollar depreciate—and erect trade barriers against the depreciating dollar. They knew, of course, that if they went on gold the dollar would go down drastically, not ten percent, but maybe twenty percent or forty percent. Who knew how far? If that happened they would have to erect tariff barriers of twenty percent or forty percent, or whatever.

This would, of course, bring retaliation from the United States. A full-fledged trade war would be set in motion. This would precipitate a depression in every country in the world.

It was exactly such trade barriers that had caused the last depression and the resulting unemployment in all countries. There was no easy answer for any country. For five years they had been increasingly at the mercy of policies made in Washington—the money created by the Federal Reserve — and consequent dollar imperialism on a global basis.

The crises had become commonplace, and they had the habit of blowing up overnight. On February 12, 1973, the U.S. dollar, after three days of wild currency trading, was devalued by ten percent. The money managers said that would cure it. Only two weeks later another currency tornado blew up and Germany was forced to absorb $2 billion in a single day. The exchanges of the world closed. They closed on the Wednesday of that week and they remained closed for the next two successive weeks. This was unheard of. Had it been prophesied a few years back, the experts would have said it could never happen.

After nearly three weeks of closure and countless high level meetings, finance ministers and the money managers simply disbanded—bankrupt of any solution at all. They merely said there was a great spirit of cooperation and they thought the crisis had been cured, at least temporarily.

President Nixon was making a show of keeping the U.S. budget at $257 billion. Even that figure meant a deficit of $12 billion. That would be $12 billion for which there were no goods and services. Unless it could be collected in taxes it would have to be manufactured by the Fed. Much of this money too would find its way into other Central Banks before the year was out.

Thus, in retrospect, the monetary troubles of 1973 can be seen, at least partially, as a consequence of a policy that started with the formation of the Federal Reserve in 1913. This policy had taken 60 years to reach its climax. Now it threatened the way of life not only of the American nation but of all the nations.

It was a problem far larger than anyone had ever dreamed. It was so monstrous that the authorities were reluctant even to verbalize it. By 1978 it was pure Frankenstein.

Throughout history there have been disastrous inflations, but they have involved usually only one country at a time. Now the inflation had reached into every corner of the planet. Unless a part of the world could suddenly stabilize itself, there would not be a safe island in the whole basin of the monetary flood. That kind of condition is an invitation to revolution, and perhaps simultaneous revolutions in several countries.

That is why it is valid to talk of the end of an era. Revolutions bring on a new way of life, and monetary revolutions are no exception.

We seldom realize what is happening until it is over. What is so clear in retrospect is hardly discernible while it is taking place. So it was not discernible to the American people or to any other people that a way of life was coming to an end. It was not even discernible to them that the inflation would get completely out of control before it was over. For, even in the fall of 1974, governments spoke boldly of the battle against inflation, while at the same time enjoying vigorous economic growth. The patient was sick unto death, but the doctors confidently expected him to win the hundred-yard dash.

And all of this can be traced to the violation of the U.S. Constitution by the Federal Reserve Act of 1913.

Congress has no power whatsoever except the power given it by the Constitution. The Constitution is the *ultimate power*. It defines the powers of Congress and the limits of the congressional power. It outlines the rights of Congress. It specifically says that any rights not specifically given to Congress may not be assumed by Congress and must, if any such rights have been overlooked, go to the states.

The Federal Reserve Act is clearly unconstitutional on the grounds that Congress did not have the *right to delegate* its authority.

For instance, if you give your son the power of attorney over your interests while you are away on a long trip, does that give your son the right to delegate this power to a friend of his own choosing? What are involved here are *two* separate rights. One is the right to coin the money of the United States. The second is the right to delegate that authority. Congress has the first but not the second.

Later on, the Supreme Court, in a time of crisis, prostituted itself by agreeing that the Federal Reserve Act was constitutional because Congress thought it "necessary and proper."

The truth is that the Constitution was designed to restrain Congress, *regardless of what it thought*. The Constitution had provided that any unanimously desired alternations or additions could be effected by a constitutional amendment, requiring the assent of two-thirds of both houses and legislative assent by three-fourths of all the states. The Federal Reserve Act would have required a constitutional amendment to make it legal. There wasn't a chance such an amendment could ever get by the people.

So the Federal Reserve System was born in 1913, a constitutional bastard.

From that date, the money of the United States and the economic liberty of the American people began to deteriorate.

The dollar, which was once backed 100 percent by gold, was later, under duress, reduced to forty-percent backing, later to twenty-five-percent backing. Then, under Lyndon Johnson, all gold backing was removed from the domestic dollar. The gold backing still applied to international claims. In 1971 Nixon repudiated even that gold backing.

The result was, of course, a continuing increase of money that was not represented anywhere by goods and services. That meant, inevitably, a deterioration of the purchasing power of the money. Every deterioraton meant stealing from those who had saved.

When President Franklin Delano Roosevelt deprived the citizens of the United States of gold ownership in 1934, the last plank under the monetary independence of the American people was removed. It has taken forty years for the house to collapse.

And now it has come to the point where either the U.S. Constitution will be destroyed or the Federal Reserve will be destroyed. These two cannot coexist.

The first article of the U.S. Constitution, in Section 10, provides:

"No state shall ... make any thing but gold and silver coin a tender in payment of debts...."

That means that no state in the union can require you to accept anything but gold and silver coin as a payment for your services or materials. And most of the states reflect this portion of the U.S. Constitution, as does the Minnesota constitution, which says: "The legislature has no power to pass any law sanctioning in any manner directly or indirectly, suspending specie payments by any person, association, or corporation issuing bank notes of any description."

In plain language that means that no legislature of any state can pass a law that sanctions Federal Reserve notes.

An explosive case came out of Minnesota. There, a courageous Justice of the Peace ruled against the big banks and the total system of the Federal Reserve — and under trial by jury.

A Minnesota attorney, Jerome Daly, gave the bank a note for $14,000, secured by some real property. When Daly failed to make final payments, the bank foreclosed and bought the property at a sheriff's sale June 26, 1967. The bank then brought action under law for the possession of the property.

Daly claimed they couldn't take the property because they had given him *nothing* in the first place. In this very touchy case two justices disqualified themselves, so it went before a trial by jury under Justice Martin V. Mahoney at Credit River township, Scott County, Minnesota.

On December 7, 1968, the jury found both the note and the mortgage to be void for lack of lawful consideration given by the bank. The bank went for an appeal to the big court. Under the law it had to pay $2 to Justice Mahoney as an appeal fee. Mahoney refused to accept the two Federal Reserve notes because they could not be required, under the U.S. Constitution and the Minnesota Constitution, as payment. Justice Mahoney ruled:

> *Plaintiff's act of creating credit is not authorized by the Constitution and laws of the United States, is unconstitutional and void, and is not a lawful consideration in the eyes of the law to support anything or upon which any lawful rights can be built.*

The bank had admitted that it had created the money out of thin air. Mahoney declared: "The Federal Reserve notes are acquired through the use of unconstitutional statutes and fraud."

But now let us read the full text of Article I, Section 10:

> No state shall enter into any treaty, alliance, or confederation; grant letters of marque and reprisal; coin money; emit bills of credit; make any thing but gold and silver coin a tender in payment of debts; pass any bill of attainder, ex post facto law, or law impairing the obligation of contracts, or grant any title of nobility.

So you see, if Federal Reserve notes are legal, New York State can create nobility; The King of New York may marry the Crown Princess of Vermont. Texas can join Mexico; and Michigan can form an alliance with Canada.

For all of these conditions are a part of the same section of Article I of the U.S. Constitution.

The enforcement of Federal Reserve notes as legal tender smashes Article I in its entirety.

If Article I of the Constitution is smashed—no other article in the Constitution has any meaning.

Then there is no Supreme Court in the United States; there are no limits on the powers of the executive branch. In short there is no orderly government. *There is no law.*

That surely will be the end of an era.

And that is at this moment a very real danger.

The U.S. Constitution can only be restored by an amendment authorizing the Federal Reserve and all its notes, or abolition of the Fed and the recall of its notes.

The sixty-year life of the Federal Reserve has marked the transformation of America into what has become, in fact, a lawless society.

27. CREDIT VERSUS DEBT — THRIFT VERSUS SLOTH

The early land of Freedonia had positive money. People accumulated credit by producing goods and services, and they either held this credit in their own possession or deposited it in banks. It was perfectly sound to lend out this saved money at interest to others who wished to expand, and to accept real property as security.

This was an era of progress. People spent after they had earned, or borrowed against what actually existed. They borrowed to produce. This production continued to expand the solid foundation of progress.

With the advent of a Federal Reserve and the evolution of fiat money (unbacked currency and credit), the life-style of any nation—Freedonia or America—undergoes a dramatic change. The change penetrates the deepest recesses of the moral structure.

People are encouraged to use now and earn later. To buy luxuries now for which they will pay at a later date. At a later date they buy more luxuries for which they will pay at a still later date. And so on forever.

The government initiates programs by borrowing money (bonds) for which it will pay at a later date. But when the later date comes, it borrows more money for which it will pay at a later date.

All of this creates an atmosphere of unrealistic euphoria. If you can have it, why not take it now and pay for it when you are dead, or let your descendants pay? The future is mortgaged to the present, and when the future becomes the present the next future is mortgaged to that. That is how it happens that the public debt of the United States is $450 billion.

The interest portion of Mr. Nixon's budget in 1973 amounted to nearly ten percent of his total $257-billion budget. By 1975, the interest portion of Mr. Ford's budget was over $30 billion. Each year the interest grows on compound interest. By 1979 it was nearly $50 billion. With a calculator it's easy enough to make further projections. In time, this compounding becomes a cancer of such size that it will involve the whole body politic, and like a cancer will kill it. The collapse of inflation is the kill.

The debt economy has another adverse, and more subtle, influence on the population. With everything so easy, it tends to produce a permissiveness, and with that a decadence of moral fibre. Thrift becomes foolish. Why should any sensible man save when he knows that his savings will be depreciated, when he knows he can get more goods by spending his money today than by spending it tomorrow? Why shouldn't *eveyone* borrow when he knows that what he borrows from his future will buy more goods today than it will buy when the future arrives? So debt mounts on debt.

For several years inflation was actually encouraged and welcomed by the bulk of the population. Of course, those on fixed incomes were suffering: their substance was being taken from them and they found it steadily harder to manage.

When spending is encouraged and consumption is encouraged, waste is encouraged. Manufacturers purposefully design their products to become quickly obsolescent. The junk piles of North America overflow with steel, tin, and rubber from obsolescent washing machines, clothes dryers, television sets, automobiles, etc.

The era of inflation produced the era of debt, and the era of debt produced the era of waste. And waste, most surely, in this finite world of ours, is not only immoral but dangerous in a world of rapidly diminishing resources.

How can we stop this senseless waste? Only by changing from a debt economy to a money and production economy.

The money that is used in the world today, as we have seen, is not money at all. It does not exist. If it did exist, all those who have savings accounts at the bank and in insurance policies, etc., would be able to get their money. But it is an admitted fact that if all the people who have this money were at once to ask for it, not more than the first five or six out of a hundred could be served; 95 would go away emptyhanded. *The money simply does not exist,* except in the imagination of the bankers and written down on some piece of paper.

We saw, in the state of Freedonia, that counterfeiters might steal from the state by adding to the money supply. The entire society would imagine that all this money existed. The same result could be reached if the politicians made it legal to create money. From the story of the Federal Reserve it is seen that the banks do exactly that. Money is lent to people on a "let's imagine" basis. This money was not owned by the bank in the first place, and it is not owned by the bank when it is paid off. What the bank does get is the interest. If "creates" an interest-bearing vehicle that does not actually exist. When the loan is paid off, that money goes out of existence again.

So it is clear that the owners of savings accounts do not own all that money; because it does not exist. The banks do not own it, because it does not exist. It is a pretense invented for the purpose of earning interest. And the Federal Reserve was given the right to "imagine" such money into existence and to reap interest.

So the lending itself is fictitious; and it is a pretense, for there is no such money. There was not before. And there will not be when it is paid back.

Now it becomes quite clear why the debt economy requires nonreduction of debt. For, you see, when people pay off their debts they are canceling out the money supply that was created when the loan was made to them. There is no greater horror for the modern government economists than the thought that people might wish, in volume, to pay off their debts—the money supply would disappear.

This must be abundantly clear to everyone. We are constantly bombarded by ads and commercials inviting us to borrow money, to spend now and pay later.

Continually increasing debt is a built-in mechanism of our credit-money system. Whenever the debt stops increasing, the system has to stop advancing. When it stops advancing, people begin to reduce indebtedness. Paying off debts reduces the money supply.

Bankruptcy is another means of wiping out debt. If a firm owes $20 million and is declared bankrupt with $4 million remaining assets, he has decreased debt by $16 million and has wiped out $16 million of the money supply.

Will it take an avalanche of bankruptcies to bring us to our senses?

28. GOLD AND
THE PHANTOM

Gold is said to have a certain mystique. Bankers and economists use the word condescendingly. The inference is that only fools or, at least, irrational people value gold as money, but, if they don't know any better, what can be done about it? The uneducated peasants are, as a matter of fact, according to bankers, largely responsible for the world monetary dilemma because of their silly attraction to gold. If only the general public could have studied economics at Harvard, the world monetary system could run smoothly and this barbarism—an echo from the uncivilized past—could be put away forever.

Yes, gold rises from the uncivilized past. But we find that, as civilization progressed, gold became even more elevated as it came to represent the condensation of wealth. An ounce of gold, the size of a small wafer, could be hidden away, and when the owner was ready he could exchange it for more than a ton of grain, which would be enough to feed him and his family for more than a year.

Moreover, it never lacked a market. It has never yet been rejected as money. No one can, by edict, destroy it, nor can it be tarnished by chemical or time.

Certainly gold has a mystique. Those who would denigrate it in the hopes that men or groups of men or nations would lose their desire to possess it—such people must be totally ignorant of human nature. For gold represents the ultimate security; and security is one of the most powerful motives of every living creature—from the gopher to the king. And it represents something more—beauty, adornment, power and even magic.

Because gold was so highly prized by men, and because it was so scarce, a very tiny amount of it could be used to represent a large amount of material possessions. And it finally came to be universally recognized that nothing was more valuable than gold. So anyone would trade you anything for gold, when they might not trade for something else. Gold would buy what they wanted. It was the *magic* medium. Unit values developed and it became the ultimate money. No Government had monetized it.

Once it became the ultimate money its desirability increased even more. It then commenced to represent the objectives of the acquisitive, the greedy, the power-hungry, the vengeful, the philanthropic. Even churches wanted gold.

Today gold has lost none of this romantic luster. The demand for it has enormously increased, firstly because the population has increased, and secondly because of the emergence of a great industrial value for gold.

Because of this element called gold, men have perpetrated the most dastardly crimes, risen to the most heroic heights—gold has led them to the ultimate extremities of all their emotions; hate, love, fear. So men will accept token money as long as they *know* it is as good as gold; but once they doubt that, they will not accept it any more. For when it is not backed by gold, it is backed by *nothing*.

Thus, I can only conclude that gold will never be effectively demonetized by edicts or by legislation, the Central Bankers of all the world notwithstanding.

The link between gold and silver is an emotional link. What may be said of one may be said of the other. Substitute the word silver throughout the above, and you will arrive at a meaning that will exist long after these words have faded; long after your most distant descendants have descended.

These are the precious metals of exchange that have existed throughout the long civilized history of man, and never in all that long history have these metals betrayed the trust that was placed in them. Yet the paper plasterers of today would have you give them up for some of the politicians' promises written with ink on flimsy paper, with a record of debasement and repudiation that goes back to Genghis Khan and his fiat money made from the bark of the mulberry tree.

THE PHANTOM WON'T GO AWAY

In 1967 the International Monetary Fund, under the leadership of the United States made the pronouncement that it would phase out gold. How successful this step was may be judged by what happened to the gold prices. The price held until 1971. The following graph shows what happened during the decade of the '70's. (Pg.176). No one ever said how gold was to be phased. out. The table gives the gold reserves of the European countries. They nearly double the gold reserves of the United States.

The most astonishing thing about these gold holdings is that although lip service has indicated that gold was finished, the central banks, other than the U.S. quite recently, have never sold any gold. In fact the bulk of the reserves of the world are retained gold. If we are to use something other than gold as a standard—or nothing at all—what do we do with the gold we've got? No one

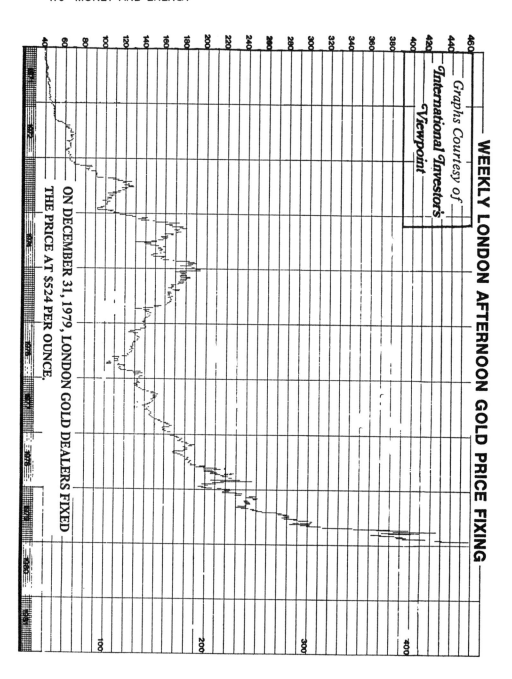

WEEKLY LONDON AFTERNOON GOLD PRICE FIXING

Graphs Courtesy of
International Investor's
Viewpoint

ON DECEMBER 31, 1979, LONDON GOLD DEALERS FIXED
THE PRICE AT $524 PER OUNCE.

has any better idea today for a way to get rid of gold than they had in 1967. Were the central banks to throw it in the ocean? The danger would be that others would recover it. Should they bury it? Certainly someone would dig it up again. They couldn't destroy it; it won't dissolve. They couldn't heat it out of existence in melting pots. It would come out in great big chunks of gold. Apparently no central bank wanted to give it away to other central banks either. So the IMF decided to give a part of the gold to the under-developed countries. They sold it at auction. But when they went to sell it, people holding dollars around the world were very happy to pay up to $200 and $225 an ounce for it. The biggest surprise was that even though so-called poor countries were taking gold rather than the money and putting it into their central banks.

This *ghost* seemed to be indestructible; a phantom that stalked the world. By the end of 1978 it began to appear that this phantom was going to take real shape as the backbone of a new currency system in Europe. The currency unit was eventually to circulate as the ECU. The European common market countries were getting ready to put this system into effect. At first, it seems, only huge inter-bank deposits would be made in the ECU. Later on there might be certificates such as Treasury bills in the amounts of $100,000 or more. Beyond that, somewhere down the line, was the idea of a regular currency to be used by the populations. That was a long way off. But behind the whole scheme lay the world's greatest hoard of gold—the indestructible phantom.

29. SILVER

Any book on monetary affairs must include a section on silver.

In relating silver to gold, the first thing one notes is the value ratio.

For thousands of years—from 450 B.C. until A.D. 1875—one ounce of gold was generally worth fifteen to sixteen ounces of silver. That was the low for silver, not the high. In the year A.D. 200 you could buy an ounce of gold with only ten ounces of silver, and in 3500 B.C., three ounces of silver were equal to one ounce of gold. In 1978 it took thirty-three ounces of silver to fetch one ounce of gold.

For 5,000 years, before silver had material and industrial uses, it held a consistently high value in relation to gold.

This relationship was upset by the development of the phenomenal Comstock Lode just before the turn of the century. Then silver dropped briefly during the Depression to where it took seventy ounces of silver to buy an ounce of gold.

But notice the quick rise of the silver curve to a ratio of 27:1 when the United States Treasury fixed silver at $1.30 an ounce while gold was fixed at $35 per ounce.

In 1967 the U.S. Treasury lost control of silver and the price rose to $2.50 per ounce, which placed silver once again near the historic ratio of 15:1.

During the turbulent times since 1967 both gold and silver have been moving violently. Silver, in 1975, was selling at a ratio of about 10:1 if related to the ridiculous price of gold as maintained by the U.S. Treasury. In actual fact, silver was moving in the area of around 40:1, with gold at $176.00.

There are some very strong reasons why this ratio is seriously out of whack, and why it will be increasingly out of whack until the price rises. The facts

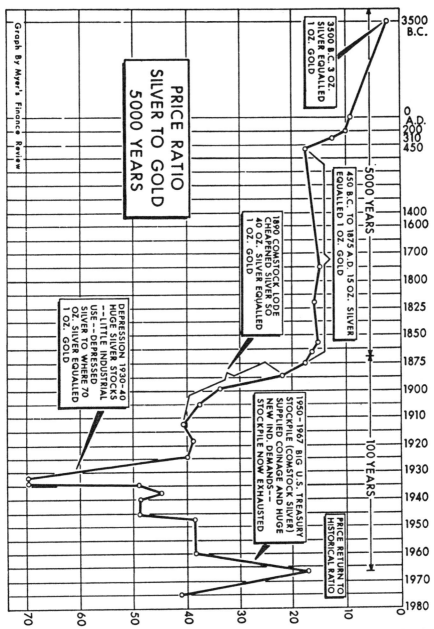

PRICE RATIO SILVER TO GOLD 5000 YEARS

3500 B.C. 3 OZ. SILVER EQUALLED 1 OZ. GOLD

3500 B.C.

0 A.D.
200
310
450

5000 YEARS

450 B.C. TO 1875 A.D. 15 OZ. SILVER EQUALLED 1 OZ. GOLD

1400
1600

1700

1800

1825

1850

1890 COMSTOCK LODE CHEAPENED SILVER SO 40 OZ. SILVER EQUALLED 1 OZ. GOLD

1875

1900

DEPRESSION 1930-40 HUGE SILVER STOCKS --LITTLE INDUSTRIAL USE--DEPRESSED SILVER TO WHERE 70 OZ. SILVER EQUALLED 1 OZ. GOLD

1910

1920

100 YEARS

1930

1940

1950-1967 BIG U.S. TREASURY STOCKPILE (COMSTOCK SILVER) SUPPLIED COINAGE AND HUGE NEW IND. DEMANDS-- STOCKPILE NOW EXHAUSTED

1950

PRICE RETURN TO HISTORICAL RATIO

1960

1970

1980

70   60   50   40   30   20   10   0

The above chart shows that the ratio of the price of silver to gold has now returned to the historic level that existed almost uninterruptedly from 450 B.C. to 1875 A.D. Development of the phenomenal Comstock Lode flooded the world market with silver so that by 1912 it had dropped to half its price in relation to gold. Since there was little industrial usage, silver was a drug on the market. The Great Depression of 1930-40 almost cut the silver price in half again. War usage of silver, plus the electronics revolution, consumed the silver at an alarming rate, exhausting the 2-billion-oz. stockpile between 1958 and 1967. While uses continue to multiply, production remains steady, resulting in an annual *demand deficit* of about 80% more than production.

weigh heavily in favor of a smaller ratio and thus a higher silver price. Here are some of the facts:

1. When the U.S. Treasury sold half a billion ounces of silver at less than $2 an ounce—the price of gold was only $35 and the ratio was around *seventeen to one.*

2. None of the world's treasuries now have any silver to dispose of. There is no *official stockpile* anywhere in the world.

3. While gold rose from $35 to $210 an ounce—a sixfold increase—silver rose from $1.30 per ounce to the present $5.90 per ounce—a 4.5 fold increase. A sixfold increase would make silver $7.80 per ounce.

4. The world's stocks and the rate of usage also seem to favor silver. There may be as much as 8 billion ounces of silver in the world—that's probably the maximum. There are 2 billion ounces of gold in the world—or a little more— and half of it is in the central banks. So there is only four times as much silver as there is gold. Additionally, the silver is being used—actually consumed— while gold, for the most part, mainly changes its form. For example, one-half to two-thirds of the industrially consumed gold has gone into jewelry, where it still exists as gold. The reason for that has been the fading confidence in the currencies. Once the currencies are stabilized, this industrial use of gold will drop off quickly; and the production of gold will be found to exceed greatly the industrial usage. And that is the difference. With gold it's *usage.* With silver it's mainly *consumption.*

In net result we face declining availability of silver, while in the long term we do not face declining availability of gold, at least to nearly the same extent. The exhaustion of the supplies of silver are foreseeable, whereas the exhaustion of the supplies of gold—apart from monetary usage—are not foreseeable.

5. The world's shortfall of production of more than 100 million ounces a year since 1968 has been catching up. The shortfall has been minimized by (a) sales of speculators, (b) coinage melt and silver from India, (c) reclaimed silver, and (d) drawing on the stocks of silver.

Probably the predominant factor in the market on silver during the past two or three years has been speculator sales. The immense popularity of silver, when it first broke loose from Treasury control, resulted in massive speculator purchases. These were later liquidated as a result of the fall of the price from above $6 per ounce to below $4 per ounce. It may well be true that the speculative acquisition of gold during 1974 exceeded the net acquisition of speculative silver — proportionate to the price. In other words, gold has been enjoying a period of enormous popularity. Silver's popularity has been moderate.

I think we are approaching the point where the pent-up discrepancies between these two metals will begin to exert themselves.

Psychologically, from having observed the market for a long time, I have noticed that there are certain strong areas of price resistance. One dollar, on

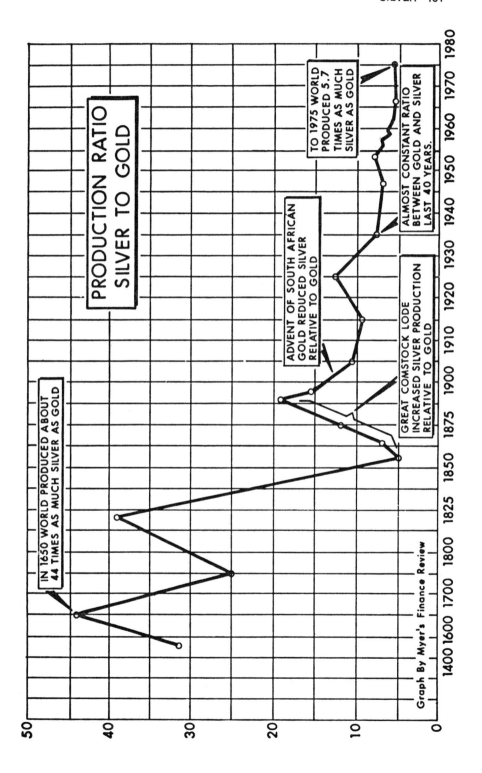

PRODUCTION RATIO
SILVER TO GOLD

IN 1650 WORLD PRODUCED ABOUT
44 TIMES AS MUCH SILVER AS GOLD

ADVENT OF SOUTH AFRICAN
GOLD REDUCED SILVER
RELATIVE TO GOLD

TO 1975 WORLD
PRODUCED 5.7
TIMES AS MUCH
SILVER AS GOLD

ALMOST CONSTANT RATIO
BETWEEN GOLD AND SILVER
LAST 40 YEARS.

GREAT COMSTOCK LODE
INCREASED SILVER PRODUCTION
RELATIVE TO GOLD

Graph By Myer's Finance Review

any quotation, is a mark of strong resistance. Each dollar up to $500 is a mark of strong resistance, and $500 is particularly strong.

I believe that the next time silver rises dramatically it will pass $7.50. Silver has shown itself to be a fast performer. Everytime in the past when it has gone up, it has gone up very fast. It is just as fast a performer on the downside.

A severe world depression would cut down on the usage. *However remember* — when that happens there will be a big decline in the mining of copper, zinc, and all silver-related materials, so that the production of silver would fall accordingly. The shortfall of usage against production would still be very large.

And remember this: *the stocks of silver are not inexhaustible.* We tend to forget that. We tend to forget how near the point we may be to when we arrive at that crunch. A bit of a silver corner developed in the spring of 1974. That was not the real silver corner because it was largely man-made. The big silver corner will come when the supplies, regardless of anyone, just are not meeting the demand. When that time arrives $10 will be a low price for silver. Another element that well may enter the scene is the fact that gold is so high priced that ordinary people can only buy tiny quantities of it. There may be a growing tendency for people to save silver as a hedge of last resort on the level of the common man, whereas the sheikhs save gold.

Only gold and silver stand apart from the other metals, and have so stood for thousands of years. That's not likely to change. The other precious metals will be priced according to the conditions. For example, platinum will remain rare, but if its usage fails to meet expectations, the price will decline. The fact that the world is going into a depression, and the price of platinum has been based on forecasts of a huge new industry of pollution control, may very well erode the price of platinum. Diamonds, which may be in much less demand due to strained economies, may fall in price, and probably will. All of the other metals fall into the same category. Of course if war or other unforseen restrictions prevent the import of a scarce metal—that metal will go up, just as oil went up under those conditions.

Gold and silver, however, are the metal stand-bys for those who would preserve their wealth.

Working strongly in favor of silver is a relative decline in silver production compared with gold production. It has declined drastically in the last 200 years.

In 1650 the world was producing forty-four times as much silver as gold. But now it only produces about five times as much silver as gold.

Yet all this time the industrial consumption of silver far outstripped the consumption of gold. So that, while the supply of gold—once the monetary situation is stabilized—can remain adequate for at least a generation, this is not true of silver. The shortfall of production over consumption continues, even under recession conditions.

It is very important to remember that, in a depression, production from copper and zinc mines will be seriously curtailed. That means an automatic curtailment of eighty percent of the source material of silver production— because nearly eighty percent of silver is mined in conjunction with copper and zinc and other metals. To increase silver production substantially, production of those other metals would have to be increased. While a depression would cut down on the consumption of silver, the shortfall would still remain.

So every month, month after month, year after year, we are eating away at the remaining store of silver.

The outlook is that the demand will grow much greater. The world must move away from pollution. Silver holds out one of the great promises not only in the control of pollution but in the huge upcoming area of batteries. As technology advances, the consumption picture for silver advances. Today photography consumes most of the silver, but tomorrow electronics and other new technologies may rival photography in their demand.

At the same time, silver is still money—regardless of what the Central Banks say. We know this because we know there are several hundred million dollars in silver holdings that plainly state on the face of them that they are money— and which are accepted without question as money—and, what is more, a money that constantly appreciates in value. It is easily proven—a silver quarter of 1965 was worth over a dollar in 1978.

Gold is the monetary Gibraltar for the larger sums of money, and for the very rich. I believe that silver still has a role to play as the monetary Gibraltar of the millions who cannot spend very much on total security—but still can spend something to know that they will have money that will always work.

Somewhere down the line silver will probably recover its ancient ratio of 16 to 1 with gold.

At present there are substantial above-ground stocks:

Commodity Warehouse stocks cannot be considered to be available at the snap of a finger. This stock is all owned by someone. Some of it is owned, or can be called upon, by the silver refiners. Much of it is owned by speculators, sometimes more respectably called investors. The price at which it will be sold is a big question mark. If silver should get really scarce, it could be that the strong speculators holding silver would not sell at all—particularly under the threat of war or worsening world monetary conditions. Or it could be that they would sell only at a very high price.

It could also be that they would let loose at a lower price. But I do not see many reasons for this.

About 200 million ounces will be produced in the Western Hemisphere each year, and that is enough to look after the needs of the United States. But no more than 240 million ounces will be produced worldwide, and other countries in the world use cameras too; and are engaged in electronics and pollution control.

The supply situation is not completely critical, but it is moving in that direction.

Over and above the visible supplies of silver mentioned we have a certain amount of storage by bullion dealers in England and Switzerland. No one knows how much that is, but it is considered to be rather smaller than the American speculative supplies. The acquisition of silver has not been popular in the last few years, and much of the silver held in London and Zurich is in long-term hands.

Beyond that we have some hundreds of millions of ounces in United States coinage. Coins nearly always carry a premium over metal. A certain amount of coinage is melted down, but smelters are not getting very large supplies from coinage; and if silver is increasingly looked upon as a "store of value," they will get less and less of the coinage for the melting pots. Or if they do get it, they will have to pay a higher and higher price.

Probably the largest supply of silver is in India, but there it is held in tiny amounts in the form of jewelry by scores of millions of peasants holding it for a last-ditch emergency.

All in all, the future for silver is subject to more influences than probably any other commodity, and certainly to more factors than gold. But whatever happens over the short term, one must not lose sight of the three major factors as far as silver is concerned.

1. The shortfall is about a hundred million ounces a year.

2. Silver is being consumed — not stored like gold.

3. Sooner or later the well is going to run dry. When that day comes there could be a panic to buy silver, and a ratio of 16 to 1 is a fairly reasonable expectation.

30. THE STOCK MARKET — INVESTMENT MANIA

A large part of the problem of inflation arises from the need to keep pace with it. Those who do not put their money on a vehicle that rises as fast as the inflation find the value of their money depreciating. It's no wonder, therefore, that an inflationary era of thirty-years duration produced the greatest bull market and the longest bull market in history.

Past periods of inflation had been relatively short-lived. That was because it was impossible to sustain them against a background of real money. The invention of the gold-exchange standard, and the circulation of debt certificates in place of money, provided the authorities with facilities to keep the inflationary machine running.

Previously, injections of *real* money would have been necessary to keep the inflationary machine alive. Since such money did not exist, the overheated economy had to come to its senses. This always had a sobering effect on the stock market and, usually, a severe although not disastrous correction.

Under the debt economy—under circumstances where debt served as money — injections of new money became relatively easy. All you had to do was to increase the debt. Presto! There was the new money.

From the end of World War II until 1966 the stock market enjoyed its greatest and longest boom. Except for corrections here and there, the curve of the Dow Jones* moved steadily and inexorably up. And as it rose its speed of acceleraton increased.

By the early 1960s inflation was beginning to be recognized by all. Brokers were quick to point out to their clients that if they left their money in cash its quality would be gradually eroded. However, they said, if clients invested their money in stocks, the stocks would rise along with the inflation, and, in the case of very good stocks, would outpace the inflation.

This popular type of buying during the sixties was fundamentally different from the investments made in our colony of Freedonia. As we understood it then, when we had real money we might invest our savings in, say, a shoe factory if we foresaw a rising market for shoes, and if the factory was run by a good manager and staff, with excellent cobblers. Our idea was that the true wealth of this business would increase, and that we would share in it.

The investment by the public in the 1960s was made for quite a different reason. Most of the buying was based not so much on visions of increased wealth of the business as on the judgment that other people would pay more for the stock later, regardless of what it was worth. Growth became a magic word. A generous expectation on earnings from share investments had been ten percent. Now people bought stocks not at a cost of ten times earnings, but often forty times earnings, eighty times earnings, 100 times earnings; on the theory that other people would get so excited about the prospects of these stocks that they would pay 120 times earnings and would take these stocks off the hands of the present buyer at a profit. The investment idea, as it had been traditionally known, became increasingly distorted. Investment gave way to speculation. Speculation gave way to outright gambling.

This kind of a market emanated from two fundamentals of human nature. One was fear; the other greed. People bought for fear that the value of their savings would disappear as a result of inflation, unless they changed cash into stocks. They bought from greed once they saw what other people were making at this marvellous new game.

Essentially, though, the massive buying by the American public rose out of fear, which itself arose from inflation. Really, without being aware of it, people were running from money.

The first factor that every investor in the stock market should take into account before he buys, is the overhanging weight of potential selling. This is true whether you are dealing in a small mining stock, a massive stock like General Motors, or the spectrum of stocks across the total economy, which is assumed to be measured by an index known as the "Dow Jones Average." Any smart stock market operator knows that the time to buy the shares of a company is before it has become highly popular. The reason for this is that

---

*Dow-Jones Average — Average price of 30 Blue Chip Industrial stocks. There is also a D.J. Transportation Average embracing 20 Transportation stocks; and a D.J. Utility Average embracing 15 Public Utility stocks. D.J.I. is probably the most quoted financial index in the world.

once it has become very popular, large numbers of former stockholders are potential sellers when it makes a healthy rise. This overhang of potential sellers is "bearish."

The point is that the more people who are involved for the simple reason of selling at a profit, the nearer we are to the top. In order for the stock to hold even, there will have to be an army of new buyers coming along just as optimistic about the future as the previous army of buyers. In order for the stock to go up, this new army will have to be bigger than the army of potential sellers. Obviously, somewhere along the line, the newest army of buyers will be smaller than the preceding army, which has by now become the "selling" army. Then we will have more sellers than buyers, and the stock will go down. This is true also for the entire mass of the stock market.

The alternating size of these two armies determines whether the stock market will go up or down. It is strictly a question of psychology. One might stretch that to say it is strictly a question of fashionable thinking. It is true that the fashionable thinking rests largely on the net overall judgment of business activity. But there is another factor that has nothing to do with the truth. The fashionable psychology can be the result of propaganda. Since the investment public tends to move on the herd instinct, even a sustained move in the Dow Jones can be entirely misconceived.

Charts try to measure what people are doing. That is, what people have been thinking, what they are continuing to think, and, therefore, what they will likely continue to do. Charts are very valuable in this respect.

But charts cannot shed the faintest ray of light on whether or not what people are doing is solidly or falsely based. If the move is falsely based it will be found out sooner or later. Then the market will go in the reverse direction.

In other words, the market is blind. It is like a blind monster trying to get out of a maze. He rumbles along in one direction and, as long as he runs into no great obstacles, continues until he smashes his head against a wall. Then he turns and rumbles in the other direction until he hits another wall.

How else can you interpret the movement of the Dow Jones from 1965 right through 1975? And on into 1979 for that matter. Look back at the graph on Page 17. You must conclude that most of the moves of the Dow Jones were purposeless—except for one thing. The blind monster never, throughout all this time, took inflation into account.

The inflation meant that the Dow Jones was not doing at all what it seemed to be doing. While it seemed to be up it was really going down, so that when it hit the thousand mark in mid-1968, and again in mid-1972, it was nowhere near the mark of a thousand that it had reached in 1965. At its peak of a thousand to 1047 in 1972, inflation had destroyed more than one-third; it was really around 650. Seven years later, near the end of 1979, the Dow-Jones was still only slightly over 800 after having suffered another 25%-30% inflationary depreciation.

The blind monster and the blind followers of the monster on Wall Street never tumbled to the fact that the whole thing amounted to the most massive bear market in the history of the world. Either they wouldn't see, or they didn't want to see that the great recovery of 1972 meant that all the massive billions invested had depreciated by at least one-third. To be even, the market would have had to rise to 1350. By 1979 the Dow Jones would have to stand at over 2000 to be the equivalent of 1000 in 1966.

Throughout all the thirteen-year period, the fluctuations of the Dow Jones were really a measure of changing psychology—first optimistic, then pessimistic. It relected the changing size of the two armies, the pessimists and the optimists. There was a seesaw battle as members of one army defected to the other. And it must be said that neither of these armies displayed any intelligent insight as to the direction in which the world was marching.

When it became fashionable to accept the cliche "We have to live with inflation, and the way to do it is to buy stocks"—the army of people holding stocks assumed massive proportions. By 1966 the army of people owning stocks far outnumbered the army of people still wanting stocks.

I don't pretend here to go into all the causes of the crash of 1966, but this was certainly a major one.

The Dow Jones averages dropped from a January reading of 1001 to a May reading of 735. It was by no means a measure of the percentage losses to the general public. The damage to the Dow Jones industrials—considered to be the big blue chips—was small compared to the depreciation in many of the speculative stocks, the growth stocks, the glamour stocks, the cat-and-dog stocks. The public took a severe beating. The big public never really returned to the market in force. It had lost confidence in its ability to invest in the right stock.

The market was turned around by injections of new money, but the self-confidence of the army of individual investors had been damaged. The climate was ready for the stellar performance of the mutual funds. Their salesmen penetrated every nook and cranny of the land.

The pitch was this: "You've been hurt in the market, sure. But why have you been hurt? You have been hurt because you have gone into a game that you do not have the background to understand. In our office we have analysts who spend their entire days examining investments. We have the finest brains out of Harvard and Yale, and our firm can draw on the expert eyes of experienced operators with proven judgment. On top of this we can apply the magic art of the computer. How could you expect to make money as an amateur against these experts? Now we offer you these services. You will pay a larger commission to buy the stocks if you do so through us. But it will give you a service that would be cheap at twice the price."

The public went for that.

The need to keep up with inflation was greater than ever. Investors would now employ experts. These experts with their noses to the grindstone, pouring over sets of tables from morning to night, would come up with the right answers, and we the investors would reap the profit.

And that worked pretty well for a while.

The investing public poured its money into the mutual funds and other institutional forms, which bought up large volumes of stocks and put new life in the market, with the result that the Dow Jones launched a rather dramatic recovery.

But now we had a new situation. The market had traded the sensitivity of feeling of the many (the public) for the feelings of the few (the experts). The feelings of the many are grass roots. The feelings—the optimism or the pessimism—of the few are academic.

By 1970 mutual funds and institutions had replaced the volume of injection of money that previously had come from millions of individuals. And whereas at one time the public accounted for eighty percent of the trading, now eighty percent was being done by institution managers.

President Nixon had decided that he would fight inflation. Apparently he did not understand that the new debt economy was like a bicycle that had to be kept in motion. If you ever stopped going forward in the process of increasing debt, your bicycle lost its momentum and, losing that momentum, would fall down. Within five months, from January 1970 to May, the Dow Jones thermometer plummeted from 995 to a new low of 631. It was a near disaster.

In the midst of the panic, two of the largest firms in the United States stood helpless before the yawning jaws of bankruptcy. In the case of Lockheed, the Bank of America was in so deep that the bankruptcy of Lockheed would almost certainly spell bankruptcy for the Bank of America. The bankruptcy of that bank, and its consequently necessary calling of loans, would set off a chain reaction that might easily result in a total collapse of liquidity.

As if that weren't enough, Penn Central Railway, one of the world's industrial giants, informed Congress that if it didn't get help immediately it would also have to declare receivership.

After emergency meetings, it was announced that the government would probably stand behind both Lockheed and Penn Central. They called out the Chairman of the Federal Reserve System, Arthur Burns; and he told the country there would be no shortage of liquidity. What Arthur Burns really said was this: "However much money may be needed, count on us to make it available." That turned the tide of the market again. In six months it sprinted from its May low of 635 to launch an assault on its old 1966 high of 1000. It got as far as 951.

By 1975, we had a different story. Mr. Burns was trying to expand the money supply and couldn't make it work. In February he testified before a congressional committee that in spite of efforts to increase the money supply by six percent or more it had actually fallen. We shall speak about this later, but it is injected at this point to show that, when inflation is nearing its end, increasing the money supply by the debt mechanism is not as simple as it sounds. While inflation is going, every offering of money by the Fed is eagerly pulled away. When inflation is about to fail, the Fed finds itself pushing a string. Eager borrowers are in financial trouble and are not wanted. Worthy borrowers, fearing to expand, don't want the money.

This results in the withdrawal of one of the principal fountains of money creation. When you go to the bank and borrow a thousand dollars, the money is at that moment created. It goes into your checking account and you begin to use it. Likewise, of course, when you come back to the bank to repay the thousand dollars, you have thereby reduced the money supply. If you go broke, the bank has to write off the thousand dollars, and thereby reduces the money supply. There is only one catch for the bank; if you go broke, the bank is stuck with the loss. That's why it has to be careful when a credit crunch looms.

The Fed, however, can inject money in other ways. By buying government securities, it creates money, which becomes available to the banks to loan out. Whether it actually becomes money in the market place depends on whether the banks feel that they can take the risk on their customers, and also whether the customers feel they want to take the risk of the loan.

But back in 1970 all offerings of money were quickly snapped up, and the market reacted like an injected filly.

As late as 1973, counting a population of something more than 200 million, and assuming that half are under- or over-age, practically one out of every three employed persons was still an investor directly in the market, with an additional unknown quantity involved in one way or another through the institutions.

Probably half or more of the public of the United States was in the stock market. Was it possible to expect that the other half were going to be buyers after witnessing the unhappy experience of their friends over a period since 1966? (Refer back to the graph on Page 18).

The age of inflation had coaxed the maximum public into the stock market. There were not enough people left on the outside of the fence to rescue those already inside. We were witnessing the transformation of the psychology of public investment. But it was generally not perceived by the investment wizards on Wall Street until too late.

The next time the sellers got scared, the Dow went to 627 in 1970. Again, in 1973, those who were "bullish on America" jumped in. The herd instinct took over, and in early 1973 the market roared up past a thousand. From then on, with some wild fluctuations, it was a downhill road to the low point of 576 in late 1974.

Once again the dumb blind giant turned around, and we had the explosive rally of early 1975.

No one stopped to think that even if this rally should reach as high as a thousand—which it did in 1972—it would still only be 600 compared with the Dow Jones standing of 1965—because of depreciation by inflation.

The bull market actually lasted only from the early 1950s through 1965.

Throughout the subsequent recoveries a very important element was being overlooked. Each recovery showed the volume to be more the work of institutions and less the volume of John Q. Public. Each of the recoveries showed more block trading than the previous ones. And most of the stock market, indeed, was being handled by the big fund managers.

If public investment was going out of fashion, so was the stock market.

Another pillar in our era—the era of credit—was beginning to crack. The warning was being flashed by growing bankruptcies.

Bankruptcies always lag behind the reality of the bankruptcy. Bankruptcy is the final *admission*. In 1974 we had the bankruptcies that were building up in 1973. The most notable was the Franklin National Bank—the eighth largest in the United States.

The dethroned millionaire was asked: "How did you go bankrupt?" He replied: "Gradually for quite a while—then all at once!"

The bankruptcies being registered in 1975 were about five times as many as those in 1974.

Few of the American brokerage houses connected the sickness of the New York Stock Exchange with the international monetary situation. Nevertheless, that was where the immediate cause lay. The lack of confidence in the dollar had swelled the reserves of foreign countries. That capital had fled to foreign treasuries because it feared a devaluation of the dollar. If it resided in a strong currency, that loss would be avoided. The capital flow proved to be correct. President Nixon devalued the dollar ten percent, the second devaluation in fourteen months.

Perhaps the surest sign of trouble, even in 1973, was a psychological phenomenon that a sharp farmer with a grade-five education might view with suspicion. It was the overdone brokerage proclamation: "We're bullish on America!"

This slogan had found wide usage about the time of the crash of 1929. When the stock market is sound and healthy, supporting slogans are superfluous. During the great bull market of 1946 to 1966 no one heard these pseudo-patriotic announcements. But in the spring of 1973 the large brokerage institutions were running advertisements almost daily emphazing their "Bullishness on America."

Even the New York Stock Exchange was running ads urging the public to get in and take advantage of the anticipated growth in the business of America.

And in January of 1975, General Motors ran large ads proclaiming that it was patriotic to "buy a car" —implying that it was unpatriotic not to buy a car. All red-blooded Americans who could afford it ought to pitch in and buy cars. It was like the wartime slogan, "Buy a bond today."

When, in April 1973 (with the Dow around 900), I predicted that the stock market would be lucky if it could bottom out in the 500 to 600 range in 1974, I was regarded not only as a nut, but the worst kind of a nut—a false prophet of gloom and doom. *Barron's* magazine headlined me as the *"bear from the north."*

But I noticed—didn't you?—that before the end of 1974 the Dow Jones actually did hit 576.

I made this assessment not on the basis of charts or great technical knowledge, but rather on the basis of psychological considerations. The most important of these was the price/earnings ratio.

If a stock earns $10 a year and is selling on the market at $100, it is said to have a price/earnings ratio of ten. The price/earnings ratio is therefore a measurement of the buoyancy factor in the investment community. When the future looks good, people are willing to credit the stocks with a larger factor of growth. When the future looks bleak they are apt to move to the extreme in the other direction. We have had price/earnings ratios of up to twenty for the Dow Jones averages as a whole. We have had them down as low as six. In the spring of 1973 they had fallen from their high of nineteen seven years before to 13. It showed that investors were becoming increasingly uncertain about growth. If they should become downright pessimistic, the figure could drop to ten or eight or even six. There is no rule as to what a price/earnings ratio should be. Although the brokers seem to assume that the market is required to be reasonable, there is no such actual requirement.

But a reduction in the effective price/earnings ratio is quite a lot more serious than a change that might develop from reduced earnings.

If, for example, General Motors earns $6 a year, and if it is selling at $78 a share, it is being given a price/earnings ratio of thirteen.

A poor year might bring General Motors down to $5 in earnings. If the price/earnings ratio persisted it would drop only to $65 per share. *But if, at the same time, a generally depressive psychology resulted in a bleaker outlook for the future, and if the price/earnings ratio were to drop to ten, the price of General Motors would recede to $50 per share.* If the earnings dropped to four — which they could in time of serious recession — the tendency would be for the price/earnings ratio to drop as well. If the price/earnings ratio dropped to eight — the price of General Motors would be $32 per share.

And that is precisely what happened. From the $60 area, General Motors actually hit 29 in the low of 1974.

Every bear market has its early period of erosion and its dramatic period of drop; then followed by another period of erosion. To me it appeared that the unusually long bull market from 1946 to 1966 had become a bear market with an unusually long first-stage erosional period (1966-1975) that was on the verge of being transformed into the second-stage dramatic slide.

But always to be added to this massive fall is the deduction for the comparative inflation.

When the distortions become serious, international traders find themselves increasingly restricted. A large oil tanker may take three years to build. How can a contract be drawn on the delivery price when the currencies are moving around like jumping beans? This puts another brake on the Dow Jones, regardless of its violent short-term convulsions.

The multiplication of the distortions themselves project the end of the age of inflation from the mere fact that the vision of economic communicators becomes blurred to the point where they can no longer perform. That leads to a collapse of international business, which leads to a collapse of business at home—which, in the circumstances of mountains of credit, can only lead to economic collapse and the total collapse of the market.

A book becomes severely dated when it deals with such transitory figures as readings of the Dow Jones. The point of all the above is to impress upon the reader the huge and overwhelming background which is leading us to the most massive crash of all time. But the significance is not the fact that the Dow Jones may fall to 400 or lower. The real meaning of this is that the recovery from such a long bear market cannot be sudden.

We had a twenty year bull market and a bear market of more than a dozen years following it. The recovery of the stock market will be a long and painful process. It will take several years to recover the lost ground, and there is a possibility it may never be recovered. The implication for the reader is not to get excited about optimistic talk of the beginnings of a great new bull market. When the final crash is finished, rallies can be expected to occur. But a real strong bull movement starts in very slowly. It progresses very slowly in the beginning. The public does not join in. It has been too badly burnt.

The era of great spending, huge debt, and a market that always goes up, has ended.

31.
EURODOLLARS SPLIT THE WORLD — BRINGING IT INTO FOCUS

We have covered a lot of ground and some seemingly disassociated subjects. However, every subject covered is intimately related with every other, and together they produce a single clear picture.

We are now in a position to see this picture in distinct focus. The elements we have to consider are as follows:

1. The monetary crisis.
2. The labor crisis.
3. The food crisis (although not dealt with previously, this is becoming an increasingly vital part of the whole world picture).

THE MONETARY CRISIS

To recapitulate: This crisis has been building up since 1968, when the world gold pool went broke. Although the dollar was theoretically convertible into gold by any country, the United States strong-armed all the nations of the Western world not to exchange the dollars they had earned for gold. The reason was that the U.S. gold pile had come down to a level of about $10 billion, apparently considered as the danger level by military and top political authorities.

It was loudly proclaimed that the dollar was as good as gold—in fact, it was better than gold—in fact, the only reason gold was worth anything at all was that the U.S. Treasury stood ready to redeem all dollars in gold. It put up a sign at the window, "Redeem your dollars for gold!"

But when you went to the window with some dollars and tentatively offered them in your hand, they slammed the window on your fingers. After about three came out with smashed fingers—the rest stopped coming. No country was strong enough to challenge the United States; and so the pretense went on—"The dollar is as good as gold."

Relieved of the necessity of putting out gold for the dollars it spent abroad, the United States continued to manufacture huge amounts of money. It spent this money on the Vietnam war, and this money infiltrated itself into various countries. It spent money on troops in Germany. It spent money on massive imports of oil and other raw materials. And it spent money on manufactured products from other countries. But the dollars continued to pile up in the scores of billions in foreign treasuries. No one could get anything back for these dollars. Of course they could buy, if they wished: American Buicks and American television sets. But they did not want to buy these things. They wanted to make them in their own countries and sell them abroad. It amounted to dollar imperialism.

By 1971 the pressure had become so great that there was a threat of a massive exchange of dollars for gold. At that time President Nixon closed the gold window and ended the pretense that the dollar could be exchanged for gold.

Soon thereafter the world went on floating exchange rates. That is to say, no longer was one currency guaranteed by the central bank of a country to be worth an equivalent value of another currency, which was, in turn, worth a specified number of dollars. Currencies fluctuated like stocks on the stock market, according to the demand. Central banks tried to buy dollars when the dollar went too low in relation to their own currencies, because, if their currencies were too high, it made their exports to the United States too high and they couldn't sell anything. But still, for every dollar they bought, they had to issue more of their own currencies—thereby leaving themselves at the mercy of the inflation of the United States.

The United States was still spending much more than it was producing, and by 1975 it had piled up more than a hundred billion unredeemable dollars.

In 1978 the outstanding claims against the U.S. were more than six hundred billion dollars. These were called Eurodollars. That was because they were still in the form of dollars. (They had never been converted into the currencies of the countries in which they resided.) They moved freely around the world still in the form of dollars. A half a trillion of these claims could, upon demand, be placed in front of the national banks of any countries. The price of these dollars would depend on what was bid for them.

With all this money abroad, the debt of the United States was piling up at such an enormous rate that it was mindboggling. As a means of self-preservation, France and Germany moved to form a new monetary union called the European Monetary Union, and planned for a currency to be called the European Currency Unit or ECU.

Their reasoning was simple: if we don't do it, we will be drowned in dollars. Either we will have to issue so much currency to buy the dollars (to keep the price up) that the inflation will kill us *or* we will have to let the dollar go so low that none of our exports will be able to compete with American exports anywhere in the world. Either way, we're dead. We must protect ourselves.

The great danger was that when those people who held the halftrillion Eurodollars found out that there would be a European currency, they would be willing to exchange those dollars for the European currency at a lesser amount. A panic in Eurodollars could develop. If that happened, no one could foretell what the price of a dollar would be in terms of a deutschmark, a Swiss franc or even an Italian lira.

That left the possibility of a monetary crisis of mindboggling proportions. No monetary authorities in the world had any idea of how it really could be solved. But they did know—many of them knew—that a monetary volcano would erupt. That was the reason behind the European Monetary Union of January 1, 1979.

Even so, it was formed with much trepidation. In the innermost circles of the central banks there was a certain amount of terror because of the knowledge that no one knew what the effect would be, and no one really knew how a solution could be worked out.

It is interesting, in the light of all this, to look back to a report I made in March 1975. It could as well have been written at the end of 1978.

Monetary Confusion Deepens

On previous visits to Switzerland over the last several years one could always find suggested remedies. Desperate perhaps—far out perhaps—some of them doubtful, and verging on the implausible perhaps—but some kind of suggestion for a remedy to the world monetary situation.   On this visit I don't even hear suggestions.

In short, the situation has worsened so much and become so inextricably complicated and entangled that the best thinkers seem to me to have given up.

Two years ago, one would hear such specific pronouncements as: "The United States debt must be funded. Otherwise we are drifting hopelessly into chaos. We must fund the debt." Or you might hear, "The Common Market countries may form a currency of their own." Or you might even hear, "We shall have to return to gold at a much higher price—perhaps $100 or more." Or you might hear, "The SDR's will have to be activated—we shall have to get rid of gold."

On this visit I hear none of these. I hear no suggestions at all.

It is as though everyone has thrown up his hands.

"I asked the Chairman of the Board of one of the very largest banks in Switzerland or the world, "Will we go back to gold?" He said, "No, we will not go back to the gold standard."

I asked the chief economist of an equally large bank, "Will we go back to the gold standard?" He replied, "We will have to eventually go to gold. There is no other way."

I asked another banker, "How is the Arab oil money to be handled?" He said, "They will have to invest on the longer term. What else will they do with it?"

"But how?" I asked. "They're only investing on the short term."

"True," he said, "ninety days or six months. They are afraid of the currencies."

I asked, "Then what are they going to do with it?" He had no answer. It has to be done—but he had no answer.

All of this would lead to the splitting of the world's monetary system in two, as the European Monetary Union emerged at the beginning of 1979.

❋   ❋   ❋   ❋   ❋

32. NEW MONETARY ERA ARRIVES

Some laws are as universal and unchangeable as the daily rising of the sun.

If I hold a rock at arms length and release my fingers, the rock will fall to the ground. If I do it 20 trillion times, the rock will always fall. Otherwise the law of gravity would not be a law.

The law of supply and demand is no different. If a mouseridden community imports 500 cats and 500 people want cats, they will sell at a certain price. If the local government imports 500 more cats, the price of cats will fall as surely as the rock will fall.

The government of the community can preach all kinds of good things about cats. Cats are lovely pets, cats are good for children, we ought to have a spare cat in case one cat dies. It will do no good; the price of cats will fall.

Now if the government has foolishly imported 5,000 cats and still wants to hold up the price of cats, it can only do so by passing a law which controls the price of cats. Then nobody will buy a cat. Sooner or later the government will have to let its cats go for what they will bring, that is to say, any price at all that people will pay for a cat. The price of a cat might fall to virtually nothing.

Today the world is awash with Eurodollars. These are American dollars owned outside the U.S. They may be in any bank in the world (including the U.S.A. Treasuries) earning interest, but they will not buy any goods except in the U.S.A. If an owner wants to spend them in Germany, the central bank will have to bid for the dollars at a price of so many marks, which it will give to the former owner of the dollars.

Well and good. But if there is a veritable flood of dollars, the central bank will have to drop its price. Other potential buyers of dollars will also drop their price. Masses of Eurodollars, far in excess of the demand, will meet exactly the same market reaction as the 5,000 cats.

If the government can persuade the people that by all means cats are a valuable asset, the price may hold for awhile. But if the government itself refuses to pay very much for cats coming on the market, the price of cats will go to hell.

In the world today there are about $600 billion outside the U.S.A. (Eurodollars). These have been floating like a satellite in space, unconnected with monetary reality. Their inflationary influence has not been felt in the U.S. and will not be felt in other countries until these dollars are transformed into those currencies. But if the holders get scared that other holders will not buy those Eurodollars, they will offer them for progressively less. This is just what happened in 1978.

The U.S. Treasury (Mr. Blumenthal) said the dollar was undervalued because it would buy more in the U.S. than its equivalent would buy in France. Alas, to no avail!

The government may tell you that cats are undervalued because cats catch mice, cats are good pets, and so on. But if they have 5,000 cats and only 500 are needed, the price of cats is going to pieces. And nobody can predict to you what will be the selling price of a cat.

The 600 billion Eurodollars floating around the world are a mythical currency; a currency with no place to land. They far exceed the reserves of all the central banks combined. And in the U.S.A. they are unredeemable for anything unless you want to spend your money there.

What will be the quoted value of a surplus Eurodollar (really an American IOU)? I can only answer that with another question: What will be the price of a surplus cat?

ECU ALTERNATIVE MAY BE DOLLAR'S PITFALL
DILEMMA OF THE DOLLAR

1. Eurodollars are claims not only on U.S., but on any currency in the world.

2. Huge offerings unsupported by buyers could bring the U.S. dollar to unthinkable lows.

3. European Currency Union is defensive - intended to relieve the necessity of buying surplus dollars. But gold backing will make it the world's favorite.

THE EURODOLLAR MASS

If an Iranian potentate has received $10 million from oil proceeds (U.S.A. buys oil for dollars), and if he quickly moves it out of Iran and deposits it in Zurich, the Eurodollar* market has been expanded by $10 million.

If the potentate invests in U.S. Treasuries or U.S. stocks, the dollars are still present. But if whoever receives the $10 million buys German bonds, the

---

*Eurodollars—Simply a deposit of American dollars on the books of any bank outside the U.S. anywhere in the world. An American with a $1,000 bank account in Ceylon is the owner of 1,000 Eurodollars.

Eurodollars become deutschemarks, and the Eurodollar market shrinks by $10 million.

However, by the transfer, the German Central Bank has issued 20 million deutschemarks. The Eurodollars have been transformed into dollar reserves in the German Central Bank.

German 1978 reserves amounted to 40 billion dollars plus 118 million ounces of gold, which was $23.6 billion at $200 an ounce.

Thus it was clear that the estimated 500 to 600 billion Eurodollars constituted a potential disaster for the currency of any country if the holders demanded that currency in exchange. For instance, *(to go to the extreme)* Germany could be forced to issue 1,000 billion marks to buy Eurodollars. If she wanted to keep the mark from rising, she would have to continue to bid for the Eurodollars to keep them from falling. This would create a tide of German inflation that would destroy the country. If she would not bid for massive offerings, the offering price of dollars would generally decline to where they matched the bids. So the German mark would skyrocket in relation to the dollar, to a point where it would be so expensive as to make German trade with its European partners impossible. The Common Market would be destroyed.

And so it goes for any currency you care to name.

Question: Why hasn't this happened?

Answer: It has been happening and on an increasing scale. The dollar, formerly worth four Swiss francs, fell to less than two. The Swiss money supply, like the German, has shot ahead very fast, ten percent to thirteen percent in 1978, because of buying large sums of dollars, much of which are probably Eurodollars.

Question: Has it nearly stopped now?

Answer: It hasn't even got started yet. The Eurodollar mass increased from $100 billion a few years ago five or sixfold by 1978. The process of transformation into other currencies accelerated. It caused the October 1979 monetary crisis.

Question: How did the Eurodollar Fund get so big?

Answer: Largely because of U.S. deficits. When the U.S.A. imports 40 billion dollars in oil this year, these dollars *(printed up by the Fed)* simply left the country adding to the pile of Eurodollars. The oil imports were not offset by other U.S. exports. Saudi Arabia, officially, (not to say anything of individual sheiks) has 60 billion U.S. dollars. A great deal of this money was invested in short-term U.S. Treasuries, helping to finance the U.S.A. This, along with large Eurodollar holdings, could be offered at any time for other currencies.

Question: Why weren't they offered sooner?

Answer: Firstly, Saudi's last wish was to see the smashup of the dollar-which is to say the deterioration of their own assets. Secondly, the volume of money was so great that this huge offering by the Saudis could not be absorbed at anywhere near par by any single country or group of countries. If they offered 60 billion dollars to several countries, the price of the dollar would drop fantastically. So they don't do it.

Question: Then why the worry?

Answer: The holders of Eurodollars are an amorphous and ghost-like mass of people, corporations, and even countries. They are mostly unidentified, completely unrestrained, and uncontrolled. They are the suppliers to the market, like any other market. The buyers in this market, who are matched against them, are the world's central banks. The sellers (Eurodollar holders) could be overpowering if they get scared.

Additionally foreign banks may lend dollars they do not have. There is no central bank control. Nobody knows how much of this has gone on.

So is it not clear that situation resembles the tulip bulb mania of Holland? If the situation is bullish for the dollar, it will rise. If it is bearish, the dollar will fall.

Bullish means a U.S. balanced budget and a positive trade balance; and preferably zero inflation.

Bearish means budget deficits such as $30 to $50 billion a year, (bogus dollars thus printed get out of the country and add to the Eurodollars); trade deficits, increasing inflation, which reduces the value of all dollars, including Eurodollars.

HUGE OFFERINGS COULD BRING U.S. DOLLAR TO UNTHINKABLE LOWS

Question: Why didn't this happen long before—say in the Sixties?

Answer: Prior to 1971 the U.S. redeemed foreign dollar holdings with gold. If there was a surplus of dollars being offered in France, for instance, the French Central Bank could bid for them at the fixed rate and issue francs. These dollars would go into France's reserves and then France would send them to the U.S. and demand gold. The U.S. paid out the gold. This kept dollar reserves in the central banks low. Thus, the central banks were always in a position to bid for surplus dollars hitting the market.

But Nixon stopped that when in 1971 he closed the gold window. This was the central support of the post World War II money system of fixed exchange rates. Thereafter central banks had to keep the dollars they held. Whereas, the German reserves were at one time adequate at $4 and $5 billion, they are now ten times that. Additional Eurodollars bought by the German bank only add to the enormous total of the German reserves.

Foreign central banks, therefore, have become constantly less enthusiastic about bidding for surplus dollars. As the offerings continued, and as the central bankers lowered their bid, the dollar fell on the International Market to where now it is only worth half as much in German marks and Swiss francs as it was.

This reduction by half in the value of the dollar has taken place during a time when the Eurodollar market was growing upwards from a hundred billion, and during a time when the U.S. balance of trade was often in deficit. Now the overhang of Eurodollars is absolutely immense.

The meaning of this can only be that, unless these deficits are almost instantly corrected, the dollar is vulnerable to a huge depreciation. No one can put a number on it, because no one knows what it is worth. In reality its price will be the accommodation established between the mass of the buyers (the central banks) and the mass of the sellers (the Eurodollar holders). In theory the dollar could go very, very low. It's all a matter of confidence.

That was the thrust of the U.S. emergency rescue of October 1978 when it borrowed almost $30 billion to become a buyer of dollars on the world markets. Generally overlooked by the public was the fact that this really didn't make much difference. The funds were currencies borrowed *short-term* from other central banks. They would have to be paid back. It was a piece of world showmanship. It had a very fancy appearance, but very little substance. In the long run, it would not do any good at all.

HOW EURODOLLAR OFFERINGS MIGHT
REACH UNTHINKABLE LOWS

In order to comprehend this, we must first fully understand what the ECU is. From this we can arrive at the more vitally important comprehension of what the ECU *will mean.*

Neither of these questions have been addressed at all by the popular press because they refuse to listen to the thought that ECU will be a gold-based money. Secondly, not recognizing that, it never dawns on them that they are missing the most historic monetary development of the twentieth century, because *it splits the world into two monetary camps.*

In my mind there is no doubt about the ultimate validity of what I am putting forward here; and in some instances it might make you a fortune to understand it, and it might cost you a lot not to.

WHAT THE ECU IS

Superficially and publicly the European countries (West Germany, France, Belgium, Holland, Luxembourg, Denmark, Italy, Ireland) will create a common reserve equivalent to $32 billion. This will be $25 billion ECU's. The currencies will not be allowed to rise above or fall below their assigned parity by more than twenty-four percent. If, for instance, the French currency sinks more than twenty-four percent below its parity, France will borrow from the Fund and buy francs. Speculation would be virtually non-existent because of the huge size of the central fund.

Similarly, for example, if the mark exceeds parity, marks must be sold to buy other currencies of the union who are at lower levels. Therefore, the marks will be absorbed in the system.

The movements of the dollar, up or down, will be completely against the ECU. *No individual currency will be affected one iota by even the wildest movements of the dollar.*

This is about as far as the news media go, and even the last paragraph is never emphasized or explained in the media. Our newsletter writers also seem to have missed the enormous significance of this point.

But there is even a greater significance, and that is the composition of the 32 billion dollars reserve fund. For the convenience of the reader, we repeat the table on page 140.

	Millions of Ounces	Gold at $200	Total Monetary Reserves
Germany	118.4	236.8	39,900
France	101.8	203.6	7,522
Netherlands	54.6	109.2	3,530
Belgium	42.5	85.	2,611
Denmark	1.9	3.8	2,636
Italy	82.9	165.8	9,446
Ireland	.5	1.	2,372
TOTAL	402.6	805.2	68,017

Additionally,

Switzerland	83.3	million ounces
U.S.A.	267	million ounces
Canada	22	million ounces
Japan	23.7	million ounces
U.K.	22.7	million ounces
TOTAL	418.7	million ounces

Total central bank reserves exceed 820 million ounces. IMF reserves in excess of 200 million ounces bring total free world gold to over 1 billion ounces.

To update monetary reserves, multiply ounces by gold price.

We have been informed that twenty percent of these reserves (gold plus monetary) will be set aside and that they will amount to a fund of $32 billion. One-fifth of the monetary reserves is $13.6 billion. Therefore, the gold component of $32 billion will have to be $18.4 billion.

One-fifth of the total gold reserves (402.6 millions ounces) is 80,000,000 ounces. Therefore, 80,000,000 ounces will have to equal $16.2 billion. That means the price of gold will have to be $230 per ounce—on the basis of what we have been told.

The gold in the reserves has to be officially revalued. Do we need to be hit over the head to realize that in one and the same breath, the entire gold hoard is thereby automatically also officially evaluated, and that we now have a set price for gold in Europe?

(This price, however, will be expressed in ECU's. The ratio is 25:32. So a $200 an ounce gold value is approximately 156 ECU's equivalent. This price would remain. The dollar price for gold would vary according to the performance of the dollar against the ECU Currency Unit.)

WHAT THIS WILL MEAN

It will mean that if the dollar should drop by one-half against the ECU, the price of gold would still be 156 ECU's per ounce, but $400 per ounce. Still the relation of the internal currencies, for example the Italian lira to the German mark would be absolutely untouched.

It means that individual currencies will no longer be pitted against the dollar. The dollar will only vary against the ECU. By this mechanism, trading among the European partners will be completely shielded from the wild monetary storms.

But this is only the mild start of what it means.

THE HUGE MEANING

There will be no reason for buyers of marks any longer to insist on marks. Since the whole thing will be one unit backed by a massive reserve, they might as well buy ECU's; even better because the ECU represents the combined strength of the union. So if you wish to change one million American currency and you are having a problem in deciding whether to go Belgium, Dutch, German, you will simply now buy ECU's. It is even likely that you would prefer ECU's to Swiss francs, because Switzerland is such a little country, and the ECU is so big.

The ECU will receive worldwide recognition. A gold-based currency will be a ready repository for holders of billions of dollars, who might want to get out of dollars. Recent history has shown there is a desperation to get out of dollars. Actual ECU's may not be available for some time, but any one of the currencies will serve as well.)

And now this brings us to the very heart of the matter.

Will the new union support the U.S. dollar? Will it put up massive billions of ECU's to meet the dollar offerings if they occur?

The answer is a threefold *no*.

1. The interrelationship of the countries is already protected from the variations of the dollar.

2. To do so would be to provide an inherent gold convertibility for

outstanding American obligations at the expense of the European gold pile.

3. Unlimited support of the dollar would amount to an offer to guarantee 500 billion Eurodollars at par, which would absolutely swamp and destroy the European Monetary Union.

(When placed against these facts, notice how silly Secretary Blumenthal's statement was. He said: " Europe has unlimited resources with which to support the dollar.").

THE FUTURE OF THE DOLLAR

If Carter reduces the budget deficit from $50 billion to $30 billion as promised, and the trade deficit from $30 billion to perhaps a dozen billion, an improvement of confidence may prevent any large offering of dollars. Some might even come to think that the dollar was making a comeback, that it would be stronger, and they might even sell ECU's to buy dollars. Doubtful, but possible.

But on December 16, 1978, OPEC raised oil prices to the equivalent of fifteen percent in one year. This is estimated to cost the U.S. $5 billion more even in the first year. The U.S. also estimates oil imports will be up ten percent. Now Carter would have to reduce the deficit to $25 billion in order to be on the same ground he would have been December 15th at $30 billion. That $5 billion extra, unless cut from the budget, means $5 billion more, adding to the massive 500 billion Eurodollars. Later oil price increases only aggravated this situation.

On December 14, 1978, Fed Chairman Miller estimated an increase of one percent in unemployment would mean a deficit of $15 to $20 billion internally. If we do get a strong recession and unemployment should climb three points to nine percent, the $30 billion target deficit would immediately go up to $75 to $90 billion—even if Carter cuts from $50 to $30 billion. Even more Eurodollars.

So if the U.S. goes into a depression or even a bad recession, the outlook for the holders of the half trillion Eurodollars is that they are only going to increase. We come to a point where there is a tendency for the holders to throw up their hands; increasingly large amounts of Eurodollars would come up for sale.

Now—can this money be refused? Of course not, but remember, on one hand, we have the sellers—the Eurodollar owners — on the other, the buyers, the central banks of the ECU itself with a total common reserve of $32 billion.

Does it make sense that they are going to expend the massive support necessary to keep on taking in the Eurodollars at par? It does not. Will they buy dollars at an artificially high price? They will not. That would be foolhardy. The surplus supply is overwhelming.

To repeat: What will be the price of a dollar. The only answer is another question: What will be the price of a surplus cat?

NEW MEANING FOR GOLD

The last thing the Europeans want is a plunging dollar. The only thing they dread more is having to issue their own currencies to keep the dollar from plunging. This explains the almost complete absence of public information about the true base and the full meaning of the ECU. Expect ECU support of the dollar in the early stages, and perhaps strong support. It will last as long as the amounts are not large. But if there should be a panic out of the dollar by Eurodollar holders, expect the Europeans to let the dollar sink.

As it sinks, the dollar price of gold rises. So for Americans (not necessarily Europeans) gold may be a better investment than ever before.

Until lately, I had resisted taking the Eurodollar market into my calculations.

It was a mass of money just floating around out there, never connected with the real world of buying goods in the market place—some kind of a free satellite that would never strike the earth. I was happy to leave it there. It posed such a mind-numbing problem, I didn't know how to deal with it.

But it cannot be kept out of the real world much longer. The entire $500 billion fund is owned by people of flesh and blood, who are just as anxious to retain value as anyone else. This fund, under the circumstances, will soon begin to exert its influence. As part of it comes for sale, it begins to resemble the story of the 5,000 cats.

The European are not apt to give up much of their gold to accommodate it. What then?

The U.S. cannot support the dollar. The sum of 30 billions is tiny against the Eurodollar mass. And even the $30 billion is borrowed. Somehow the U.S. has to earn it and pay it back—or pay it back in gold.

Now the governments appear to have come to the limit of lending the U.S. their currencies. The U.S. has gone to the German public to raise Deutschemarks with a $3 billion bond offering. The Germans went in and bought like crazy. They did not understand the U.S. has no way to pay them back, except by a positive balance of trade some years down the line—or by selling gold to do so. Their own governments wouldn't lend the U.S. anymore currency. Now they are going directly to the citizens.

It is a good deal for the German Government. Instead of issuing marks (thereby aiding inflation), the U.S. banks actually take marks out of circulation in Germany.

But this is no answer at all for the Eurodollar colossus. What then?

I believe the U.S. will be forced to put up its gold to redeem its outstanding deficits around the world. It has 275 million ounces. For easy arithmetic, let's call that 250 million ounces. Against $500 billion, that means a price of $2,000 per ounce—to make good. I do not know how this will be resolved. I simply do not believe the dollar would go so low. That would be one-tenth of what it is worth today. Instead of being worth two deutschmarks as of today, the dollar would be worth one-fifth deutschmark.

If the ECU quintupled the price of gold, one dollar would be worth one deutschmark.

Perhaps the ECU will lend the U.S.A. gold or currency at a very low interest rate for 30 years or so. But acceptance of the loan will mean the greatest austerity in the American history—a deep, deep depression.

Without such a helping hand, though, I can foresee nothing but a total monetary disaster.

We cannot wish the $500 billion away!

Perhaps a combination of such steps would occur.

In any case, the ECU of January 1979 is nothing more than a first step. The price of gold will go much higher. An eventual price of $1,000 in dollars as noted earlier, and $300 in ECU is a very real possibility.

Some financial writers have talked such figures from time to time, and I have always branded them quite unrealistic. And so they were! They were pure hunches and guesses. No logic was advanced to support them.

Here are basic facts which could bring such prices into the realm of reality.

No one has dared to face the unavoidable conclusions that naturally arise from these facts.

DEFLATION AND THE FALLING DOLLAR

How does this effect the deflationary scenario? I don't think it changes it. Just because the U.S. dollar will be worth much less in terms of gold and ECU's, does not mean hyper-inflation in the U.S. In my opinion, the group of people, who have preached that we will have hyper-inflation for the simple reason the Fed has a license to issue as many dollars as they want, have not thought very deeply into the question. I said the Fed would be *blocked by the international situation.* I think it now shows up clearly.

If we have large deficits already, which are adding to the huge overhang of Eurodollars — and if the Fed continues to print up masses of bogus money*, that will only make the U.S. dollar plunge faster on the international markets. Any effort by the Fed to solve this situation by printing more dollars is courting disaster.

The bankruptcies are no less likely to occur because of the worsening position of the dollar in the international markets. In fact, they are more likely to occur. Bankruptcies have a habit of triggering one another. Whenever they start, you can expect a flock of them.

---

*Federal Reserve notes are printed by the Bureau of Printing and Engraving of the U.S. Treasury Department for the Federal Reserve System. They form the largest share of the liabilities of the Federal Reserve Banks. Until the Smithsonian Agreement broke down in 1973, these notes were twenty-five percent gold-backed. With gold officially pegged at $42.22 per ounce, Congress eliminated the gold backing, because it had reached the point where no more notes could be issued unless the price of gold were increased — which Congress refused to do. These notes are now backed by paper assets of the U.S. Government.

PRICE INCREASES AND INFLATION

Everyone seems to take it for granted that higher prices inevitably means higher inflation. That is not so. The alternative to higher prices (barring inflation) is less consumption. In other words, a lower standard of living.

For example, the oil bill will be $5 billion more. The government automatically assumes and so does everybody, this will add to inflation. However, a reduction in the consumption of $5 billion worth of oil would leave inflation exactly where it is.

As a nation we have been conditioned to thinking that the standard of living is not negotiable. Everything else may change, but not our accustomed indulgence.

Now we find the pie is smaller. Our answer is to strike. Unfortunately, that will not make a bigger pie. The huge labor unions and laissez-faire management as yet have no comprehension of this natural law. But a natural law does not yield.

Therefore, increased prices of imports can be met in either one of two ways: (a) Increased inflation, which makes the dollar an international disaster, (b) A realistic readjustment of the living standard.

In the second case, the prices of imported products do go up, but the prices of services come down. The consumption is reduced. Business profits are reduced. For a certain time unemployment will be drastically increased.

These are the birth pangs of a new era. We are about to enter it.

33. TWO CRISES

Some pages back (Chapter 30) we listed three current crises — the monetary crisis, the labor crisis, and the food crisis. Now let's examine the last two.

THE LABOR CRISIS

The labor situation is not necessarily intermixed with monetary affairs. Nevertheless it is a crisis that has helped to produce this vast inflation, and that continues to aggravate it to the point where corporations find themselves helpless against further wage increases—beyond productivity—and politicians do not have the nerve to stop issuing the necessary additional money.

Even in stable times, strong and militant labor unions tend to demand wage increases beyond any increase in productivity. The moment such extra money is injected into the monetary stream we have an element of inflation. That is clear if, again, we go back to the state of Freedonia and find that a certain group is getting money beyond what it is producing. It is watering the money supply. Which brings us back to the foundation of all society, "Thou shall not steal."

If the labor union of Freedonia demands money in excess of what it produces, diluting the value of all other people's money, then it has taken from the people. They have suffered the loss — just as if the money had been counterfeited.

Every time a group of people gets more money than its production justifies, the other members of the public pay the bill. They don't realize it, of course, until the situation becomes serious.

So we can live with strong labor unions for quite a long time if inflation is modest. The big trouble is that, once inflation gets going, the demands of the labor unions become ever more excessive. Management acquiesces and ups prices, adding to the inflationary spiral. Those workers who do not have unions and who are unable to enforce their demands, and all other people on fixed incomes, pay the bill for the excessive demands of the strong labor unions.

By the 1960s, and particularly in the '70s, the strong unions had become monopolies. Policemen would strike, threatening the loss of law and order if their demands were not met. Firemen would strike, leaving the population open to the danger of death and destruction. This, of course, was pure blackmail. But there was no possibility of negotiation with these unions if they wanted to hold out.

They had become monopolies through the device of the *closed shop*.

With the beginning of the seventies, negotiations with labor unions became a joke. You didn't negotiate. You just gave them what they wanted—or very close to it.

So a company like General Motors, or U.S. Steel, would agree to a large rate increase. During the sixties they merely tacked this on to the price of the goods and their profits remained the same—or were even more. They cared very little.

However in the seventies, as purchasing power began to shrink, the corporations were running into a wall on the other side. As long as they had room to retreat, they could yield to the labor unions. But when they hit the wall of buyer resistance, they were finding difficulty in selling their products. Now the demands of the labor unions were beginning to come out of profits—not out of additional costs. As profits shrank, the confidence in the ability of the companies to pay dividends undermined the value of their shares.

In 1975 Consolidated Edison shocked the whole investment world by dropping its dividend. When a utility could no longer pay—where was an equity that could be counted upon for an income? The flagship of all equities was sinking.

But the workers for utility companies had an even more powerful blackmail weapon than any other group. If they quit, the country would be crippled. As unions keep on striking, employers keep on paying.

Of course inflation could have been stopped by the government, in any case, if it had simply refused to increase the money supply. That should have happened long ago in the sixties. Then the corporations, unable to sell their products, would have had to close down some of their factories. The workers would find themselves without work, and would turn against their leaders who had demanded the excessive increases.

But that didn't happen. The Federal Reserve continued to issue whatever money was necessary. There was no brake anywhere on the demands of the labor unions—and therefore on prices—and therefore on the growing inflation.

By 1978 inflation had gone so far as to justify many of the demands of the labor unions. But it was a sickness that had been generated to a large extent by themselves. Nevertheless, we had now reached a stage where inflation was feeding upon itself, and there was really no way to stop it—except *to stop issuing more money.* The government would absolutely have to stop increasing the money supply unless it was matched by increased productivity. But in 1979 inflation was worse than ever, running over thirteen percent.

Of course no government *had* the courage, and no government *will have* the courage to deliberately stop increasing the money. Once again, increasing inflation becomes inevitable until it smashes itself. When it does, the labor unions will be smashed with it.

That is why declining inflation is not even a possibility. When the politicians talk about reducing inflation they are just "whistling Dixie." Once inflation is feeding on itself, there is no remedy except to kill the beast. Like a dandelion stimulated with a chemical growth-stimulant, it must grow until it dies.

So, once again, inflation must continue until eventually it demands such enormous issues of money that the money either becomes worthless or the social order is hit by mountains of bankruptcies that will wipe out the greatest portion of the money supply. In either case you end with a terrible deflation and depression.

Thus organized labor has brought upon itself a crisis that will help to destroy the social order that supports it and might then have to end with a dictatorship of either the left or the right. The only hope that such a dictatorship could be avoided would be if the deflation would set in at once, rocking corporations from one end of the country to the other and throwing millions out of work.

Unfortunately, those are the hard and unalterable facts.

THE FOOD CRISIS

We haven't said much about this, and not much will be said, because you can find it in many popular magazines. But there are a few stark facts that need to be brought to your attention. There are now millions on the verge of starvation, and many millions are already starving. Huge volumes of food must be provided if these people are to be kept alive. There are now a few less than four billion in the world, and the expectations are that we will be up to nearly seven billion by the year 2000. We have been told that technology will perform the miracle of feeding all.

Well, technology doesn't have a very good record in that respect. We have been applying ever more and more technology. When I was a boy we plowed the land with a single-furrow plow and, later on, when I was a youth, with three furrows and ten horses. At first we could cut fourteen inches of sod, and then we could cut forty-two.

Today they cut it up in swaths more like forty feet than forty inches. Monstrous machines pull huge earth-tilling equipment so that one man today produces the wheat that was produced by scores of men fifty years ago.

But we have not kept up with the food demand of the world. Population has grown faster than production in spite of the constant stimulation of advanced technology.

And this is going to continue. We might as well face the fact that it will be utterly impossible to feed the growing multitudes of human beings on this planet. Since most of the planet is too unsophisticated to practice birth control, there is not much chance that the population will stop growing. Even if they began to practice birth control now, and there was zero increase, the present youth of the world would still bring a food crisis upon us.

The world must face inevitable mass starvation.

The question is, where will this starvation take place? The advanced industrial countries have big pulpits from which the politicians preach of the necessity of sharing with the rest of the world. To bring this down to a practical application, you could then expect the following situation. The citizens of the United States would say: whereas today we consume 500 pounds of grain, and 100 pounds of meat, and 50 pounds of sugar, we know that many people in the world have hardly any of these foods; therefore to help the others survive, we must then, next year, eat only 100 pounds of grain, ten pounds of meat, and two pounds of sugar. We shall have a referendum on this, and we shall vote to dispose of our food supply in this manner—because, after all, we are generous people.

It wouldn't come to pass *exactly* that way, but it would happen in reality *just about* that way.

Politicians who intended to make this kind of a division would be voted out of office. Politicians who voted to retain the food supply for the United States would be retained.

If you wish to be a realist you cannot avoid the logic and the truth.

Then how are the increasing hundreds of millions to be fed? Not by technology. Not by the advanced countries. Not at all.

Then comes a very important moral question facing a hard-headed decision. The question is this:

If the increasing hordes cannot be fed, is it wise, or even humane to provide the present hordes with just enough food to allow them to reproduce new hordes facing certain starvation?

Are you doing them a favor by teasing them along at a bare subsistence level by virtue of a program that you know you cannot continue?

What can the developing countries do about it as their populations increase? What can the industrial countries do about it? And what will happen to the leaders of the industrial countries that do something about it to the point where it begins to pinch their own populations?

And how can anything be done as long as world money remains in its present chaotic condition, moving toward a state of collapse?

And the next and final question is: what can you do about it?

34. WHAT'S THE BEST WAY TO FACE THE PROBLEM?

The first thing you can do about it is to recognize that you can do little more than look after yourself and yours. You will be doing society a favor if you do that. If there are enough people who can remain healthy and self-sufficient, there is still a chance that able leadership will emerge.

In doing so, the first and most important question you must consider is whether we are faced with another wave of inflation, or whether, indeed, deflation is now on its way. These answers call for completely opposite reactions.

If there is going to be another wave of inflation, you should load up with debt and then pay off with cheaper dollars. If, on the other hand, we are now heading into deflation, you should get rid of every dollar of debt and hold cash and hard-core asssets.

Another wave of inflation presumes the Fed has the will and, what is more important, the *ability* to inject new billions into the money stream.

An increase of the money supply depends mainly upon borrowing. Unless the psychology of the American consumer can be turned around, consumers will not start new borrowing that will create more new money. Until consumers start to demand more and buy more, business will not expand more. Therefore business will not borrow more. Therefore, in spite of the great increase in the money supply caused by the Federal deficits, the total money supply will continue to shrink. As it shrinks it will bring about bankruptcies, and these bankruptcies will cause others, which will end in a great domino display of deflation. The destruction of money will far outpace the manufacture of money by the Fed, and we shall be plunged into the worst depression in the history of the world.

But even if inflation should continue unabated for some time, gold and silver holdings remain the answer. Deflation or inflation, the end is a wreck.

It is as though you are driving a car down a steep and icy mountain road. You are going fifty miles an hour, and you have a mile to go. If you put on the brakes you will go spinning over the cliff. If you don't put on the brakes you will be going so fast that you will end up a junk heap at the bottom of the road. Your mistake was that you got going at that speed on this road in the first place. It is too late now for you to rectify the situation. The further down the road you travel, the icier it gets and the steeper it gets—and already you dare not touch the brakes.

This is a true analogy to our extended money system. I do not believe it can be successfully denied or refuted.

In the event of deflation, cash itself would be a very good thing to hold. You will have to watch the developments, and if the present budget deficits do not result in growing inflation, you can be pretty sure we are headed on the road to deflation.

That means the bankruptcies of many banks. It seems that the Federal Reserve would stand behind the first banks. But the question I have asked, without getting a satisfactory answer, is this: What happens when people, terrorized by the failure of a major bank supported only in the nick of time by the Federal Reserve, get scared that the Federal Reserve might not back the next failure. Wouldn't they draw out their money in massive amounts, causing a run on all banks?

Even a greater danger, as pointed out by John Exter*, might be the large holders of funds in banks—in other words, banks. If a large bank were in danger, it is quite possible that the other banks holding deposits in that bank would withdraw their funds, as would the big holders of Certificates of Deposits in the hundreds of thousands of dollars. What you would have when the deflation actually arrives would be a debacle and a destruction of money unimaginable.

So if you have cash, certainly keep a close eye on the situation, and, if you see danger developing—not necessarily just in the United States, but with large banks in other countries—you ought to be withdrawing that cash and changing it either to gold or silver, or actually holding it in greenback form in your own possession or in well-guarded safety deposit boxes.

I am reproducing here a concept devised by John Exter but drawn by me that shows you the hard core of the money pyramid—the last-ditch-stand of hard money when everything else goes to pieces. At the top you have the instruments of credit and the stocks, and then the bonds, and then the treasury

---

*John Exter, the former Governor of the Central Bank of Ceylon, Senior Vice-President of First National City Bank, New York, economist for the Federal Reserve Board, and Acting Chief of the Far Eastern Section of its Reserve Division

bills and the cash, and at last the silver and the gold.

If and when worst comes to worst, you must dig to the bottom of this pyramid for utter security.

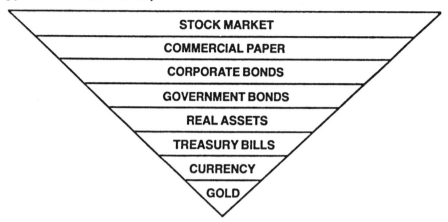

THE UPSIDE DOWN PYRAMID OF CREDIT. The above graph is qualitative and illustrative only and represents the author's concept of safety.

There is growing evidence that people have begun to head for the bottom part of the pyramid already. The rising price of gold and the heavily oversubscribed auctions of gold at the U.S. Treasury and the I.M.F. show it clearly. Also the fact that the price is strongest when large quantities are offered indicate that very big money has entered the picture. Trying to buy such quantities on the open market would be self-defeating because it would only push the price very high, and the quantity just isn't there.

There's also growing evidence of a rush to the second lowest part of our inverse pyramid—cash itself.

Actual currency in the hands of the public is increasing at record rates. Every week of 1978 saw an increase in currency of approximately 10% over the corresponding weeks of 1977.

This is most surprising since the rash of credit card buying has increased by leaps and bounds, and hardly anyone uses cash for purchases anymore.

Yet currency increased ten billion last year. With a twenty million population, that amounts to $500 for every man, woman and child—$2000 per family of four.

Total greenbacks in circulation is now $103.8 billion.

I find it hard to believe that these great increases in currency are in general circulation. Rather, it seems to bear the earmarks of currency hoarding. That's quite a reflection, because, if true, it means a growing belief that real currency, even if inflated, is better than figures in books. As Will Rogers said: "I'm not worried about the return on my capital, I'm just worried about the return of my capital."

And now to get quite specific.

35. WHAT CAN BE DONE BY THE GOVERNMENT

It is clear that money and energy are inextricably intertwined. Our weakened energy situation is one of the direct results of our weakened money.

In the beginning, money was a warehouse receipt for goods. Whenever money became less than that, it bought less, always in proportion to the amount it had been watered down. We saw that demonstrated in our mythical state of Fredonia.

Adulterated money in itself would be bad enough, but after the adulteration occurs, another factor enters which accelerates the process. That factor is *expectation* of further adulteration, resulting in higher prices.

The *expectation* is the real disease.

Prices and labour demands rise according to the degree of the *expectation*. The only way the government can cure the disease is to cure the root cause by getting back to the pure *warehouse receipt. Enter energy.*

The most basic material we have is energy. All goods require energy to produce, from flour through clothing, shelter, to automobiles and airplanes. The fundamental building block for our industrial society is *energy.*

What has happened is that the United States (issuing the world's money) has issued warehouse receipts for goods (energy) which are in somebody else's warehouse. The Arabs' warehouse.

This won't work any longer. What are we to do? Pay for energy with real goods or warehouse receipts for real goods. How can we convince people that our warehouse receipt is valid? Only by offering to produce the real goods upon presentation of the receipt.

216

What goods shall we offer?

We can't offer something our suppliers don't want. *We must then offer a warehouse receipt for something that our supplier can present to any person anywhere for his real goods.* The warehouse receipt must always represent our guarantee of "value" in redeemable goods. Over the course of centuries the only universally acceptable commodity to stand this test is gold.

Only by offering real, gold-backed money can we expect to continue to obtain adequate supplies of foreign energy.

But in order not to deplete our stockpile of gold (whatever the price per ounce) we must also work hard to produce goods that others want, and that are exchangeable for true warehouse receipts from other governments. All warehouse receipts must be convertible into the universally acceptable gold.

This means, initally, a drastic deterioration in our standard of living. We must *conserve more, consume less,* and *sell more.*

Or we must produce energy ourselves so we will not have to give up so many warehouse receipts to get it.

As a nation, we must:

1. back our money with gold.

2. utilize the energy abundantly available at our feet - the most plentiful supply of energy in the world — *Coal.*

Until the U.S. government gets up the courage to take the first step and the initiative to take the second, we are on a downward spiral. The end of that spiral, is the ruin of our system.

How much longer can we put off facing the truth?

THE PRACTICAL STEPS

The U.S. will have to get together with leading industrial nations in a new monetary agreement that will numerate all the money by weight in gold. As a result the price of gold will have to be somewhere in the broad area of $500 to $1,000 per ounce.

The price will depend on how much of the present money evaporates into thin air as a result of bankruptcies and defaults in the coming depression. It depends on the degree of capital deflation. The more deflation, the less floating money, the nearer we may approach the $500 price. The less deflation, (or the more continuing inflation) the nearer we will have to come to the $1000 mark. The higher mark is more likely.

As for energy, the U.S. Government will have to join hands with industry much as it did during the synthetic rubber crisis of World War II. Surely the government must be aware that our energy vulnerability is far more serious to our existence than the rubber crisis ever was. It must also see that *volume potential* far outweighs *price* as a criterion. (If you need a certain amount of air per hour to live in a confined cubicle, your prime consideration is volume, let the price be what it may).

In consequence, the government will have to change those laws that now shackle the coal industry. It will have to authorize and encourage coal slurry pipelines, encourage electric generating plants to switch from oil to coal. It will have to back up the railroads, and help them refurbish their tracks.

It must use as much coal as possible on stationary energy. If we can save our indigenous oil for transportation, we'll get through.

The government must push mass transport, busses, railroads--even for short runs.

The life of our nation is at stake. The *KEY* to survival is volume. The answer to survival is *COAL.*

36.
WHAT YOU CAN DO ABOUT IT

No one can say how much further inflation will go before the bust. But we really do not need to know. As far as our personal preservation is concerned, what we should do is already quite clear:

1. In general we should convert our surplus assets into either energy or gold.

2. We must prepare our personal lives for the bust and its aftermath. To be specific:

Convert bonds and financial instruments of all kinds, including outstanding credits, as well as money from the sale of properties, to gold. Avoid conversion into any currency. Some currencies are better than than others (those countries who have warehouses stocked with gold or energy) but none are as good as gold.

Your home should not be sold. You always need a home. If you have a retreat it should not be sold.

Gold should be bought in a form and size that is easily disposed of. For example, if you have $120,000, and gold is $300 per ounce, you don't want to convert your $120,000 into a 400-ounce bar of gold. If you wanted $2,000 you would have to sell the whole bar or place it in custody of someone from whom you would borrow. Never jeopardize your gold by letting someone else hold it as collateral. They might go broke.

Your $120,000 should be converted into coins which you can use one by one without disturbing or moving your major holdings.

What coins?

Those coins which have the lowest premium over gold content. As of latter 1979 this was the South African krugerand, exactly one ounce of gold.

If you buy gold coins such as the "American eagle" carrying a large premium over the gold content, you have entered the field of numismatics. That is an entirely different field. We do not wish to contaminate our warehouse gold with imaginary or psychological values that may or may not endure.

The Austrian kroner is also a coin which comes at relatively low premium. The krugerand is probably the better because it is legal tender of a sovereign nation.

In buying coins the price may vary from dealer to dealer. To test the offering price you should check with a large and responsible institution such as a bank. You may find it hard to get a solid price from many U.S. banks. It would therefore be advisable for you to phone the Bullion Department of the Bank of Nova Scotia in any major Canadian city and ask them for both their selling and buying price of krugerands on that day. The Bank of Nova Scotia is the official bullion dealer in Canada. It works right off the London gold market.

If the Bank of Nova Scotia's price is better than any coin dealer's price, after you add freight and insurance charges for sending it to you, then of course have it sent. The international movement of gold is free. It may well be, however, that after you add these charges you can do just as well with a reputable coin dealer.

WHERE TO KEEP YOUR GOLD

This gets back to temperament and conditions. Some people like their wealth nearby. Some don't. Some are suitably equipped. Some aren't. If you live in an apartment block in a large city, your best bet is probably a safety deposit box. Make sure that your wife (and, in the event that the two of you should die simultaneously, another member of your family), are registered with the right to enter the box. You could even put it in your joint three names.

There is no law that says you must disclose where you keep your personal and private property or how much you have. Theoretically, at least, that privacy is part of our system. You don't have to note it down as part of your estate. Your successors or partners in the box may wish to declare your share as part of the estate. This is a moral matter, and outside our discussion.

If you live in a house with a back yard you can safely bury your gold in a plastic container. The coins will never deteriorate no matter how much it rains or snows. Paper money must be absolutely sealed so that it is completely air - and moisture-proof.

Make sure that your wife and at least one other member of your family knows exactly where the gold is kept.

Some people can't see paying the fee for a safety deposit box on something that can be just as safely held at home.

However, if you have any reservations, you should not keep gold at home. If you talk about it at all, someone might force you, at gunpoint, to hand it over.

Therefore if anyone knows that you do keep gold coins, or is even apt to suspect that you might have such holdings at home, you should by all means use a safety deposit box; the security will be better than your own.

YOU SHOULD BUY SILVER

Silver is also a warehouse receipt and compared with all else except gold, platinum and diamonds, can be stored in the smallest space. It is much weaker concentration of money than gold. Silver takes up about thirty times as much space in equivalent value. It is comparatively unwieldy.

You need silver, though, for smaller purchases. A pre-1965 silver quarter is worth $1.00 to $1.50. You can tell at any given time what the approximate price should be. A quarter was worth twenty-five cents when silver was $1.33 per ounce - so if silver is $13.30 per ounce your coin should be worth about ten times as much as its face - that is $2.50.

For a number of years I have advised people to keep two or three thousand dollars (face value) in silver coins. This will take a fairly large safety box. If you store it at home it will take up about the same amount of space as $60,000 to $90,000 in gold. Additionally it will tarnish. Of course that is not serious. The value is not impaired. It will not rust. Probably the best way to buy silver coins is in bags of $1,000 face value, called junk silver, on the Mercantile Exchange in New York. At least you can get the true market quote on value. You can also buy these coins from several reputable coin dealers. Always check on the New York bag price before doing so. If you buy in smaller quantities than the $1,000 bag you will probably have to pay a little higher price per ounce from a dealer.

The same scale holds for relative values. The $1,000 bag was worth $1,000 in silver when silver was $1.33 per ounce. So if silver is over $13.00 per ounce, a $1,000 bag ought to be worth over $13,000. These figures serve as a rough guideline.

Some silver should be kept at home rather than in the safety box. It's always possible that a crisis could come up over some weekend and banks would be closed for a few days. In these uncertain times we don't know what might happen.

In the event of the banks closing, your safety deposit box is still okay. Banks, even if they go broke, cannot take over the contents of the rented boxes.

What you do, of course, depends on your personal circumstances. You will have to use your own common sense with respect to:

a. The amount of gold and silver you wish to hold.

b. Where you will keep it so that you can get at it in an emergency. Keep it in mind that we could be overtaken by such chaos that even travel might be hazardous over temporary periods.

I do not advise that you buy platinum, even though it may hold its value, because *exchangeability* is just as important as value. The exchangeability of silver coins is unquestioned anywhere. The same is true of gold. If you have a platinum bar you might have to hunt around a while before you can realize your money on it. Not everybody buys platinum. Certainly your grocery supplier would not want to exchange groceries for a piece of platinum of unquestioned quality but unquoted value.

I do *not* recommend that you buy diamonds. Here again we come to the convenience of the marketplace. If you want goods from a clothing store, you will have to use cash or silver; you could even use gold. A diamond is a different matter. You would have to take it to a dealer to appraise and to exchange for cash. Normally the retail price on diamonds is so much higher than the amount you could realize, that your loss is likely to be very serious. If you buy from a reliable diamond wholesaler you may be getting proper value together with a certificate.

I mistrust certificates. When diamonds are changing hands, the certificates change hands with them. What is to prevent someone in the course of exchanges from substituting the certificate for an inferior diamond and then taking the perfect diamond and getting another cetificate? Quite possible. If things get to the point where silver and gold are vital and necessary, you don't need any more complications. You want something that is instantly acceptable as value.

Nor is there any reason to think that the value of diamonds will increase faster than the value of gold, or that the value of platinum will increase faster.

Keep in mind we are not doing this to make money. We are doing this to preserve what we have. In any case, we are comparing oranges and apples because when we buy gold we are buying from a monetary standpoint and when we buy platinum we are buying mostly from an industrial standpoint. When we buy diamonds we are buying something comparable to art or to numismatics. Inherent in the price of diamonds is what people are willing to pay for them. They are apt to reach their highest price at the top of the inflation spiral when people are scrambling to get out of cash into something of real value. But within the depth of the bust the bidding for diamonds would, in my opinion, cool down considerably. I would think that you might very well stand to lose, even if you got the full price of the certified and accredited diamond.

I think diamonds find their greatest use when times are so bad that people have to flee their homelands. The value of diamonds is so concentrated that it can be effectively concealed whereas even gold cannot.

THE QUESTION OF GREENBACKS

Apart from your silver and gold, you should have cash money instantly available. The amount again depends on your situation. If your savings are small—let's say you have one or two thousand dollars in the bank—you should probably keep at least a quarter of that in cash at home at all times. You never know when you may need instant cash. If banks are closed, you are just out of luck.

If you are in the bracket where you have cash savings of $20,000, your gold and silver holdings should be at least $80,000. For instance, one-fifth of your money should be the maximum you hold in cash.

It is prudent to have enough real cash—actual greenbacks—to serve your needs for a period of three to six months.

Today, banks prominently advertise the F.D.I.C. insurance coverage. To me this is a danger signal. Ten years ago they had the same coverage, but I never saw it mentioned anywhere. Now I see it displayed in every branch of every bank and savings and loan, large and small. That fund amounts to about one percent of the total savings deposits. It couldn't handle more than two or three large banks, if that. The insurance fund would go broke at about the same time a fourth bank went broke - maybe even a third bank. It is a nerve pacifier. It is meant to instil confidence in every depositor when he walks into the bank. The fact that we need this confidence is not a good sign.

We have different money today than we had 30—50 years ago. Today we have check-book money. Of more than a trillion dollars of such kinds of money, we have only one hundred billion dollars in cash. In the case of bankruptcies, figures in books can disappear; wiped out as with a magic ink eraser. They're simply gone. Actual greenbacks, whatever they may be worth, cannot be made to disappear by that kind of magic.

Getting your bank account might not be simple. It's not really payable on demand.

This is not *news* in the sense that it's new. It's *news* in the sense it's known.

You have $10,000 in the bank. In case of a national emergency, you could not go in and draw it out. At their discretion, the banks or the S & L's may give you a portion of it and a portion at further stated dates.

S & L 's need not pay on demand anymore than $1,000. Your remaining $9,000 goes to the bottom of the list and will be paid if the money holds out, and when it is available.

Commercial banks can invoke a *withdrawal moratorium system*, and might pay you one percent, or twenty percent, or as their ability provides, holding up the remainder indefinitely.

I went into my bank to see exactly what the rule is. Here it is: *"The "depositor" may at anytime be required by the bank to give notice in writing of an intended withdrawal not less than thirty days nor more than six months before such withdrawal is made. If it is not made within five days after the expiration of such withdrawal notice, withdrawal rights pursuant thereto shall be considered waived and a new notice shall be required."*

There must be a reason. The *reason* for this provision signifies recognition of the unpalatable proposition: Demand could exceed the supply of money; then the demand would have to be curbed.

The Federal Depository Insurance Corporation has $9 billion. In the event of a panic it would have to reckon with $980 billion. One bank okay. Many banks—no good!

So I foresee the possibility where greenbacks will be money but bank deposits may not be money, and where all kinds of promises such as bonds and notes may not be money.

The next best thing to greenbacks are treasury bills. They are direct obligations of the U.S. Treasury. In every respect they have the same value and the same guarantee as the greenbacks. But there still remains the intermediate catch. If cash is rationed and you have a $100,000 Treasury bill you are not nearly in the same position as if you had the $100,000 in the safety deposit box. The bill you have will be recognized, but the teller may very well inform you that you can get only $1,000 on it today.

The storage problem for greenbacks is more difficult than for gold and silver. If placed in the ground, unless they are absolutely sealed, moisture will in time penetrate and dampen them. They have been known to be destroyed by rot. That doesn't mean they can't be stored this way. It's just that you have to be a lot more careful. Thermos containers are okay if tightly sealed. They should be examined once every few months.

I don't want to give the impression that I am recommending that you take everything you have and put it in the ground. I am merely trying to put enough in your hands so that you will be able to meet any emergency without difficulty and without depending on others.

(I suggest these measures because they have been used by man in the face of war, revolution and chaos for a long, long time. They are methods that go back to the hard lessons learned in troubled times. They are basic survival thoughts, and as such they belong in this discussion.)

The biggest danger with holding greenbacks is that continuing inflation shrinks them, whereas if they are in a Treasury bill the inflationary result is reduced. But if you are in the fifty percent tax bracket it is by no means eliminated. If you have $100,000 in Treasury bills at ten percent interest, and if the inflation is ten percent, you might say you are even. You are, until Uncle Sam gets in for half the ten percent. You still lose five percent.

People seem to be greatly impressed because Treasury bill interest rates are so high. They're not high at all. The result of a substantial Treasury bill is in the end a loss - no interest at all. The point is that with the greenbacks your loss would be the full ten percent.

You must weigh, depending upon how much money you are talking about, what the net difference is to you if you keep the emergency cash in greenbacks or in a Treasury bill. If the amount is so small that the net result is only $50 or $100 a year, why take the risk? If it's a large amount it will probably be worthwhile holding until such time as you see things deteriorate to a point where the banking system is in danger.

PERMISSIBLE PAPER

Money will always be made. To succeed in life you don't have to be cleverer than the next fellow, you just have to be a day earlier. If you are a year earlier, so much the better. Money will be made from those industries and commodities which serve the new situation. The opportunities for profit will be much less numerous than the chances of loss, but if you can pick these opportunities you will not only survive, you will profit. This may at first sight seem selfish and immoral. Quite the reverse. What's moral about losing your money? If *everybody were to lose*, the total society would be so much the worse off. Those who survive and profit will provide the foundation for the recovery. Because you have survived, or even profited, does not mean you have harmed your neighbour who may have taken a different route, and been less successful.

For those who have enough money to ensure their survival and who wish to speculate on the growth possibilities of the new era, I offer here some suggestions. Like all our other conclusions they arise right out of the body of this book.

I believe those who are in gold will profit handsomely from their holdings of the solid metal in the form of coins. But the shares of profitable mines will increase a great deal more percentage-wise. If you buy a share of a company which is paying a $1.00 dividend with gold at a price of $200, and if gold doubles to $400, the gold itself has increased 100 percent; but in the case of the share, the basic production costs have already been written off at the $200 figure, and most of the increase is profit. Therefore the $1.00 dividend may very well become a $3.00 dividend, or even more. Accordingly the price should rise 300 percent or more as compared to the 100 percent increase in the gold price. This applies in the production of any commodity whose price is on the rise. When you buy a share of a producing property, you buy an ownership in that property; an ownership in the reserves owned by that corporation.

We have narrowed our principal problems to money and energy. If we are going to take part of our capital and try for a more speculative increase, we should concentrate on these two opportunities.

We have to be careful here that we do not simply buy ideas or high sounding new schemes. Dealing first with the subject of money, you should not speculate beyond the purchase of shares in gold mines with known reserves. This limits us almost at once to South African gold mines. It is unwise—and indeed it would be foolish at this writing—to make specific stock recommendations. I can only give you guidelines:

Two reliable bell-wether stocks in South Africa are East Dreifontaine and West Dreifontaine. The first is a mine of long life, over thirty years, with the lowest production costs per ounce of any in South Africa. Its ore is quite rich. At the time of writing the stock is selling at about $14, and the dividend for the current twelve months ought to be between $1.70 and $2.00. The South African stocks have been paying seventeen percent and better in 1979. This stock is already up from a low of $8.00 in the fall of 1978. The gold to produce $1.70 dividend was selling at about $230 per ounce. A gold price of around $300 ought at least to increase the dividend—perhaps $2.50 to $3.00 per share. Because of the prospects of gold rising much higher (See the chapter on Thousand Dollar Gold) I expect this appreciation to continue over the long term. Therefore it is difficult to guess what the price of East Dreifontaine might be if indeed gold rises to a price of $500 to $1,000 over the next few years. The beauty of the situation is that the production cost is so low and the life of the mine is so long that you could wait anything out.

West Dreifontaine has been like a flagship of the South African stocks, always leading the pack. Its life is probably 10-15 years, but its gold quality is very high and it has the second cheapest cost of production. Because its veins are richer, it pays an even better dividend than East Dreifontaine. Also it reacts faster to an increase in the price of gold. West Dreifontaine was selling at about $22.00 when East Dreifontaine was selling at $8 to $9. In June of 1979 West Dreifontaine had risen to $48, more than double, while East Dreifontaine had risen to $14. The West Dreifontaine semi-annual dividend for June 1979 was $4.11 per share with gold selling in the $235 range most of the period.

If, when you read this book, you decide to put a portion of your wealth in shares, I suggest you look at these two stocks closely, but that before you buy you make a very thorough study of the rest of the stocks. You should be in touch with a broker who is somewhat of a specialist in the South African stocks.

You must be aware of a risk here which you do not take with solid gold. Nothing is quite as good as the real thing.

South African gold stocks are dependent to a large degree on the political stability of South Africa. The weakened position of the west in the Middle East would seem to dictate an increasingly friendly attitude towards South Africa. The fuel supplies of the Western world have to pass around the Cape. Only the friendly ports of South Africa can be a haven to them. For this reason I believe that confidence in South Africa will increase rather than decrease. Its problems may turn out to be fewer than the problems of the United States itself.

Nevertheless, when you buy these stocks, you must be fully aware that they are less secure than gold itself.

Silver should also be mentioned. It acts quite differently from gold, when we come to monetary fundamentals. Gold has no business rising above $250 unless it is to represent the world's money. Industrially, we are consuming about eighty percent of the world's gold production. We are using it for gold jewelry, which is just another form of hoarding gold. It is not needed for photography or for important industrial processes. It is principally important in the monetary situation.

Silver is a mixed bag. It will never lose certain monetary aspects, and these will help to buoy it up. But the monetary influence will be much less significant than with gold. As we run into a choked down economy, the industrial use of silver will decline. People will not be buying and exposing as much film in very hard times as they are now.

To offset that, silver will remain a coveted store of value. Its monetary aspects will still, I think, cause it to rise in price, to make it highly desirable as a metal of adornment and of rock-solid pocketbook security. But I think it will lack the flamboyance of gold. Therefore you should be a little more careful about selecting silver stocks than gold stocks. If you do buy silver stocks the best are those in the Coeur d'Alene area. But be careful to buy only stocks with known substantial reserves and to investigate thoroughly their dividend records, their production in ounces, their management. At the moment of writing the most often referred to are the Coeur mine, Hecla, Callahan, and Sunshine. This is not meant to be a comprehensive list, merely a guideline.

I would place silver stocks definitely secondary to gold and only a small percentage should be put into the silver stocks, if used at all.

Platinum is a very scarce and a very prized metal but if the production of automobiles falls drastically, the demand is bound to decrease from present expectations. It is these expectations which give platinum its present price of around $400 per ounce.

In short, when it comes to buying paper, restrict yourself to the stocks of the monetary metals, silver and gold—with one exception—energy.

ENERGY INVESTMENT

Gold and energy are each a store of value. Gold is an exchangeable store of value providing the recipient with a means to avoid a cumbersome system of barter. The store of value which is energy is less flexible until it has been transformed into gold. A relationship is developing between these two which can make them almost interchangeable from the standpoint of long-term investment. There are two prerequisites for a long-term investment. The first is the protection of the asset. We want to be quite certain to eliminate any danger of shrinkage.

The second prerequisite is growth. We want to invest in something that is going to be worth more. We want to do the same thing that the public will do, but we want to do it a day earlier, a year earlier, maybe five years earlier. It must be energy and it must have a future. Our previous discussions can nail that down to one word—coal.

These investment prospects can be broken down into three categories:
1. The owners of the coal
2. The processors of the coal
3. The service companies of coal

The big owners are the major oil companies. Very quietly they have acquired coal properties as they have foreseen in advance the end of the petroleum era. Initially, this prescience will not cause appreciation of those oil company shares. What it does do is put a foundation beneath them. Considering the future of coal, and considering the size of the companies, they begin to qualify as outstanding blue-chip investment prospects for the future. They have already put behind them the confiscation of their properties in foreign lands. Controls are coming off in North America. To save itself, the country will have to turn them loose. Their future in oil production will be a dwindling one, but that will be more than offset by their future in the mining of coal and in the processing. Two giants stand out.

Exxon Donor-Solvent system can handle a wide range of coal seams and at the same time accommodate a wide flexibility of product production. The naphtha yield can be as low as twenty-five percent or as high as fifty-five percent of the total liquid product. The less naphtha taken, the more heating oil produced. The naphtha potential is important because it is the foundation of gasoline.

Gulf is in the picture not only with properties but with its subsidiary *Pittsburgh and Midway Coal Mining Company*. This company's process mixes coal with a solvent, then introduces hydrogen under heat to form liquid hydrocarbon. Sulphur is side-tracked, processed and sold. Products include pipeline gas, liquified gas, naphtha and fuel oil. The elimination of the sulphur problem is very important because it opens up sulphur coal reserves which are far more plentiful than low sulphur coal. The fact that the U.S. and West German governments are jointly sharing a cost in the perfection of this process places it among the top candidates for large-scale commercial production.

Once a company like *Gulf* and its subsidiary got going on the practically unlimited sulphur coal reserves one could expect phenomenal growth over at least two decades. The fact that Germany with its huge sulphur coal reserves has chosen to enter the picture is an added plus.

Combustion Engineering is working on a third highly promising technology that involves siphoning off the gas from burning powdered coal and treating it electrically to make petroleum products while directing the hot gases to steam boilers for the generation of electricity. A partner in the situation is *Avco Everett Research Laboratory Inc.* which is now designing a 100 MHD plant.

The above are sort of double headers, both owners and processors. But there are many companies which own large coal reserves. It is not my place here to give you a financial rundown of these individual companies. You can hunt them down yourself. One example though, is the *North American Coal Corporation*. Its coal reserves are the equivalent of 20 billion barrels of oil, about two-thirds of the total oil reserves of the U.S.A. Its five billion tons of coal are located in Pennsylvania, Ohio and the huge open pit potential in North Dakota. Producing about ten million tons a year and selling at $25 a share in mid-1979, the company was expected to pay a dividend of $2.50 to $3.00 per share. At present production rates North American Coal would have enough to last it for 500 years.

In the service end of the business, the biggest is the *Fluor Corporation*, now engaged in building the biggest coal gassification plant in the world in South Africa. South Africa is approaching 75% self-sufficiency in energy including synthetic gasoline and gas.

Other large companies involved in this kind of work are *Foster Wheeler, Ralph M. Parsons, Dupont, Dravo Corp.*, a specialist in coal gassification.

The service industry for this new giant of the next twenty years will have to be developed. It hasn't really got started but you will find many companies getting into the picture. Just as *Schlumberger, Dowell* and *Hughes Tool* were record-setters as service companies to oil, so you will find service companies to coal. A whole new family will spring up. The first and most obvious are the railroads.

Santa Fe Railroad moved five million tons of coal in 1976, 5.7 million in 1977, 9.2 million in 1978, 18 (expected) in 1979.

Burlington Northern increased from 50 million in 1977 to 63 million in 1978, expects a larger increase in 1979.

Best railroad prospects for coal freight are those who will carry the low sulphur coal from the west.

The purpose of all of the above is no more than to open up for you a new vista of investment opportunities in the coming age of capitalized coal.

It would require a whole book to analyze and present these opportunities. My purpose is not that. If a person is blindfolded you do not lead him around by the arm where he wants to go. You take off the bandage so he can see for himself. I hope I have turned on the lights. I leave it to others, and there will be many, to amplify the energy opportunities that lie ahead of us.

As our old way of life approaches its end, out of the ashes will rise new industry—a new Aladdin's lamp for America. Just as we had the great sweep of *steel*; then *railroads*; then *automobiles*; then *oil*; then *aeroplanes*; then *chemicals*; then *electronics*; now we shall have *coal*.

We shall go through a deep valley. At the end of it we shall come out in the sunshine.

The most important part of it now is to get through the next five to ten years unscathed, and maybe to come out even stronger.

THE NEXT FIVE YEARS

There will be other fields of opportunity. New ideas and new companies will spring up to make use of the wind, of geothermal energy, and particularly of solar energy. None of these, however, for the next twenty years will be more than helpmates to coal. Many upstarts will bite the dust, more than will succeed. Investments in these companies will usually be highly speculative. Some fortunes, of course, will be made. The greater risk involved the higher the rewards. The trouble is that too often there are no rewards at all—nothing but loss. You will hear of countless new marvellous ideas which will fade away with their promoters. Only use money that you are prepared to lose on most of these schemes.

But there will be other profitable fields. Whenever circumstances change drastically, new needs arise. To those who are first to see and satisfy these needs come fame and fortune. Once penniless entrepreneurs even in our generation have built empires. Some of you younger people who read this book will be among that class I am sure, in the next five to ten years. It is just the penniless entrepreneur who is the man to do it. Fired with an idea and great ambition, he will take any risk; fortunately he has nothing to lose.

Beyond that, certain existing industries will do well during the coming depression. People always need to escape their troubles. There will be a lot of reading, so the publishing industry will be good. There will be a lot of walking and that should mean something for the shoe industry. There will be a lot of cycling, and I recommended as long as three years ago stocks in bicycle companies which I understand have done exceptionally well. Small motor bikes and motorcycles will increase in great numbers. Home entertainment devices including fascinating games and new television schemes will prosper. Garden equipment companies will enjoy major growth. Seed companies and do-it-yourself devices of all kinds will come into their own, as the service industry now employing half our people withers on the vine. You should be alert to these opportunities. *They will be there.*

But your first consideration must be your security—your fortress to endure.

PERSONAL SURVIVAL

The subject itself suggests disaster. Guard against over-reacting to the suggestion. It can be as harmful to go overboard in panic as to remain passive.

First, remember that we are not talking about war. We are not talking about the end of America. The country will still function. People will walk the streets, drive the highways, and go to work. Secondly, we are not talking about prolonged paralysis. We are talking about a temporary paralysis which will be bad enough to justify extensive preparation.

In essence we are anticipating a paralyzing initial shock resulting in a massive but temporary dislocation. We are talking about arriving at a *realization* that our way of life has changed and will never be quite the same again.

Following that, we are talking about a painfully slow convalescence. It will take a lot of time to adjust to new austere conditions—to face a reality we have refused to face for so long. We are like a rich man who is over his head in debt, shutting his eyes to the inevitable bankruptcy; paralyzed for a time after it happens, finally picking himself up and beginning to rebuild his life on a reduced scale. He can still enjoy the sun and the flowers, his family and his friends, his intellect, his body. Gone are the servants and the pomp, the cars and the boats, the furs and the flowers, and above all the grand feeling of power and wealth. Rebuilding and re-adjusting will take a lot of time, probably years.

I use the analogy because it is dead on. America is bankrupt. We are hopelessly in debt. We never can pay. The only reason we have been able to avoid the truth is that our creditors haven't closed in yet. Our creditors are ourselves.

Our creditors are foreigners as well but the biggest credit resides in the liabilities of banks, and the bonds of corporations and government— municipal, state and federal. This kind of situation always comes a cropper, and when it does the nation will go into a state of financial and monetary shock similar to the bankrupt individual. The federal insurance corporation (one percent of bank funds insured) will be swept away like a dike made of straw.

That's the day the shock will hit; pandemonium at first, and for a while chaos. You cannot rule out widespread violence and looting. I doubt that the chaos could last as much as six months. Even a wild bronco, put in ropes, eventually reaches a period of exhaustion. But that six months, or three months, whatever, may be the most crucial period of your life. I do not want any reader of this book to wake up one Monday morning to a bank closing and say: "I meant to get money out yesterday."

Your principal elements of concern are money, physical protection, shelter, transportation, food.

MONEY

This has been pretty well covered already. I want to emphasize emergency cash at home, well secured, and totally secret. Cash can be kept anywhere from beneath a floorboard in a tenement to a concealed concrete vault in a mansion, or in a sealed container under the garden. This also applies to your silver coinage and your emergency gold coinage, if you are in that bracket.

My main objection to safety boxes in banks miles from where you live, or in the heart of populated areas, is that if things get bad enough, you would not like to take the risk of getting there and back.

If you wanted to fly out of the country or drive to a retreat you might want to do so quickly, by-passing the city and by-passing the bank which might be closed for a few days in any case. The logic of this survival money rests on a personal decision and is likely to differ according to circumstances.

So much for money.

PROTECTION

The first consideration is security. That means first of all good locks and strongly bolted doors. In suburban residences a strong floodlight at entrances, automatically triggered by light conditions, is an effective deterrent. Thieves and looters would rather see the place in darkness. Exposure worries them.

A good apartment block will probably increase its own security, but your door lock is your own business.

Where practical, a good dog is also a deterrent, especially one of the big breeds, Great Dane, St. Bernard, Newfoundland. One bark out of these monsters will send all but the bravest robbers scurrying. A German Shepherd can be much fiercer but the problem with that is it may be fierce to your friends as well. The big dogs are mainly bluff, but the robber can't be sure and their bluff is often enough.

Firearms are tricky. If you don't know how to use them, you are probably better off without them. Never show a firearm you don't intend to fire. It could get you killed. Never aim unless you are prepared to pull the trigger. If a warning shot doesn't spur the intruder to flight, you have no choice but shoot to kill, if your life or the life of your family is threatened.

Don't monkey with firearms unless you are *completely* familiar with the piece you are using. You might, in the excitement, forget to release the safety catch and end up shot.

You should have your door equipped with a peephole, your windows fully blinded. Allow no entry unless it's someone you know. And don't buy the firearms and forget to lay in the ammunition. You don't need a lot.

SHELTER

Some will be able to have a retreat and some won't. If you do have a retreat, don't take your safety any more for granted than you would at home. Hoodlums will spread far and wide from the big cities and these will be the most dangerous. In an isolated retreat you should take every precaution outlined above and you certainly should have firearms. You should have only one main entrance, and you should be equipped to floodlight it.

In making the shelter (home) secure, each person must use his own common sense according to his circumstances. In certain cases neighbours can team up for security. In other cases you have to go it alone. In the shelter you should have candles, kerosene lamps or coleman propane lamps. There are bound to be power failures. You should have propane or high-test coleman stoves. Propane is probably better because you can easily store half a dozen cylinders.

You should have lots of warm clothing and blankets in case of heat failure which is very likely to happen occasionally. You should have a fan for summer.

You should have books and games on hand and devices for the amusement of small children such as coloring books etc. By all means you must have one or two battery radios and some spare batteries.

All of these things, so plentiful now, could become scarce in a matter of a few days. Why should you be part of an anxious lineup, and probably near the end of it?

Don't be caught without proper shoes and winter clothing. Even if you have only a modest amount of money in the bank it will be worth more to you in the form of these essentials which you can always use even if there isn't the crisis we anticipate. You should be prepared to stay in your shelter, tenement or castle, for at least a week, hoping of course that it won't be necessary.

Fuel is vitally important. For suburban communities I prefer oil heat with a full 1000 gallon tank buried in the yard. Natural gas lines can be blown up. I don't think the difference here is great, but given the choice I would go for oil. Only a few people will be able to afford or to house their own gasoline generating plants, but where possible this is a good idea. Power failures are almost certain. Wood fire places are fine if you have a supply of wood or live in a wooded area. New wood stoves are very efficient.

TRANSPORTATION

All the means without the fuel are useless.

I expect service stations to be closed. Under these conditions, there will be a complete breakdown of truck transportation. It could last a few weeks or a few days. There is no accurate way to predict its duration.

Transportation fuel can range from jerry cans in small garages to 1000 gallon tanks in yards, acreages, or retreats. Already it is getting late for the big tanks, at least for the filling of them. Probably you will run into times when it can be done. If you have the tank installed I think you will get the fuel if you are willing to pay the price. But the time is getting late — maybe very late.

In the case of a buried tank it should be well concealed, overgrown with lawn or garden and the outlet should be equipped with a standby hand pump inside an adjacent building, shed, or disguised by an ornamental fixture. Tell *nobody* about the fuel. You will simply defeat your purpose or make enemies of those friends who have been grasshoppers instead of ants.

Everyone should have two to four metal jerry cans (5 gallons) full. You might want to leave in a hurry at a time no service stations are operating. I realize there is a certain danger in the case of rearend collision but under the circumstances you will have to decide which risk you would rather take.

You should have at least one bicycle, more for families, as well as a moped, and a small Honda equipped with a carrying basket might be a great asset.

I have already dealt with the fuel situation sufficiently to make these conclusions obvious. Diesels are best but everyone can't go out and get a diesel. Having only a gas guzzler will be bad, chaos or no chaos. Nevertheless, for those who can afford it, one big car could come in mighty handy if a family is to be moved.

It all gets down to your personal circumstances. I could wish we might prescribe the same remedy for all. But it doesn't work that way. This book is for the pragmatist. We must take things as they are, and work from there.

As a last word, those in the country might find some use and much pleasure from a saddle horse.

FOOD

The first priority is storage security. That knocks out freezer food. A power failure and you are finished. That leaves you canned foods and dried foods. This problem is as old as the world.

North American Indians picked wild berries in the summer, smashed and mixed them with buffalo fat, bound the whole mass up in a buffalo stomach, tied with a sinew from a buffalo leg. That was pemmican, on which they could survive during long, severe winters.

In Africa, natives dry meat from freshly killed game animals on great racks in the direct sun. The volume is greatly reduced, but the nourishment remains. This is concentrated food.

On an Alberta homestead we lived forty miles from a railroad. Our only form of transportation was by horseback or lumber wagon on an often snowbound prairie trail, in temperatures that might reach thirty below, a twelve hour trip one way, and always the danger of a killing blizzard. You didn't count on getting to town.

We lived on salted sow belly and beans and the vegetables and fruit my mother had canned, supplemented by dried apricots, raisins, and such. Add sugar, baking powder, baking soda, salt and pepper to a few hundred pound sacks of flour and you didn't need much more. We had our own cow but today you have powdered milk and bottles of vegetable oil for fat.

So food survival is not all that difficult and nothing to be afraid of. The only thing to be afraid of is not having it when the time comes.

Of course you can go as elaborate as you like. Our position here is that we are preparing for 3 to 6 months. My suggestion to those whose surplus cash is limited is to make a start on three months. Draw up a list. Start out. Add as you go. When you have completed three months, begin to add the next three months.

I am not going into this problem at length, but here are the essentials of a simple and pragmatic plan.

CANNED FOODS

Their drawback is that they have limited shelf life, but in all cases it exceeds six months. The trouble is we don't know when the emergency will come. What if it doesn't happen for a year, two or more? Easily overcome. On your shelves you have three or six months' supply ranging from coffee through canned peaches and beans. Each week you do your shopping as usual. At the one end of the line you remove the stored can for use and add the new can at the starting end of the line. The line is always moving forward. You are always using food that is three months old, but is absolutely as good as if you had bought it yesterday. The key to this program is making sure that you always use the old cans. At any point in time you have a new three to six month supply in good condition.

As to the elements of this supply the best suggestions are your own preferences (for example, honey, jam, syrup, or all three).

Howard Ruff devotes a section of his book, *How to Prosper During the Coming Bad Years* (Times Books, Three Park Avenue, New York, NY 10016 $8.95) to the food you should store. Look into it. It will probably be worth your while to buy the book. It won't be a duplicate of this one. Ruff's ideas and mine differ substantially, but we converge on the *conclusion* that we face somewhere down the line a national emergency and a resulting temporary paralysis. I tend to think it is nearer than Ruff does, and he believes that it will be longer than I do. No matter. His work on food, nutritional value, vitamin needs is very good.

My conceptions are more limited because I don't think it is necessary to go all that far. I survived many winters on the farm and we had never heard of vitamins. Carbohydrates and proteins were not in our vocabulary.

The point I make is that *you can get by* simply and cheaply. The more affluent, of course, can probably do better.

Make sure the canned goods are fresh when you buy them. For that reason it's probably wise to stay with the big supermarkets where turnover is very fast. Be watchful though of tempting *sales*. It might be old stock.

DRIED GOODS

No doubt these are, if less tasty, more reliable, and I certainly recommend that part of your supply be in this form. There are several good outfits who specialize in this field but for starters I suggest that you write for *The Storage Food Catalogue*, Food Reserves Inc., 710 S. E. 17th Street, Causeway, Ft. Lauderdale, Florida 33384.

Apart from all the foregoing be certain that storage is dry and in as cool and constant a temperature as possible. Don't talk about it.

If you are well off it would be nice to have something else extra to help out friends or relatives in an emergency, but don't let it be known that you have a supply. Word gets around and you might find yourself at the wrong end of the gun in the hands of a hungry stranger.

37. THE STORM

By now we must have arrived at the conclusion that there can be but one end to the present worldwide inflation. That is a collapse of the *value* of money followed by a collapse in the *quantity* of money (deflation). Such a collapse usually comes in the form an an exponential curve, rising rather swiftly to a crescendo near the end. We do not know exactly where we stand on this graph today, and there is no means by which we can predict the time of the final flourish.

But it is not always necessary to predict time. It is often enough for us merely to know that a thing will happen, without exactly knowing when.

Among my earliest memories are memories of *the storm*. It was a small frame house of perhaps 500 square feet and it sat alone (so it seemed to me) on a vast and endless plain. Far beyond my known horizons lay a town. And in that town you could — if you had money — buy coal and lamp oil, sugar, even some preserves. The town was a reality only when the weather was right. It was a day's journey. We were as far from the town, in time, as Los Angeles from London.

When the deep winter set it, when the storms came, the town might as well have been London. Anything you needed from the town must have been laid in store long before *the storm*. You knew the storm would come. And you took it for granted. And you laid in the store of goods, with such resources of money as you had.

Long, long before any sign of snow we were getting ready for *the storm*. The early frosts brought us to our knees, plucking potatoes from the soil, pouring buckets of red spuds into sacks, and storing these in the dark cellar. There was canning of beans and beets; and even peaches — if we could afford them from the town. As the frosty mornings moved in, and long before the daylight, I could hear the rattle of the wagon as my father set out for the mine to lay in the winter's store of coal.

When it was all done, it was a pretty safe feeling. There was oil for the lamps, sacks of flour and sugar, dried prunes and raisins. The chicken house had been thatched; the hens were comfortable on the straw. The cows were in the nearby pasture. The barn was ready. When it was all done we read by the evening lamp. And we didn't worry. We knew *the storm* would come. We didn't have to know *what day*. And we didn't worry.

When, at length, the sky grew black in mid-afternoon and the wind began to whistle round the eaves and the temperature started to drop we were almost glad. The snow fell. The winds howled. The darkness settled, and the drifts piled high. So high, sometimes, that a boy could not see over them. Even when it went to twenty degrees below, forty degrees below, and the chill factor stood at ninety degrees so that three minutes would freeze your nose off, we made our quick trips, as necessary, to the well and the barn. The warm milk was in the pails. The pot-bellied stove glowed its heat. And as the storm increased in fury, my father would say: "Let her come. We were here first." He would say it on the third day, and if need be, say it on the tenth day: "Let her come. We were here first."

The storm always blew out. And the sun shone again. And eventually there was spring.

Had we not known the storm was coming, of course, we should have perished.

I feel very strongly that we have had all the signals we could ask for in predicting the monetary and economic storm. Already the skies in the north are black, and the winds are rising. The temperature is dropping. This may be a preliminary storm, or it might be *the big one*. On the farm we didn't worry if the storm came a little later than we expected. The important thing was to be ready for it. It came when it came. Why should we wish it before it came? Or why should we conclude that because it had not yet arrived, it would not happen at all?

We are now entering the period of winter. If we are ready for it, we need not fret, nor hope that it will happen tomorrow, nor hope sooner or later; because we have no control. Our situation is simply this: To the best of our financial and economic ability we have stocked our cellar, boarded up our house, and we might as well relax. "Let her come. We were here first."

And now we must touch on the most unpleasant possibility of all. That is virtual revolution in the United States.

This book is concerned with the end of an era. That means the end of an era of permissiveness, the end of an era of the spoilage of people, the end of an era of credit and waste, the end of an era of something for nothing, the end of an era to buy now and pay later, the end of an era of dependence on someone else.

Americans aged forty years and younger have become so accustomed to the idea that the country owes them at least a living that the withdrawal of this presumed privilege could result in widespread rioting across the nation. Empty bellies produce inflamed minds. When it comes to considering the possibility of violent protest, it's difficult to project either the upper or the lower limits. The lower limits could be rioting throughout the large cities. The upper limits could be organized revolution.

In preparation for the time that will inevitably fall upon us—sooner or later—every man must rely upon his own imagination, his own projection, and his own initiative. You will be able to come up with your own solutions particularly applicable to your personal conditions in *the storm*.

One thing is certain. You will see the collapse of this inflation and that will mean the end of the era you have known. But you and your country can still be saved.

The storm *can* be weathered.

NOTES

NOTES

NOTES

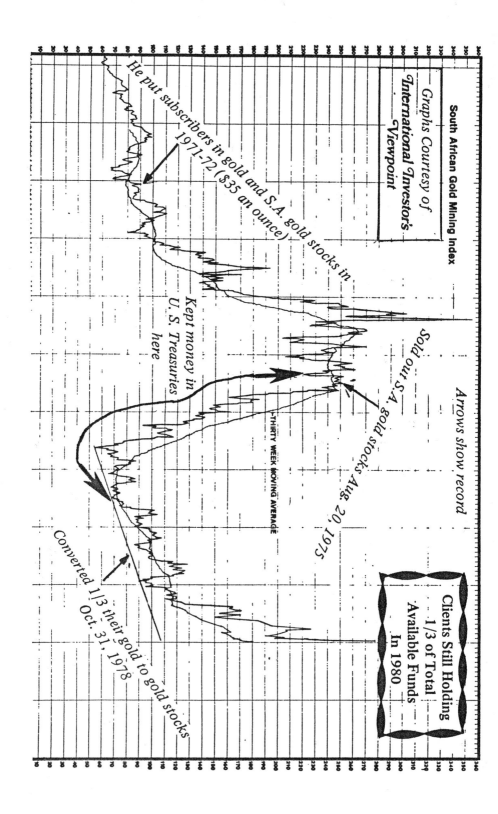

South African Gold Mining Index

Graphs Courtesy of
*International Investor's
Viewpoint*

He put subscribers in gold and S.A. gold stocks in
1971-72 ($35 an ounce)

Kept money in
U. S. Treasuries
here

Sold out S.A. gold stocks Aug. 20, 1975

Arrows show record

THIRTY WEEK MOVING AVERAGE

Converted 1/3 their gold to gold stocks
Oct. 31, 1978

Clients Still Holding
1/3 of Total
Available Funds
In 1980

THE MYERS FORECAST RECORD ON GOLD

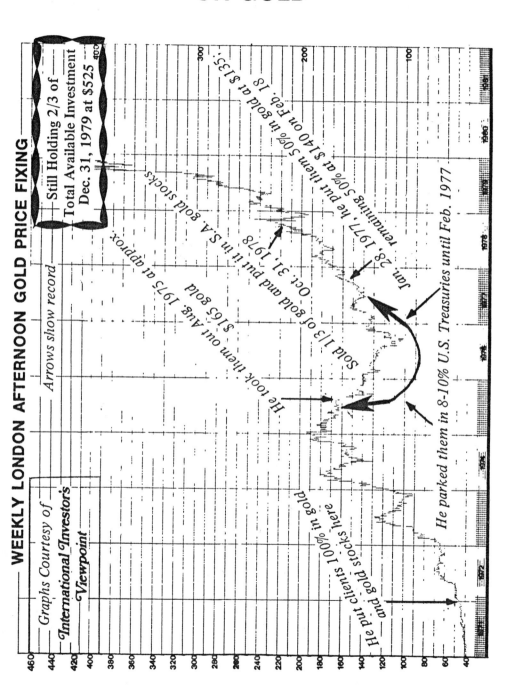

C. V. Myers' newsletter,
MYERS FINANCE AND ENERGY
is published at
642 Peyton Building, Spokane, WA. 99201
(See charts on preceding pages.)